Learning, Teaching, and
Musical Identity

COUNTERPOINTS: MUSIC AND EDUCATION

Estelle R. Jorgensen, editor

Learning, Teaching, and Musical Identity

VOICES ACROSS CULTURES

Edited by Lucy Green

INDIANA UNIVERSITY PRESS

Bloomington & Indianapolis

This book is a publication of

Indiana University Press
601 North Morton Street
Bloomington, IN 47404-3797 USA

www.iupress.indiana.edu

Telephone orders   800-842-6796
Fax orders   812-855-7931
Orders by e-mail   iuporder@indiana.edu

∞ The paper used in this publication
meets the minimum requirements of
the American National Standard for
Information Sciences—Permanence
of Paper for Printed Library
Materials, ANSI Z39.48-1992.

Manufactured in the United
States of America

Library of Congress Cataloging-
in-Publication Data

Learning, teaching, and musical identity :
voices across cultures / edited by Lucy
Green.
    p. cm. — (Counterpoints. Music and
education)
  Includes bibliographical references and
index.
  ISBN 978-0-253-35603-1 (cloth : alk.
paper) — ISBN 978-0-253-22293-0
(pbk. : alk. paper) 1. Music—Instruction
and study. 2. Folk music—Instruction
and study. 3. Identity (Psychology)
4. Group identity. I. Green, Lucy.
  MT1.L52 2011
  780.71—dc22

                          2010033182

1 2 3 4 5 16 15 14 13 12 11

Contents

Acknowledgments

I would like to thank Estelle Jorgensen for her warm encouragement when I once mused about an idea for an edited book on learning, teaching, and musical identity; and Jackie Wiggins for her support and enthusiasm about the initial plans. Jane Behnken and all the team at Indiana University Press have made the publication process as pleasurable and smooth as it could be. When I took on the task of putting the book together I imagined much of the work would be arduous, and that the "donkey-work" would be tiresome. This has by no means been my experience. It has been a pleasure and a joy to work with every one of the authors represented here, and my heartfelt thanks go to them all for their enthusiasm, efficiency—and willingness to answer all my e-mails extremely quickly! But most of all I thank them for carrying out and sharing their fascinating work.

LUCY GREEN
Institute of Education
University of London
London, UK

Learning, Teaching, and Musical Identity

Introduction

The Globalization and Localization of Learning, Teaching, and Musical Identity

LUCY GREEN

THE AIMS AND APPROACH OF THE BOOK

From an early age, in most if not all parts of the world, an individual begins to acquire a musical identity, or rather several musical identities, which are liable to develop and change over time. Musical identities are forged from a combination of personal, individual musical experiences on one hand, and membership in various social groups—from the family to the nation-state and beyond—on the other hand. They encompass musical tastes, values, practices (including reception activities such as listening or dancing), skills, and knowledge; and they are wrapped up with how, where, when, and why those tastes, values, practices, skills, and knowledge were acquired or transmitted. By "acquired" I am referring to any kind of *learning*, whether it arises naturally from mere interaction with the physical world, or from enculturation by the family, friendship group, or mass media, or whether it results from conscious application and study, or from "being taught." By "transmitted" I am referring broadly to any kind of *teaching*, whether it is formal and intentional or not, which involves the transmission of tastes, values, practices, skills, or knowledge from one person to another.

The main aim of this book is to investigate aspects of the interface between learning, teaching, and musical identity by "giving voice" to a range

of adults, teenagers, and children engaged in different music learning-
and-teaching practices, situated in different localities around the world.
Each chapter is grounded in qualitative research involving case study,
observation, interview, diaries, biographies, or a mixture of these. The
data are interpreted in relation to the immediate locality where they were
collected, with implications for wider national or global sociomusical and
music-educational issues. Thus, whereas each chapter is socially, historically, and geographically situated, taken together the chapters reveal differences and commonalities in musical identity formation, learning, and
teaching practices across a range of contexts, along with many potential
implications for music educationalists and others.

The researchers followed standard ethical procedures, including giving participants the right to withdraw and to remain anonymous, seeking
permission or providing written information where relevant, and sharing
findings with participants whenever it was reasonable to do so. Any further explications of methods or methodologies are included within each
chapter only when this is absolutely necessary in order for the reader to
understand the research or findings; and such explications are woven into
the discussion rather than being presented as separate sections. Similarly,
there is no separation between the presentation of data and the discussion of findings: the presentation of data *is* the discussion of findings.
Examination of literature, likewise, is largely undertaken in relation to
discussions of data and findings, rather than being presented as a separate
literature review. Thus, each chapter keeps the discussion of data and findings at the forefront of its narrative, in a way that we hope readers will find
enjoyable and accessible.

The chapters can be read in any order. But insofar as a book has to
present its chapters in one order or another, I decided to arrange them in
a rough geographical line. The line starts in the southeastern corner of the
world map, zigzags up, down, and across to the southwestern corner, and
ends in cyberspace. Beginning in Australia and moving north to Japan, it
then follows a diaspora from the Philippines to Hong Kong, stops in Bali,
Malaysia, South India, takes in another diaspora spanning the North Indian area of Gujarat to the UK, then goes to Cyprus, Greece, southerly to
South Africa, northerly to Ghana, through the Scandinavian areas of Lapland, Sweden and Iceland, to England, Scotland, and Ireland, and across
the Atlantic to the United States and Brazil. The final chapter, although

inevitably socially, historically, and geographically situated, addresses a virtual learning-and-teaching project. There are of course no claims here to have covered a representative sample of the entire globe, but the book is designed to offer a range of grounded perspectives, each from a different location. While we hope that each chapter will be of interest in itself, as I mentioned earlier, their combination can throw up some interesting overarching issues.

Next I will give an overview of the chapters, and situate each one within the overall aims of the book; then I will pull out some of the overarching issues that connect them.

A PREVIEW AND REVIEW OF THE CHAPTERS

Firstly, Kathryn Marsh examines the musical identities of children in a remote region of Australia where the population is almost entirely Aboriginal. She emphasizes the fluid nature of learning, teaching, and identity construction within and between the classroom and the playground; and she understands learning as a part of family, friendship, or kinship networks, as well as a reflection of cross-cultural or global influences. In Marsh's case study school, Aboriginal identity was maintained through strong kinship affiliations and cultural practices, including language maintenance programs; but it was challenged by two factors. One was the influence of the global media which, despite the remoteness of the region, affected the musical environment of the students. The other was contact with non-Aboriginal members of the community, who were in positions of power within the school and wider society. These factors were overlapping, as evidenced by the ways in which participants would switch between different musical styles or different spoken languages and by the equal acceptance of both global and indigenous markers of identity.

During the postwar era of the twentieth century, popular music became a major symbol of youth rebellion against the older generation in many parts of the world. However, nowadays it is common for children and young people to enjoy not only "their own" music, but also the music of their parents' generation. To this extent, what was known as "the generation gap" in the 1960s, and with it the rebellious connotations of popular music, seem to be receding. In chapter 2 Kyoko Koizumi explores some of the reasons for this with reference to Japan, where, after a postwar period of musical rebellion, many young people today respect and even follow their parents' musical tastes. This transmission of shared musical taste through the family started with the second Japanese baby-boomer generation, born between 1971 and 1974. Through interviews and life-studies of Japanese music-listeners across the generations, Koizumi illustrates the nature of these changes in taste and identifies various reasons for the phenomenon. These include new types and uses of musical media in everyday family lifestyles, such as car stereo equipment and *karaoke*; changes in parents' own musical tastes; and gender-specific ways of passing on tastes from mothers to daughters and from fathers to sons.

In chapter 3 Annie On Nei Mok investigates the relationships between music-learning and identity formation through the musical practices of a diasporic group of Filipino women who were born and brought up in the Philippines, then moved to Hong Kong to work as domestic maids. There are many thousands of women in this role living and working in Hong Kong. Among Mok's participants, their childhood and teenage musical enculturation had involved regular music-making in churches and social gatherings, where among other skills many of them had learned informally, by ear, to sing in spontaneous two-part harmony. Since moving to Hong Kong they have continued to maintain this kind of musical involvement through groups organized among themselves, but they have also been eager to absorb new learning within this wealthier society. They made use of the internet and audio resources and listened to a range of music they had not heard before, often by raiding their employers' CD collections. One particularly interesting finding is that they took steps to benefit from the instrumental lessons given by private music tutors hired to teach their employers' children. The maids would observe and even take part in the lessons, including learning for the first time how to read notation. Their homeland enculturation processes had given them a profoundly personal musical identity and a deep love of music, along with a set of musical skills many classically trained musicians would envy. Yet they did not place high value on these factors, but rather wished to reject them in favor of what they saw as more advanced, Westernized musical identities, skills, knowledge, and opportunities.

As with many countries around the world, the teaching and learning of music and dance in Bali intersects with tourism, economic pressures, religious identity, gender issues, and community expectations. In the case

of Bali, the pressures of increasing reliance on tourism, nascent independence, and a fragile existence as the only Hindu island within a Muslim ar-
chipelago add to the complexity of music learning-and-teaching processes
and musical identities there. Independent learning studios, as opposed to
traditional village-based teaching groups, are among a range of responses
to such pressures affecting the transmission of traditional music, which
are explored by Peter Dunbar-Hall in chapter 4. Both national (Indonesian) and local (Balinese) agendas for the use of music and dance as
commodities of cultural tourism mean that learning to play music or to
dance can become a means to personal, family, and group economic gain,
as well as affecting individual and group identities. Dunbar-Hall's analysis
draws upon his long-term association and ongoing fieldwork mainly in the
village of Ubud, which he views as a microcosm of movements to affirm
Balinese identity through the performing arts.

One of two reprinted chapters in the book, Roe-Min Kok's autobio-
graphical essay analyzes the postcolonial influences which the British
instrumental grade-exam system had on her identity formation while
taking classical piano lessons as an ethnic-Chinese child in Malaysia.
Her analysis reveals the processes involved in the transmission and reception of Western classical music in late twentieth-century Southeast
Asia. These include the informal, complex, and influential relationships
between the institutions of family and society, and between ethnicity,
local culture, and colonial history. For her, learning to play Western classical piano bridged both lived and imagined ways of being. It was an avenue for articulating and exploring changes in self-perception, a way of
expanding experience, a tool for the construction and even the disruption
of values—in short, a flexible, open-ended, and powerful element in the
formation of a mixed and complex ethnic identity.

Ethnomusicological studies of Indian classical music, tending to focus on the Hindustani tradition of North India, suggest that despite the
difficulties of maintaining certain aspects of traditional music transmission processes in the ever-changing cultural landscape of modern India,
musicians consider the unique communication between a master, or *guru*
(who may be male or female), and a *shishya* (student) to be fundamental. In chapter 6 Sophie Grimmer explores the *guru-shishya* relationship
across a range of participants in the South Indian Karnatic tradition of
advanced solo vocal performance. Her findings demonstrate how deeply

felt is the relationship for both parties as she explores the concept of the *shishya's* total "surrender" to the *guru's* or the tradition's particular ways of approaching technique and musicianship. She touches on a range of pedagogical principles: for example, musical intent and invention appear to be given priority over the vehicle of expression; the development of vocal "technique" occurs via exploration of the music itself, rather than via a separate pedagogical process; and the prominent mode of communication in the lessons is vocal rather than verbal, and imitative rather than explanatory. Underlying all this are the role of discipline in the *guru-shishya* relationship, the overwhelming respect and even awe that *gurus* can be expected to muster in their *shishyas,* and the emotional attachment that develops on both sides. Almost more than musical skill, enormous significance is placed upon commitment to the process of learning, and upon a *shishya's* identity as a follower of his or her particular *guru.*

The other one of two reprinted chapters is by the ethnomusicologist John Baily (chapter 7). In the past, he explains, members of the Muslim Khalifa community in Gujarat, North India, held a low position in the social hierarchy, and this status was closely bound up with two of their hereditary occupations—that of barber and that of musician. While Khalifas have historically acknowledged and actively pursued their connection with hairdressing, music-making has been an area of contestation, with competing claims, on one hand, that "music is in our blood," and on the other hand, that music is not fully endorsed by Islam. Through his study of Gujarati diasporic groups in two cities and one town in England, Baily examines participants' changing attitudes toward their previously stigmatized occupations now that they are members of a well-established and relatively successful community in the UK. He suggests how Khalifas conceive their own musicality and illustrates how they pass on music through informal learning. Unlike North Indian classical musicians, and unlike the South Indian Karnatic musicians in the previous chapter, the *guru-shishya* relationship has no relevance for these musicians: in their own much-used phrase, they learn music by just "picking it up"—and they express considerable pride in being self-taught, which they regard as a sign of inherent musicality and a fundamental aspect of their collective identity.

In chapter 8, Avra Pieridou-Skoutella discusses the construction of children's musical identities and practices in the Republic of Cyprus, with particular reference to Greek popular music in the Greek-Cypriot context. Greek popular music spans a continuum, from local or traditional musical characteristics at one end (Byzantine, *rembétiko,* and *laïka* musical styles) to global characteristics reflecting Anglo-American popular music at the other. Pieridou-Skoutella explores children's processes of transmitting and/or learning these musical styles in a range of urban and rural, school-based and out-of-school contexts, revealing aspects of globalization, local empowerment, ethnic identity construction, and the effects of Eurocentric ideology on the children's musical identities and practices. The issues are particularly pertinent to how music intersects with the formation of national as well as ethnic identity, since the data were collected over a period when, after a lengthy process of application, Cyprus was finally granted membership in the European Union.

The island of Corfu in western Greece has a long history of "Philharmonic Societies," which offer music education for free to anyone interested. There are eighteen Philharmonic Societies on the island, dating back to the 1840s, when Corfu became a British Protectorate. Among the societies, there is a particularly strong presence of wind bands, which involve both adults and children, many of whom remain active members throughout their lives. In chapter 9, Zoe Dionyssiou examines music-learning, teaching, and the formation of local identity through these bands. The bands tend to be marked by militaristic principles in their hierarchical organization, performance style, and repertoire, and the education students receive under their auspices is frequently criticized by participants and commentators as being conservative and "out-of-date." This involves a mix of authoritarian conductor-lead instruction, with ways of learning now often described as "non-formal"—that is, somewhere between the formal and the informal—such as learning by watching, listening, imitating, peer-interaction, and ear-playing. Such approaches mark brass band practices in many other Western or Westernized contexts around the world. Wind bands are regarded as second nature by Corfiots, characterizing the musical identity of the locals and raising the status of everyone who participates in the flamboyant street-marching festivals that take place on the island.

Chapter 10 examines the musical play of South African township children in the Soweto area of Johannesburg. Susan Harrop-Allin focuses on a clapping game played by a group of girls, based on the pop song "Barbie Girl." She illustrates various ways in which such games can be understood as "multimodal" practices in relation to cultural hybridity, and how music and dance function for children as semiotic resources. She also considers the musical capacities that children's games demonstrate and develop, and the implications of their play for music pedagogy in South Africa. She proposes that recognizing, incorporating, and developing learners' songs, dances, and clapping games should form a bridge between local musical practices and the country's official Arts and Culture curriculum. This position responds to the current dislocation between the richness of children's musical play and the formalized content of Arts and Culture lessons in township schools.

In Ghana a number of cultural groups are involved in music/dance activities, sometimes intertwined with story-telling, drawn either from a specific locale or a wider Ghanaian background. The study by Trevor Wiggins (chapter 11) focuses on three such groups: the Brotherhood cultural group based in Alajo, Accra; the school *bewaa* group at Mary Queen of Peace Catholic Primary school in Cape Coast; and the Kukyekukyeku Bamboo Orchestra based in Mosmagor. They contrast with each other, particularly in relation to the tensions in Ghana between state education and regional cultural differences. The Brotherhood is based in an economically deprived area of the capital. It is led by an Ewe master drummer but uses material from around Ghana. The Cape Coast primary school is in a relatively affluent area of a coastal city, but it teaches a style of music drawn from the north of Ghana, partly because there is a significant population of Dagara people in this Fanti-speaking area. The Bamboo Orchestra is a response by a whole community in the Kakum forest to try to preserve some aspects of their tradition, but it also draws on a wider range of musical idioms from other Ghanaian regions. Each ensemble trains group members in the acquisition of performance skills and passes on an aspect of Ghanaian culture in a way that is not found in most schools there. The chapter suggests that insiders' perspectives shed light on the balance between a personal, "tribal"/linguistic identity, and a national identity, through examining how these groups relate to contemporary popular music, both indigenous and international.

The Lapland region of Scandinavia includes the northernmost parts of Norway, Sweden, and Finland as well as the Kola Peninsula in the northwest of Russia. In chapter 12, Sidsel Karlsen studies three major music festivals across the region, all of which are geographically situated at some distance from their respective countries' capitals and cultural and economic centers. She illustrates some of the ways in which these music festivals foster collective as well as individual dimensions of identity through, for example, the telling and retelling of existing community narratives and the continued regeneration of collective self-images. By participating in such stories and their associated musical practices, festival audiences learn, through music, what it means collectively and individually to be inhabitants of their respective municipalities. At the same time, the festivals promote a broader collective identity crossing the boundaries of individual towns, municipalities, or local regions; two of the festivals joined Lappish culture together in a way that transcended official national borders. Karlsen calls for more research by music educators on how music-learning, teaching, and identity formation occur through festivals.

Chapter 13 concerns the formation of a "music-teacher identity" by five upper-secondary music teachers in Sweden. Eva Georgii-Hemming's main aim is to describe how the participants' identities have been forged biographically through their musical and educational experiences, and yet how they can come into conflict with the demands of the institutions in which they work. All the teachers wish to pass on to their students what they have themselves derived from their own musical experiences: pleasure and play, skill, a sense of community, and an outlet for emotion. In trying to negotiate this they tend to invoke a concept of individual need that is considered distinctive of contemporary Swedish life—and life in many other nations—where values such as individual freedom of choice have acquired greater importance than collective orientations. Georgii-Hemming discusses the negotiation between personal and professional spaces, individual and public discourses, and she puts forward an ideal view of the school as a space for reflective dialogue between the familiar and the unfamiliar in relation to the individual's "life world" and musical and cultural preferences.

It is widely accepted that gender is locally as well as globally constructed, and that its practice is complex and often contradictory. Nevertheless, the study of music's role in the construction and representation of masculine gender identity has often focused on global, "accepted" male or masculine musical behaviors and genres. This overlooks the potential multidimensionality of men's musical lives in different cultures and parts of the world, and the ways in which local identity can impact on men's gender identity. In chapter 14, Robert Faulkner investigates the construction of masculinity through men's musical practices in Iceland, where the activity of group singing has long been regarded as "masculine." He illustrates some of the ways in which Icelandic men construct and represent masculine identities through their musical practices, including the embracing of emotion, physical proximity, and touch; the use of a wide range of musical genres and vocal expression; cross-generational issues; the representation of mothers, love, and relationships in Icelandic lyrics, culture, and lore; and the role of Icelandic landscape and locality in musical meanings. Stereotypical views of Western masculine identity are in many ways challenged by these musical practices and the cultural associations that go with them.

Extracurricular musical performance has long been a defining characteristic of English music education, as Stephanie Pitts makes clear in chapter 15. She argues that participants' experiences are often powerful, even life-changing, and that they remain some of the most vivid memories of their education years later. For teachers as well as pupils, participating in a stage production or a large-scale concert can be a source of musical satisfaction, personal confidence, and social connection within the school community. Yet remarkably little attention has been given to this central feature of music education, and to its long-term consequences. Focusing initially on a case study of the musical *Anything Goes* produced in a secondary school, and then on some new forms of extracurricular engagement within English schooling, she considers the role of extracurricular music-making in the musical identity formation of teachers and pupils. While voluntary music-making within an institutional context may bring new dimensions to school life, she suggests that questions remain about how such teacher-directed projects link with new demands for student autonomy in music-making; and about the particular ways in which extracurricular participation may be a preparation for lifelong engagement with music.

Along with many other countries, Scotland has seen a huge increase in the numbers of young people engaging with "their own" ethnic musical heritage in recent years. As well as the informal sphere, in many parts of the country tuition is now provided on traditional instruments such as the chanter, clarsach, fiddle, and whistle, and increasing numbers of courses and modules in Scottish traditional music are being developed. In chapter 16 Charles Byrne investigates the views of five undergraduates and recent graduates of a bachelor's degree in applied music at the University of Strathclyde in Glasgow. Many of them work and perform across formal and informal settings including *cèilidh*-type sessions in local bars, and in successful professional and semiprofessional ensembles in large cities or farther-flung locations such as Orkney, Skye, and Fife. They are products of an ongoing musical genesis whereby the characteristics of traditional Scottish or Celtic music mingle with the sounds of jazz and hip-hop to create new musical fusions. Byrne explores when and how the students learned their instruments, what aspects of musical communities impacted their learning, and the contributing factors to their own musical identity. A rich and diverse Scottish musical heritage emerges, which coexists alongside cultural influences from across the world.

Marked by possibly a slightly longer revivalist history than its Scottish counterpart, Irish traditional music has had a major presence both inside and beyond Irish borders for many years, whether as a symbol of national identity, part of a unique heritage, or as representative of a distinct way of life. However, the past twenty years or so have witnessed the forging of close links between traditional music and mainstream contemporary popular culture in Ireland. In chapter 17 John O'Flynn explores the musical practices and perceptions of a generation of young adults who have become traditional musicians within this more recent phase of Irish musical history. The chapter centers on young musicians' activities as performers, listeners, composers, learners, and teachers, and on their perceptions of these activities in relation to wider sociocultural contexts. O'Flynn provides insights into musical, social, pedagogical, and phenomenological aspects of the participants' individual and collective experiences, and into the potential interface of musical, national, ethnic, and youth identities in the social experience of traditional musicians.

Chapter 18 by Sharon Davis explores the music-learning processes of children in a fifth-grade beginning band class in a US public school. Davis took part as both teacher and participant-observer in the study, during which she endeavored to bring about two main conditions. One was to foster a learning environment in which students could incorporate informal practices in the context of a formal band classroom. The other was to give students the opportunity to have what she calls a "musical say" in expressive decision making within the ensemble. By a "musical say" she means something that incorporates identity, ownership, agency, relevance, and the personal expression of the individuals involved, as well as the required pedagogical accommodations. She describes some of the ways in which the students expressed themselves individually, collectively, and musically when given free rein to do so. Their interaction was not without tension, but negotiation among peers provided the possibility of developing students' investment in the learning process, in the ensemble, and in their own musical growth. Identity construction became a negotiated experience, and those students who felt marginalized used strategies to continue to have their voices heard. Allowing time for such negotiation and for incorporating group decisions into the final product revealed aspects of beginning musicianship that, Davis argues, were pedagogically transformative.

Heloisa Feichas's chapter considers the musical identities of students in a Music School within a major Brazilian federal university. The context of learning and teaching in most Brazilian music schools has been strongly influenced by the European conservatoire model in terms of pedagogy, repertoire, and concepts of musical meaning and value. Recently, however, due to governmental measures to expand opportunities in higher education, students with more informal backgrounds in popular musics and jazz have been entering the schools. Thus, while the predominant soundscape of the corridors and classes continues to be mainly classical, some sounds from the worlds of popular music and jazz are now beginning to be audible. Feichas investigates how students from different musical backgrounds construct their own identities and their conceptions of each other, showing how this intersects with course choice and specialization. For example, students from popular music backgrounds are seen as having inferior skills in some respects, but superior skills in others; course choices lead to particular identities, such as "bachelor of music" or "music education" student, each of which carries a higher or lower status depending on the views of the beholder; and specialization in piano, guitar, string, wind, voice, or composition leads to the construction of often competitive identities between and across different groups of students.

As mentioned earlier, all learning is of course socially, historically, and geographically situated. This applies to "virtual learning" no less than to any other learning practice, since the persons undertaking the learning—and the teaching if there is any—are always already situated beings themselves. But virtual learning also affords some level of dislocation, at least from the literal ground of a particular learning site. In the final chapter Sheri Jaffurs offers a case study of some ways in which a particular computer-mediated environment opened possibilities for music education and the construction of musical identity. Jaffurs's public school, in the Midwest of the United States, purchased a "virtual island" named SIMPhonic Island, which is open to teenagers from thirteen to seventeen and to approved adult teachers. It became the venue for a pilot online immersive music technology course for high school students who wished to develop the skills and techniques needed to become virtual musicians. Jaffurs describes her "netnographic" investigation of how the students' musical identities were formed on the island, through their virtual representations of themselves as avatars and their interactions with her as a researcher/teacher avatar. The investigation of teenagers inhabiting a virtual island, creating their own environment, their own music, and even their own embodied representative, allows for particularly candid discussion between the researcher and the participants concerning how teenagers develop their musical identities in this virtual space of learning through imagination and play.

EMERGING ISSUES

Many of the overarching issues that emerge from the discussions in this book concern the push-and-pull effect of globalization versus localization. In the case of music, globalization can on one hand be understood as an electronic cultural, musical colonization by powerful nations or regions at the metaphorical "center" of the world over smaller or less powerful ones at the "periphery." The ready availability and profitable marketability of music, through not only the mass media but also the internet, by mp3 downloads and other electronic means, have added new dimensions to cultural imperialism. As illustrated in this book, young children in places as far apart as a remote Australian Aboriginal village, rural and urban areas of Cyprus, and the townships of South Africa are forming their musical identities in relation to global mass-mediated popular music, based on sounds that originated either actually, or stylistically and historically, in the United States. Such children are negotiating these globalized identities with other identities formed at both the local and the national level.

For centuries, musical cultural imperialism has also taken place through the export of Western classical music as a status symbol and cultural icon. This is illustrated here through the exportation/importation of British classical piano grade exams in Malaysia, for example, and the conservatoire-influenced music schools of Brazil. In such contexts, families, educational organizations, and governments have wanted to "modernize"—also known as "Westernize"—their status and societies, and have found music a convenient means to help in that endeavor. Very differently, Western music has also entered many regions as an inseparable aspect of the missionary work of various Christian churches, as illustrated in this book by the Filipino maids' childhood experiences of musical enculturation. Western music and Western teaching-and-learning practices also mark, for example, the case of Corfu, where the brass band tradition harks westerly to Italy and Europe rather than homeward or easterly toward the modal and rhythmically complex roots of Greek traditional music.

On the other hand, in many countries or regions, perceived threats from musical globalization, along with the expansion of the industry category of "world music," are causing a vigorous renewal of interest in ensuring the survival of local, traditional, and national musics. At the same time as the colonizing effects of "central" world superpowers occurs through musical globalization, many moves are afoot from governmental, educational, and other cultural organizations to encourage musical localization and nationalism in "peripheral" regions. In this book, the cases of Bali and, in different ways, Ghana offer examples of various organized attempts to maintain local or national identity through music. Some such attempts can be regarded as involving a struggle to hold back globalizing trends, while at the same time affording the possibility of capitalizing on the touristic attractions and global marketability of indigenous music, and indeed in some ways, the cultural export of local identity. This can in turn put them in tension with issues of cultural preservation and "authenticity." Such issues tend to occur more vigorously in "small" countries or regions, such as Bali, Cyprus, or Corfu; and/or in countries with long histories of colonization or some level of subordination under a larger power, such as Ghana, Scotland, or Ireland. In India, Karnatic music, with its long scholarly history, specialized and highly intense learning-and-teaching practices, still holds on to its identity as an emblem of South Indian high culture; and yet modern life is forcing some major changes in its transmission processes, and participants are concerned to hold on to the practices of the past in as many ways as are feasible.

Not only governments, educational bodies, and cultural organizations, but also children and young people themselves, as well as older people, are feeling the pull of musical identity formation as a way to express their local, ethnic, or national selves. In the case of *musicians'* identities, this book offers some illustrations of how this works through music-making practices in different places. These include Scotland and Ireland, where it is "cool" for young people to play traditional music, although less than fifty years ago this was hardly the case; Iceland, where national identity is reproduced through diverse local musical practices with strongly felt national connotations; Corfu, where a long tradition is upheld through the wind bands, which carry strong Corfiote identity; and in India, Bali, and Ghana in ways just discussed. In the case of *listeners'* musical identities, the discussion about Lapland, for example, illustrates some of the ways in which people respond differently and with more strength of feeling to their local music than to imported or globalized music. Yet local musics in many countries are experiencing struggles between the retention of tradition, in some sort of "pure" or "authentic" sense, and the fusion of traditional sounds with popular, jazz, and "world" influences. Within this book are accounts of struggles or accommodations between local, indigenous, and globalized musical identities in areas as far-flung as Australia, Bali, India, Cyprus, Ghana, Lapland, Iceland, Scotland, and Ireland.

While the construction of localized musical identities occurs within national borders, musical identities are also carried across borders through diasporic groups. This is illustrated in the present book by two contrasting cases. One is the above-mentioned diaspora of female Filipino maids to Hong Kong, and the other, the diaspora of male Gujarati barbers to the UK. Many interesting contrasts can be illustrated through these two cases. In each, members of the diaspora have strong musical identities arising from their enculturation in their familial ethnic groups, and from the informal music-learning practices of their childhoods. But for the Filipino women, their removal to a different society resulted in a rejection of these identities and a search for new, more formalized, and as they saw it more advanced ways of learning; whereas for the Gujarati men, their new overseas status enhanced their pride in both their ethnic musical identities and their informal learning practices. Furthermore, the Filipino women were engaged with Western, not indigenous Filipino, music, whereas the Gujarati men were engaged with a music very much identified as ethnically and culturally "their own." These two cases alone can illustrate the complexities of musical identity formation, and the need to avoid generalizations about this challenging issue.

Having said that, it is tempting to put forward a hypothesis, which could be worth testing perhaps in future work. This would be that the local and national musics of "central" or powerful countries with imperial pasts may be relatively more problematic as markers of identity for their indigenous, national people, while the local and national musics of "peripheral" or previously colonized countries or regions may be relatively straightforward and inviting for their populations, as well as their governments. For example, in England, although there is a history of folk or traditional music at least as strong as that in Scotland or Ireland, and although the government and educational system have for over a century included English folk music in the school curriculum, arguably, English folk music is not receiving the same level of interest from either musicians, listeners, teachers, learners, or the mass media as its Scottish, Irish, or Welsh counterparts. The same could be said of Japan, where far more attention is given to Western or Westernized forms of both popular and classical musics than to Japanese traditional music, which has only recently entered the music curriculum there.

Two major, contrasting ways in which early musical identities are formed occur through children's informal games and their formal educational experiences in schools. Within this book, aspects of children's unsupervised playground activities are examined in Australia, South Africa, and Cyprus, where they reflect a mix of the children's local and global musical identities. In the two chapters located in the United States, teacher-researchers, acting in relatively more formal environments, encouraged children to make music-learning an expression of their feelings or a part of their "own" individual identities, rather than being either a means to affirm local or national collective identities, or a response to a set of instructions. The value of self-expression and enjoyment as music-educational aims are also echoed here by teachers in Sweden and, through organized extracurricular activities, England. Interestingly, and again in need of further research, it is tempting to suggest that where children's games or children's approaches to self-expression are supervised by adults, and/or where they occur in metaphorically "central" as distinct from "peripheral" regions of the world, the emphasis may be placed more explicitly on individual expression or identity, rather than on the affirmation of ethnicity, locality, or nation.

At the local level, family, friends, individual teachers, schools and other institutions, and the community all foster musical identities. Several chapters in this book illustrate different processes through which this occurs. They include: the passing down of taste and knowledge through family values and practices in Japan (concerning popular music), and through family values and the provision of private tuition in Malaysia (concerning Western classical music); informal music-learning practices passed down through the family and/or community, as in the Philippines, Gujarat, Scotland, and Ireland; informal games or formal, expressive learning activities in the school playground or classroom as in Australia, South Africa, Sweden, and the United States; intense relationships between teachers and students as in the South Indian context; and extracurricular, independent, or government-funded music organizations such as those in Bali, Ghana, Lapland, England, Scotland, Ireland, and many other places.

How individuals construct and conceive their own identities, as well as the identities of others around them, can involve conflicts between their "personal" identity and a more "public" or professional identity required of them by an institution. The institution could be a school, where teachers are required in some ways to drop their individual musical identities in order to fulfill the demands of their jobs, as the case of Sweden illustrates in this book; a conservatoire-based music school containing the often conflicting and competing identities of students from different backgrounds, as shown here in the case of Brazil; or the time-honored *guru-shishya* relationship of the Karnatic tradition of South India, which puts heavy demands on loyalty as well as time and commitment that are not easily met in contemporary life.

Only two chapters in this book have a subsection specifically devoted to the topic of gender identity: one concerning the construction of masculinity through Icelandic musical practices, and the other examining the gendered demarcation of instrumental performance in Bali. Yet all the chapters to some extent implicitly or explicitly address this vital area. The Gujarati musicians, for example, are all male; the Filipino maids are, of course, all female; the playground games of children tend to involve not only gendered but sexualized concepts of identity coming through the mass media; the passing on of taste in Japan occurs from father to son, and from mother to daughter; teachers of different sexes as discussed in Sweden have accordingly different musical backgrounds; and so on. How gender identity and sexuality are constructed through formal and informal music transmission and learning practices, and how issues of globalization and locality impact this, are areas calling for more research.

Finally, many of the authors point to the implications of their findings and discussions for the future of music-learning and teaching, whether conceived as formal, informal, or somewhere in between. Many echo recent moves in countries right across the world, in which educators are respecting and incorporating the informal music-making and music-learning practices that take place outside the school or other formal educational institutions, and are developing new teaching methods that aim to reflect such practices, as well as the values and identities that go along with them. Such areas also contain implications for understanding different types not only of teaching but of learning, and suggest that more knowledge about music-learning is needed to enhance the ways music educators think about teaching.

All the contributors to the book would agree that, as music educators and music-education researchers, we should approach issues connecting musical identity, teaching, and learning tentatively. Among them, the chapters show how different are the *processes* of musical identity formation, and how varied the *contents* of musical identity for individuals and groups in different places; and they illustrate how closely woven musical identity formation is with music-learning and/or music teaching. They point to a need for music educators and researchers to deepen our understanding of the complexity and multiplicity of the influences on children's, teenagers', adult-learners', and our own musical tastes, knowledge, and skills. They suggest that music education can gain in many different ways when it acts in parity and interchangeably with both global and local musical traditions and practices; and that global and local musical traditions and practices can complement and fill many gaps left by more formal approaches to music teaching and learning. These issues have implications for curriculum and pedagogy within and beyond schools, conservatoires, universities, community schemes, and other education providers, and suggest the continued importance of opening up what we conceive to be "music education."

ONE

The Permeable Classroom

Learning, Teaching, and Musical Identity in a Remote Australian Aboriginal Homelands School

KATHRYN MARSH

From many recent explorations of children's musical lives, it is clear that children's musical identities are influenced not only by formal music-learning activities within the classroom, but also by informal music-learning experiences beyond. These include learning in the playground and learning through exposure to various media, as part of a network that may be familial, friendship, or kinship-based, or that may reflect cross-cultural or other global influences. At the core of this mix of influences are issues of cultural contact through multiple sources, and the ways in which children (and their teachers) negotiate musical identities in the light of this contact. This applies to children living in urban environments no more or less than to those living in remote regions. In this chapter I describe and explore the varied influences on identity formation that are enacted through both formal and informal music-learning experiences at a small, remote primary school in the arid landscape of the Northern Territory, the least densely populated area of Australia.

CONTEXTS FOR TEACHING AND LEARNING

Since 1990 my research has centered on ways in which elementary school children use musical play as an expressive practice within and beyond school playgrounds. My explorations of this phenomenon have occurred through ethnographic fieldwork in schools in Australia and internationally (Marsh 2008). In each location I observed and interviewed children in the playground and nearby areas during recess times within the school day. I employed non-participant observation and reflexive semi-structured interview techniques, whereby children were engaged in discussion about their play *in situ* as it occurred. Observations and interviews were video- and audio-recorded and supplemented by field notes. Through these means children in urban, rural, and remote school settings provided a rich source of varied experiences and perspectives.

As an ethnographer I also collected a large amount of contextual data relating to the school and wider community, the functioning of the school itself, and school policies, programs, and teaching practices that affected children both inside and outside the classroom. I therefore occasionally recorded activities within the classroom environment, and the observations of classroom teaching and learning, as well as discussions with teachers and interested adults, further informed my understanding of influences on playground teaching, learning, and performance.

In urban Australia the locus of my investigation of musical play was a study of a multiethnic school in Sydney, the most populous and ethnically diverse Australian city. In contrast, the schools that I next investigated were located in remote localities in the Barkly Tablelands region in central Australia. In this area of arid grasslands, schools are found both in small towns, such as Telford Spring (with a population at the time of approximately 3,000) and Auston (a town of 500 people, 250 kilometers north), and in small Aboriginal homelands communities such as Bradford Well, ten kilometers north of Auston. (Pseudonyms are used for all school areas and individual research participants throughout the book unless otherwise stated.) Bradford Well School, with a population of 25 students, mostly aged between 4 and 12, forms the focus of the discussion in this chapter. I visited the school during two month-long periods of fieldwork over two subsequent consecutive years, and observed children engaged in play, lessons, and whole school and small group activities. In addition, I conducted interviews with children, the two teachers, and members of the school community, including the language workers and a respected elder. With the exception of the teaching principal and her son, all students and members of the school community were Aboriginal.

Aboriginal people in central Australia are identified by language groups that have close cultural, religious, economic, and ecological connections with particular geographical areas, though such links have been ameliorated by the movement of Aboriginal groups into new settlements as a result of white pastoral and political interests, particularly over the last century (Nash 1984). For many years, two Aboriginal language groups, Jingili and Mudburra, have coexisted in the Bradford Well and neighboring Auston areas; and the languages and cultural practices have to some extent coalesced through language borrowing, intermarriage, and co-location of ceremonial and social activity (Chadwick 1975; Pensalfini 2001). Over recent decades the traditional owners of this area have successfully campaigned for land rights. As a result, the homelands settlement of Marlinja, a significant site from the Dreaming (the beginning of time, central to traditional Aboriginal beliefs), has been excised from a large cattle property for exclusive habitation by the Jingili-Mudburra people (Dunbar-Hall 1997). Programs to maintain culture and language in the face of previous dispossession and resultant social and economic dislocation have been initiated in both Bradford Well and Auston schools. During the fieldwork periods, Aboriginal elders and language workers were being employed through the Community Development Employment Projects (CDEP) Program to share cultural knowledge and teach the prevailing Mudburra language.

TEACHING, LEARNING, AND MUSICAL IDENTITY AT BRADFORD WELL

Ethnicity and culture might seem to be of greatest significance in the construction of musical identity in such settings. However, it is evident that many factors influence musical identity formation, including age, gender, musical preferences, and the "cultural, ethnic, religious and national contexts in which people live" (Folkestad 2002: 151). Slobin (1993) has disputed any monolithic account of musical culture, and Campbell (2002) has elaborated on the multiple subcultures and intercultures with which children may have an affinity as they construct a personal musical identity at what Keil terms the "idiocultural level" (Keil and Feld 1994: 297). In establishing a musical identity, children may indeed be both reflecting and representing a "confluence of cultures" (Lum 2007:

4), with individual "choice," "affinity," and ways of "belonging" all being implicated (Slobin 1993: 55–56).

At Bradford Well, the multiple affiliations between children, teachers, and the community, and the locations and modes of teaching and learning, meant that the boundaries between formal classroom activities and informal music (or other) learning were highly permeable, both physically and figuratively. Rather than concentrating on the playground, my attention became focused on all forms of music-learning occurring within this domain. A liminal zone for learning was provided by a large paved and roofed area adjoining one of the two classrooms and open to the playground on two sides. This area contained a wealth of play materials (toys, ball game equipment, dress-up clothes, a toy kitchen, and other regalia) and was used by the children for pretend play during recess times and for assembling in readiness for formal school activities. During such times, when children were waiting before or in the interstices between formal "work," both boys and girls could be observed playing clapping games and other hand games involving rhythmic movements.

This space also functioned as a teaching location for whole school formal learning activities. In particular, at the time of my second field visit, it was used for language maintenance lessons in the Mudburra language. Music was used as a primary vehicle for this activity, with several songs being taught or practiced in whole-group sessions during my time at the school. These songs reflected the multiple musical and cultural influences on the language workers, who included an Aboriginal teacher at the school, her sister, and their mother, a knowledgeable elder who sat silently near the children to oversee the activity and who was consulted regarding appropriate vocabulary periodically during the teaching sessions.

One song was based on the model of the well-known children's action song "Heads Shoulders Knees and Toes," with verses relating to various body parts sung first in English and then in Mudburra. Interestingly, the grouping of body parts diverged markedly from the English original, with combinations such as "Hair (Wijalma), Head (Damang Ka), Forehead (Wirdurru), and Eyebrow (Ibidjibidgi)" and "Arm (Nungkuru), Elbow (Munjuna), Bones (Karda-Karda), and Hands (Marnda-marnda)" perhaps more indicative of an Indigenous taxonomy than a "whitefella" one (which has typical groupings of "head and shoulders,

Table 1.1. Text of Gospel Song in English and Mudburra

English	Mudburra
Standing up, Hallelujah	Kurdij karrili wanya
Standing up, Hallelujah	Kurdij karrili wanya
Standing up, Hallelujah, whoa oh	Kurdij karrili wanya, whoa oh
In the name of the Lord	Ngayinya kirda nginyi Ini
Kneeling down, Hallelujah	Jird-wandili wanya
Kneeling down, Hallelujah	Jird-wandili wanya
Kneeling down, Hallelujah, whoa oh	Jird-wandili wanya, whoa oh
In the name of the Lord	Ngayinya kirda nginyi Ini
Sitting down, Hallelujah	Dakwandili wanya
Sitting down, Hallelujah	Dakwandili wanya
Sitting down, Hallelujah, whoa oh	Dakwandili wanya, whoa oh
In the name of the Lord	Ngayinya kirda nginyi Ini
Clap your hands Hallelujah	Marnda marnda barlkij karri
Clap your hands Hallelujah	Marnda marnda barlkij karri
Clap your hands Hallelujah, whoa oh	Marnda marnda barlkij karri, whoa oh
In the name of the Lord	Ngayinya kirda nginyi Ini

knees and toes," and "eyes and ears and mouth and nose"). There were seven verses in total, outlining a broad range of body part vocabulary with matching actions.

Another of the songs also aligned action to language but drew on a completely different stylistic source for inspiration. This song was in gospel style, the English version (again sung first), consisting of the text, with a performance of the Mudburra version following, as shown in table 1.1.

The religious beliefs and musical background of the language worker Ellen were clearly evident in this song. Ellen was a singer, previously a member of a local Aboriginal band who created and performed original country, rock, and gospel songs in both English and Mudburra, many of the songs celebrating the return of the traditional homeland of Marlinja to the Jingili people. One of Ellen's songs on her band's album *You're Not Useless* seemed to illustrate the strong disposition to use song for cultural maintenance with children, a practice that had permeated the learning environment of the school from the community:

Now I'm sitting round the campfire
With my family round with me
Telling stories to the young ones
For the time we'll come to know
Singing songs and clapping hands
For the one I love so well [referring to the Marlinja homeland]
Staying happy at my home called Marlinja
(from "Oh! My home Marlinja," 1993)

Song creation as a form of cultural transmission was also evident in the other two songs that were used for language teaching that I witnessed at Bradford Well school. The first of these, *"Karu lungkarra"* (translated as "Kid Crying") told a story about a child sick with hunger being fed by his mother. The song, performed from a typed copy of the text pasted into the children's language books, had been co-constructed by the children, together with Ellen, and her brother, Richard, as discussed with the Anglo-Australian teacher Rhonda and several of the children:

KM: Where did the song come from?
NINA: Our aunty.
RHONDA: Well, they worked together as a group and Ellen worked with them, and . . . Richard came down and worked with Peter and Ellen, like, working out the chords and how they were going to put the song together.
KM: How you were going to make the tune of the song?
RHONDA: The tune of the song; and then so that's how it [went].
KM: So who's Richard?
RHONDA: Richard is—
CHILDREN: Tom's dad.
RHONDA: Yeah, Tom's dad. Yeah, and he came down and gave us a hand with it.

The network of relationships outlined in this discussion was integral to the nature of music teaching, learning, and creating in this school and to the consequent formation of musical identity. The community served by this school, as with all Aboriginal communities, was composed of an intricate web of kinship ties that have social and cultural significance and that are associated with particular behaviors and obligations. At Bradford Well immediate familial relationships were evident, but terms such as "aunty" and "cousin" are also used to denote the more extended kinship ties in Aboriginal communities.

What was signified in this instance was a level of familiarity emerging from the multiple identities of the community members working with music in the classroom. Ellen, her sister Julie (the Aboriginal school teacher), and her brother Richard had close familial or extended kinship ties with many of the children in the school. There was thus a relatively seamless movement between formal and informal classroom relationships and, therefore, ways of teaching and learning. Ellen and Richard were known as musicians, performers and creators of popular music, but they were simultaneously parents or kin and also teachers of language, culture, or music.

Similarly, the place of other members in this music teaching-learning-performing-creating continuum was also fluid. Peter, the non-Aboriginal teacher's son mentioned in the above interview, was known in the community as a talented musician, who sang and played country and rock standards regularly on stage in country music venues and competitions, despite his young age of ten years. During the first morning of my field visit, his performance of what was evidently favorite repertoire, "Ghost riders in the Sky" and "Sweet Home Alabama," was greeted with cheers and loud applause by the assembled children. He accompanied the children's singing of the Mudburra language songs *"Kurdij karrili wanya"* ("Hallelujah") and *"Karu lungkarra"* in an accomplished fashion on his guitar, and his skill had evidently been recognized in the collaborative process of devising the accompaniment to the latter song. He was therefore included as a musician within the framework of musical activity in the school, elevated by his status as a performer. However, he had an often uneasy relationship with the Aboriginal children in the school, and his inclusion in the school community was sometimes tenuous. His participation in formal or informal musical activity therefore entitled him to membership of a *musical* community of practice within the school, by nature of participation in the "joint enterprise" of music making, "mutual engagement" in music and a "shared repertoire" of musical outcomes (Wenger 2000: 229) but this did not always extend to complete social acceptance.

While the teaching or rehearsal of new or known songs was enacted in a formal manner, often through lengthy repetition indicative of traditional Aboriginal modes of learning (Harris 1990), the creation of new songs, as shown in the discussion of "*Karu lungkarra*" above, was a much more informal and interactive process. I saw this process at work in the construction of a new song from a story of traditional Aboriginal life that had been taught as part of the language maintenance program. The song, titled "Long Ago" ("*Larrpa-Ngi-Nyi*") was created to accompany a video made by the children, enacting the traditional practices outlined in the story, which was to be shown at the Darwin Festival (in the state capital city, Darwin) later in the year. Two older girls, Emma and Nina (both age eleven), sat out in the playground with Ellen and Richard, who provided some initial country-style melodic and harmonic ideas, Ellen singing and Richard playing a chordal accompaniment. Although the process was also reiterative, with repetition and revision of different phrases sung within the context of the whole song, Emma, along with the adults, made suggestions regarding melody and text setting, and her contributions were incorporated naturally as part of the process. For more than half an hour the song ideas were created and tested through performance by the four participants, and the song gradually developed into a complete entity with which they were all satisfied.

In the subsequent teaching of the new "Long Ago" song to all the children after lunch on the same afternoon, Emma and Nina demonstrated the song, with Richard accompanying. In this sense, they had taken on the identity of music performers and teachers, age and perhaps knowledge being equated with expertise. This was certainly the case with Emma, who was quick to learn the songs and sang confidently and tunefully, but Nina's performance was much less confident and accurate. Nevertheless, they both took on this role in response to expectations of their position as older children, assisting in the instruction by Julie, Ellen, and Richard. They were brought forward to model the songs from the front when the other children's attention began to flag as the teaching session continued (for nearly an hour of repeated renditions of the song).

As with all of the language-learning experiences, the language workers directed the learning while the non-Aboriginal teacher sat to the side as a facilitator, clearly indicating the knowledge and power as belonging to the Aboriginal culture-bearers in this field of endeavor. The elder sat at the front of the room with her two daughters, her son, and the two older girls, occasionally issuing instructions and urging the children to sing more loudly. It seemed that participation and enthusiasm (as indicated by dynamic volume) was viewed as the most important indicator of successful learning and performance of this song, as with the performance of the other language songs in the morning. In this regard the social aspect of participation, signifying belonging, was of prime importance, with inaccuracies of pitch being unremarked. In discussing "participatory performance" Turino notes that "quality of the performance is ultimately judged on the level of participation achieved . . . with little thought to how the music might sound," indicating that the concentration on mutual participation creates a "strong force for social bonding" (2008: 29). In this session the only points of accuracy that were continually corrected and reinforced related to the Mudburra language. The cultural marker of standard English was also used very sparingly for most of this session. Instructions were nearly all in Kriol, a pidgin language used as a lingua franca among Aboriginal people in parts of the Northern Territory (Walsh and Yallop 1993), Aboriginal English (a dialect of English), or Mudburra.

It was notable, then, that traditional Jingili or Mudburra songs did not appear to be part of any school activities, reflecting a general decline in their transmission to younger generations, particularly those with a genesis in Jingulu language. In a news article recounting a journey to sacred Jingili dreaming sites (Holland 2004: 15), linguist Rob Pensalfini noted that, though "[b]asic initiation ceremonies are still performed every year . . . as none of the youngest people speak Jingulu or know the songs by heart, there is a distinct possibility that soon the knowledge will be gone." It is also evident that, because a great proportion of traditional songs have usually been learned in a ceremonial context, as part of traditional initiation and other ceremonial practices, it is not appropriate for their transmission to take place in the context of the school.

Mudburra language was also not included in performance of playground games at this school because it was reported by two playground performers as "a bit hard to speak," despite the fact that it was a language spoken at home. However, it may be that all models for playground games have been in English and that there was not an Aboriginal tradition of musical play in this area. In an interview, the elder who supervised the Mudburra language maintenance program at the school told me that, as a young child, "a wild one" (initially without contact with Europeans) she stayed close to her mother and listened to the women telling stories or accompanied adults to collect "bush tucker" (food from naturally oc-curring plant and animal sources in the local environment). As an older child employed on the cattle station in this locality, she worked from 5:00 in the morning to 6:00 at night and therefore did not have much time to play. Because girls were married at the age of fifteen, female playmates were also limited. Although she remembered one game of skill, she had no memory of playing games involving singing or rhythmic movement. In this respect, practices appeared to differ in this location from those of the Warumungu people in the town of Telford Spring to the south, where a number of older women and men had shared with me songs and games they had played as children, involving chanting taunts to the moon, finger plays, tickling games, and song stories invoking the names of Dream-ing animals (I have discussed these in more detail in Marsh 2002 and 2008).

In contemporary times at Bradford Well, games were frequently learned from relatives, either on the playground, at home in Marlinja, in neighboring Auston, or far afield in Darwin or Borroloola, a favorite holiday destination for fishing. They were reportedly also "pulled up" from television programs (with *Playschool,* a national program aimed at preschool children being cited), but regardless of their derivation they seemed to retain their genesis as games originating from non-Aboriginal sources. This echoed the situation at another small homelands school, Maringa. There, playground games learned in the more populous town of Telford Spring were always played in English, though intervening in-structions were given in Kriol. At Bradford Well the only possible ex-ample of localization of text occurred in the clapping game "Down by the Billabong," which may have referred to the local water source that gave its name to the area. Though the players inserted their names and those of playmates into this song, it, like other games, seemed to be a marker of inclusion in a non-Aboriginal world, firmly associated with non-Aboriginal identity.

It is interesting that playground games in this school have not under-gone the transformation that I have witnessed in other localities, though the appropriation of game content from the media, and small structural adjustments—largely truncation of text and changes in the rhythmic emphasis in word setting associated with performing in a less familiar language (see Marsh 2008)—indicated that some dynamic processes of oral transmission were in evidence. Whereas games in a number of other field schools, both in Sydney and international locations, clearly marked ethnic identities, this was not the case at Bradford Well.

There was no playground corollary to the way in which some adult popular music styles have been used as vehicles for the expression of Aboriginal culture, even though there were models for this within the local Marlinja community (Dunbar-Hall 1997), both in the form of popular music recordings and language teaching songs. It may be that these musical games are a relatively new genre in this school, as attested by the Aboriginal teacher, Julie, who had only played musical games learned in the classroom in her own childhood (rather than the playground clapping games played by her daughter, a current student). Children may therefore have had limited opportunity to stamp them with their own imprimatur—a theory backed up by discussion with several of the game players, who all told me that they did not make up new games. Only markers of individual identity, in the form of players' names, denoted nascent forms of composition in performance at Bradford Well.

Despite the remoteness of this location, many musical influences shaped the musical identities of the children in this school. These ranged from children's songs through to the global popular music industry, filtered through local Aboriginal popular music and the performance experiences of the non-Aboriginal child, Peter. Through participation in various musical activities, different children could identify in multiple ways: as performers, composers, learners and teachers, but also as individuals and as members of the school and the Aboriginal or non-Aboriginal communities, supported by cultural and kinship ties and open to a wider world of music. At times their participatory membership in the music-learning community was enhanced, for example, by virtue of age (in the case of Emma and Nina) or performative prowess (as with Peter). However, at other times, different factors, such as Aboriginality, prevailed to endorse inclusion, as with the creation, teaching, learning, and performance of the Mudburra song "*Larrpa-Ngi-Nyi*."

The variable identities of the indigenous teachers of language through music at this school—as culture-bearers, popular music band members, teachers, parents, and kin—also contributed to quite fluid modes of teaching and learning, both formal and informal, teacher-directed and interactive, with recognition of indigenous knowledge, either through direct instruction or esteem (as accorded to the elder) being given due importance. The non-Aboriginal teacher's role also changed according to activity, from one of authority to one of participant in or facilitator of indigenous learning, where authority was ceded to the knowledgeable culture-bearers. It was evident that processes of consultation with the members of the larger indigenous school community were ongoing.

Environments for learning were also permeable, with formal music-learning and musical play activities both occurring in the liminal covered area and moving between the playground and classroom at different times. Playground games were learned at school, at home, and through association with friends and relatives in towns both close by and at a great geographical distance, though they seemed to largely retain their non-Aboriginal characteristics. My discussions with children at this school did not extend to an exploration of musical preferences, though children at the neighboring Auston school had a well-developed knowledge of, and expressed preferences for, current popular music hits (Marsh 2002 and 2008). The impact of current global popular music repertoire on the musical identities of children in this school is an area for further investigation.

This study illustrates in microcosmic form ways in which the classroom can be permeable in nature, and how the roles, relationships, and identities of the children and adults who inhabit the classroom are also quite fluid. Too often the supposed boundaries between, for example, the classroom and the playground or other informal learning environments, and the fixity of relationships between members of a community within and surrounding a school, are maintained, to the detriment of music-learning possibilities. Enabling opportunities for differing roles of students and teachers to emerge—for varying forms of musical ownership and engagement to be enacted, and for recognition of the multiple musical identities of students, staff, and community members and the resources on which they draw—can only result in enrichment of the school music-learning environment for all participants.

Acknowledgments

I wish to acknowledge the assistance of Papulu Apparr-kari Aboriginal Language and Culture Centre, L. Dixon, E. Dixon, J. Dixon, R. Dixon, and the children and staff of the school about which this chapter is written. I also wish to acknowledge the funding for this study provided by research grants from the Australian Research Council, Australian Institute of Aboriginal and Torres Strait Islander Studies, and the University of Sydney.

References

Campbell, Patricia Shehan. 2002. The Musical Cultures of Children. In *The Arts in Children's Lives: Context, Culture, and Curriculum*, ed. Liora Bresler and Christine Marmé Thompson, 57–69. Dordrecht, the Netherlands: Kluwer Academic Publishers.

Chadwick, Neil J. 1975. *A Descriptive Study of the Djingili Language*. Canberra: Aboriginal Studies Press.

Dunbar-Hall, Peter. 1997. Music and Meaning: The Aboriginal Rock Album. *Australian Aboriginal Studies* 1: 38–47.

Folkestad, Göran. 2002. National Identity and Music. In *Musical Identities*, ed. Raymond A. R. MacDonald, David J. Hargreaves, and Dorothy Miell, 151–162. Oxford: Oxford University Press.

Harris, Stephen. 1990. *Two Way Aboriginal Schooling: Educational Survival*. Canberra: Aboriginal Studies Press.

Holland, Miguel. 2004. A Walk in Jingili Country. *UQ News*, no. 538 (October 2004).

Keil, Charles, and Steven Feld. 1994. *Music Grooves*. Chicago: University of Chicago Press.

Lum, Chee-Hoo. 2007. *Musical Networks of Children: An Ethnography of Elementary School Children in Singapore*. PhD diss., University of Washington.

Marsh, Kathryn. 2002. Observations on a Case Study of Song Transmission and Preservation in two Aboriginal Communities: Dilemmas of a "Neo-Colonialist" in the Field. *Research Studies in Music Education* 19: 4–13.

———. 2008. *The Musical Playground: Global Tradition and Change in Children's Songs and Games*. New York: Oxford University Press.

Nash, David. 1984. The Warumungu's Reserves 1892–1962: A Case Study in Dispossession. *Australian Aboriginal Studies* 1: 2–16.

Pensalfini, Rob. 2001. On the Typological and Genetic Affiliation of Jingulu. In *Forty Years on: Ken Hale and Australian Languages*, ed. Jane Simpson, David Nash, Mary Laughren, Peter Austin, and Barry Alpher, 385–399. Canberra: Pacific Linguistics.

Slobin, Mark. 1993. *Subcultural Sounds: Micromusics of the West*. Hanover, N.H.: Wesleyan University Press.

Turino, Thomas. 2008. *Music as Social Life: The Politics of Participation*. Chicago: University of Chicago Press.

Walsh, Michael, and Colin Yallop. 1993. *Language and Culture in Aboriginal Australia*. Canberra: Aboriginal Studies Press.

Wenger, Etienne. 2000. Communities of practice and social learning systems. *Organization* 7 (2): 225–246.

TWO

Popular Music Listening as "Non-Resistance"

The Cultural Reproduction of Musical Identity in Japanese Families

KYOKO KOIZUMI

Popular music was once a symbol of youth rebellion against the older generation and its received traditions. Japan is no exception. In the 1960s, there was an extensive student movement, on whom the Beatles had a strong impact when the Fab Four gave a concert in Japan in 1966. The then postwar-born youth was called the *bītoruzu sedai* (the Beatles generation) as well as *sensou o shiranai kodomo-tachi* (the children who do not know World War II). For them, to listen to rock and protest folk song meant taking up peaceful "arms" against their parents' generation, who they thought bore the responsibility to stop incessant wars around the world.

However, there has been a recent tendency in Japan for young boys and girls to no longer rebel against their parents by listening to youth music. Instead, young Japanese people today seem to respect their parents' favorite music and even follow their parents' musical tastes. This reproduction of musical tastes involves a type of informal learning whereby children are nowadays acquiring their tastes and musical knowledge as listeners, partly from their parents, as well as from each other, the media, and the school. Why does this reproduction of musical tastes in the family occur? When did young people quit rebelling against their parents' generation through defiant listening to music? What does this cultural reproduction bring about, and how does it change the ways of listening and identities of Japanese youth? Finally, what are the implications of these changes for popular music studies in Japan?

In this chapter, I will show how popular music in Japan has transformed its meaning from a symbol of youth rebellion to a communication tool between young people and their parents. Mainly using qualitative methods, I investigated recent music-listening choices among young people in relation to their families. In this chapter I trace the life-histories of my informants in terms of which generations their family members belong to; then I analyze the transgenerational musical identities constructed within the family and by the media. As my research focus is not on special education or provision for the gifted but on ordinary listeners in everyday life, I excluded the families of professional musicians in my fieldwork. This research is a successor to Crafts et al. (1993) and DeNora (2000). While the former interviewed forty-one (from one-hundred-and-fifty people in total) listeners from children to middle-aged adults in New York State, the latter observed and interviewed fifty-two female listeners in Britain and the United States.

Before recounting my qualitative research, I first elucidate the characteristics of each generation, distinguishing between those born before the war and those born after. Then, based on the data from my interviews, I analyze the transgenerational musical identities constructed by the media as well as within the family.

JAPANESE BABY BOOMERS, "*DANKAI SEDAI*"

I conducted interviews with Japanese music-listeners aged 16 to 67. There were seventy informants, fifty from my ongoing fieldwork since 2007 and twenty from my previous fieldwork (1998–2001, Koizumi 2002, 2003). I first interviewed combinations of the children and parents of five families. During the interviews I asked either the mother or father, or the daughters or sons about family influences on their music-listening. Snowball sampling was then used to find informants to cooperate with my study on the *dankai* generation's musical styles. Interviews were conducted in Osaka, Kobe, Tokyo, Nagoya, Fukuoka and other Kyushu regions, as well as in the Tohoku region.

Findings suggest that the aforementioned tendency of nonresistant young listeners nowadays seems to start from the generation called *dankai junia* (junior). In Japan, "*dankai sedai*" corresponds to "baby boomer," and "*dankai junia*" indicates the children of the baby-boomer generation. As I will go on to show, Japanese young people's listening choices are recently attributable not to their class or particular family upbringing but to their generation.

As distinct from the United States, where baby boomers were born over a twenty-year period from around 1946 to 1964, in Japan the *first* baby-boomer generation (*dankai sedai*) was born in the space of three years from 1947 to 1949. As this generation's cluster is much larger (8 million in total) than other generations (the population of Japan as of 1 September 2009 is 12,754,000 persons),[1] this first baby-boomer generation is called *dankai*, which literally means "nodule" in Japanese. *Dankai* junior is the second baby-boomer generation, which occurred as a result of the "baby boom echo" of the first baby-boomer generation. Whereas the second US baby-boomer generation was born after 1978, the Japanese second baby-boomer generation (*dankai* junior) was born between 1971 and 1974. Having investigated young people's listening practices in postwar Japan, it seems likely that the emergence of the *dankai* junior generation has converted their ways of listening from resistance to obedience to their parents' generation.

CULTURAL REPRODUCTION AND THE CONSTRUCTION OF MUSICAL IDENTITY IN THE *DANKAI* FAMILY

The cultural reproduction of musical taste in the family is important to youth musical identity in contemporary Japan. In this chapter I regard musical identity as being "produced by means of repetitions of 'performative' or 'representational' practices," as Nicola Dibben discusses on gendered identity, quoting from Judith Butler and Teresa de Lauretis respectively (Dibben 2002: 119). She takes identity as "something we *do* rather than something we *are*" (ibid.: 120). This social-constructionist view of identity corresponds with Stuart Hall's views of cultural identity. In his essay on Caribbean identity, Hall considers identity as negotiable in various situations rather than as stable or unchanging (Hall 1990/1997). I will show how Japanese young people have negotiated their musical identities within their families since their childhood.

The transformation of ways of listening in Japan seems to start in 1989, which corresponded with the high-school graduation age (eighteen) of *dankai* junior.[2] Since this time, changes within Japanese contemporary society have emerged in various spheres of consumption and culture. The inheritance of musical cultural capital, or "inherited capital" (Bourdieu 1984), has given rise to what is known as the *dankai* family, which consists of *dankai sedai* parents and *dankai* junior children. In particular, musical tastes are frequently inherited between same-sex family members, that is, from a *dankai* mother to her daughter, and from a *dankai* father to his son. Through my fieldwork, I found it important to take into account this cultural reproduction of musical taste in the *dankai* family when investigating the social and cultural meanings of popular music in Japan since 1989.

Although Japanese sociologists have tended to analyze musical identities horizontally through youth networks (e.g., Minamida 2006), I would like to emphasize the significance of vertical networks in the family, that is to say, family members' transgenerational influences on the musical choices of young people in Japan. Before examining the reproduction of musical cultural capital in the family, we need to define *dankai* family more precisely. For Atsushi Miura, a Japanese marketing analyst, *dankai* juniors are different from *shinsei dankai* juniors (real second baby boomers), who were born over an eight-year period from around 1973 to 1980 (e.g., Miura 2007). Miura emphasizes a difference between these two categories of baby boomers, that is, *dankai* juniors and "real" *dankai* juniors. While the second baby boomers (born between 1971 and 1974) were defined by how many of them were born to *dankai* mothers (over 2 million each year), *shinsei dankai* juniors were defined by how many were born to either *dankai* fathers and *dankai* mothers, or both. Miura turned his attention to age gaps between husbands and wives in Japan. In general, women marry men two or three years older than they are. This is why *shinsei dankai* juniors were born, on average, two years after so-called *dankai* juniors.

Therefore, in this chapter, I regard *dankai* families in a broad sense. That is to say, I categorize my young informants' parents into five generations; prewar-born (born before 1940), pre-*dankai* (born between 1941 and 1946), *dankai* (born between 1947 and 1951), post-*dankai* (born between 1952 and 1959), and *shin-jinrui* (a new type of young people).

Shin-jinrui were born between 1958 and 1967, and correspond to the US Generation X in its status and value. Likewise, I will categorize my young informants into five groups: dankai, post-dankai, shin-jinrui, besides dankai junior (born between 1971 and 1980) and post-dankai junior (born after 1981).[3]

THE DANKAI FAMILY AND THE HEISEI ERA

There has been a change in ways of listening since 1989, because this was the last year of the Shōwa Era[4] and the first of the Heisei Era. For most Japanese the Shōwa Era (1926–1989) brought back bad memories of the country's defeat in World War II. When the Shōwa Emperor ended, most Japanese people thought a new, peaceful, and revitalized Japan would begin. However, the reality of the Heisei Era was quite different. Japan experienced an economic bubble that burst in the early 1990s, and, on the contrary, people were nostalgic for the Shōwa Era as an age of rapid growth for the Japanese economy, especially in the 1960s. In spite of this, the start of the Heisei Era marked the introduction of innovatory social and cultural values among young people in Japan today.

The shift from the Shōwa to the Heisei Era had a strong impact on the media, school culture, and the relationships among friends and family members in Japan. On the one hand, the dankai family has been problematized in Japan because it introduced serious social issues for young people, such as "parasite singles" as a result of friend-like relationships between dankai parents and dankai juniors. Parasite singles are single men and women aged between twenty and thirty-four who still live with their parents after graduation. It is said that parasite singles have become accustomed to a comfortable lifestyle in the home environment of the dankai family (Yamada 1999). On the other hand, the dankai family has elicited strong attention from the advertising industry because of the sheer size of the first and second baby boomers' populations as well as their eager desire for consumption. The negative and positive sides of the dankai family arise from the friend-like relationships between dankai parents and their children, called tomodachi oyako (see, e.g., Aim Creates 1996; Yomiuri Kōkoku-sha and Hai Raifu Kenkyū-sho 1999).

The reasons for the transformation of the social background of music listening styles in Japan since 1989, which corresponds with the graduation age of *dankai* junior from high school, are threefold: first, changes of musical media in everyday family lifestyles, such as car stereo equipment and karaoke; second, the end of visible school violence in around 1985 and the increase of invisible *ijime* (bullying) in school since then; and third, changes in favorite musical styles among *dankai* families and younger ones. These three changes surrounding young people have major implications for rethinking the musical culture of the Heisei Era in Japan.

Japanese marketing strategy has shrewdly encouraged this Heisei *dankai* family style, which is different from the previous relationship between parents and children in the Shōwa Era. The change of values after the appearance of the *dankai* family has been reflected in TV commercials since the middle 1990s (Dentsu Shōhisha Kenkyū Sentā 2005). For example, in 1994 Honda's family-type van, the Odyssey, became a commercial hit using the characters of the US film *The Addams Family* (directed by Barry Sonnenfeld 1991), and was consequently promoted as a marker of a new special friend-like bond between parent and child in the *dankai* family. Friend-like *haha-ko* (*dankai* mothers and *dankai*-junior daughters) have appeared in food commercials since 1998. Around the millennium, Toyota used car commercials to play on the image of the ideal father as family-oriented, having common interests with his children, and being loved by them. Correspondingly, the old image of the reticent, stubborn, and awkward father had disappeared from Japanese TV commercials by 2000.

MEDIA STRATEGIES FOR SELLING THE *DANKAI* GENERATION'S "CLASSICS"

Since 2000 the music industry in Japan has started to follow the *dankai* family phenomenon. For instance, the reuse of parents' generation's songs as repertoire for their children's favorite artists has come into prominence. The following are examples of songs revived from the parents' generation since 2000, all of which were mentioned by my informants in the interviews, who are fully aware of this musical recycling. The most famous example was a hit by a *dankai* male singer, Kenji Sawada, titled *"Tokio"* ("Tokyo" 1980), which was sung in SMAP's concerts and album in 2006. SMAP is now the most popular male idol group of Japanese pop music (J-pop). They are popular not only among young girls but also among their middle-aged mothers. Such transgenerational popularity encourages mothers and daughters (*haha-ko*) to go to SMAP concerts together. Sawada was the vocalist of the Tigers, one of the "group sounds" bands that imitated the Beatles in the 1960s. Sawada was popular among *dankai* female fans, while "*Tokio*" is nostalgic for teenage girls' mothers in their thirties or forties. It is obvious that SMAP performed "*Tokio*" for the mother-daughter combination of concert-goers. When I introduced Sawada's version of "*Tokio*" in my class, one of my female students came to me and said "I know '*Tokio*' because SMAP sings it. My mother likes it and she was delighted to listen this song when we went to a SMAP concert together."

Another example was a revival of "*Amairo no Kami no Otome*" ("The Girl with the Flaxen Hair") in 2002, sung by Hitomi Shimatani. This song was originally sung by the Village Singers, a Japanese group sounds band in 1968. One of my female informants (born in 1957) said, "This is my generation's song." The success of this song triggered off a chain of cover versions of 1960s and '70s hit songs to attract both parents and their teenage children in the *dankai* family.

In addition to 1980s hit songs and group sounds hits, 1960s and '70s Japanese protest folk songs by Wataru Takada, Takuro Yoshida, or Shigeru Izumiya are also covered. The repertoire of the indie band Gagaga SP, who emerged in 2000, is distinguished from other bands of their generation by its enthusiasm for covering the *dankai* generation's hit songs. The band's particular feelings about 1970s folk songs were cultivated through their musical socialization in their home town. Kozak Maeda, the vocalist of Gagaga SP, born in 1979, belongs to *shinsei dankai* junior. Maeda was influenced by his local folk song pub, in Japanese, *fōku kissa* or *fōku sakaba*. Folk song pubs have been popular among Japanese businessmen in their forties and fifties (in Japan, *fōku sedai*, the folk generation, is the post-*dankai* generation and the first half of *shin-jinrui*) since around 2000. Here they can play acoustic guitars and sing 1960s and '70s folk songs. The guitarist Gagaga SP, Satoshi Yamamoto, born in 1981, post-*dankai*, used to listen to his father playing and singing folk songs (*Asahi Shimbun* 2002). It is interesting that while Yamamoto reproduces his father's cultural capital *inherited* as band repertoire, Maeda reuses his cultural knowledge *acquired* at the folk song pub. When I visited a folk song pub in Fukuoka city in 2008,[5] a young woman of twenty-three (born in 1985, post-*dankai*) played guitar and sang Takuro Yoshida's folk songs from the 1970s. Among middle-aged visitors, she was the youngest and looked like the other visitors' daughters. I asked her how it was that she knew songs by Takuro Yoshida, whose fans are mainly in their fifties. She told me that she had been an enthusiast of Gagaga SP since she was eighteen and had become interested in Yoshida's and Shigeru Izumiya's 1970s folk songs through going to Gagaga SP's gigs. It is worth noticing that the musical identities of Heisei youth have been constructed by listening to and playing Shōwa folk songs.

> I even sing 1970s folk song at karaoke that my friends don't know, but it's OK because they usually focus on which songs they will sing next, and don't listen to what other members of karaoke actually sing.

Finally, in a Japanese hit film titled *Waterboys* (directed by Shinobu Yaguchi 2001), hit numbers from Western European pop songs (*yōgaku*) such as the Ventures' "Diamond Head" (1965), Sylvie Vartan's "*Irresist-iblement*" (1968), and Japanese hit songs (*hōgaku*), such as Mina Aoe's "*Isezaki-cho* Blues" (1968) and Finger Five's "*Gakuen Tengoku*" ("School Heaven") (1974), were effectively inserted into the soundtrack to enhance the comic mood of the film. According to the producer, he chose songs for this film from the "classics" of "eternally loved pop music across the generations."[6] This film was made as a tribute to the *dankai* generation's musical idols, Tadao Inoue (a member of a group sounds band and the composer of "*Gakuen Tengoku*" mentioned above) and Mina Aoe, who both passed away in 2000. Through this film, which is a story about a male synchronized-swimming club at a high school, young audiences became familiar with 1960s and '70s hit songs of the *dankai* and post-*dankai* generations. My male informant (age forty-four at the interview time, born in 1964) said, "My son (then seventeen) is familiar with Sylvie Vartan because it was used in *Waterboys*."

WHAT IS "STANDARD" AFTER THE MILLENNIUM?

Does the reuse of the parents' generation's songs, as described above, become "standard" in musical culture in 2000s Japan? In my previous ethnographic studies (Koizumi 2002 and 2003), I found that the musical identity of Japanese youth is not fixed. Rather, they tend to change their "favorite songs" just as they wear different clothes in everyday life depending on where they go and who they meet. Three categories of popular music that have emerged from my fieldwork can be used to explain how young people vary their favorite songs to communicate in different relationships, such as with friends or family members. This tripartite categorization of popular music—personal music, common music, and standard music—is not equivalent to particular styles of popular music. "Personal music" equates to private musical tastes. "Common music" is shared within the same generation, but not with older generations such as parents or teachers. The karaoke repertoire is representative of common music. "Standard music" is shared across different generations, including parents and children. When I did my fieldwork before 2000, only standard music could become shared popular music between parents and children. However, after the millennium, as a result of the appearance of the *dankai* family, children's personal musics seem to be "promoted" as standard music to be shared with *dankai* parents and *dankai* junior children. Thus standard music can be reproduced not only through the media but also at home. In fact, new standard numbers can be made from the *dankai* junior children generation's songs, such as SMAP's "*Sekai ni Hitotsu dakeno Hana*" ("The One and Only Flower in the World," 2003), *dankai* classics are not the only resources to be upgraded to the representative standard of the Heisei Era. In the last two sections, I explore forms of communication among family members in order to consider what is regarded as standard at the micro-level after 2000.

THE REPRODUCTION OF MUSICAL IDENTITY FROM MOTHERS TO DAUGHTERS

In this section, to analyze the reproduction of musical cultural capital from mothers to daughters, I categorize the combined ages of mothers and daughters into four types. The first category comprises mothers born before the war in the 1920s, and *dankai* daughters, who were born in the late 1940s. According to *dankai* daughters, they can still sing the military songs (*gunka*) that their mothers used to sing. As these mothers experienced World War II, the postwar *dankai* daughters knew military songs by ear. The mass media, such as radio and television, were listened to and watched by all family members, sometimes with neighbors. Television was so expensive and such a rare "treasure" in the 1950s, but it spread into ordinary homes after the marriage of the Heisei emperor (1959) and the Tokyo Olympic Games (1964). Through their family environments, *dankai* daughters have developed a broad range of musical tastes from *enka* (a traditional Japanese popular song, usually concerning sad stories about the separation of adult lovers) to the United States–originated oldies by, for instance, Paul Anka and Neil Sedaka. The cover versions of English and Japanese oldies from the 1960s, which are frequently sung on television, make *dankai* daughters nostalgic for their families, because they were familiar with them in their youth.

The second category comprises pre-*dankai* mothers, who were born in the early 1940s, and *shin-jinrui* daughters, who were born in the mid-1960s. My informants said that if pre-*dankai* mothers used to like the theme songs of American or European films, their daughters acquired an interest in musicals or other incidental music.

The third category is *dankai* mothers, who were born around 1950, and *dankai* junior daughters, who were born in the mid-1970s. As *dankai* mothers like music from *enka* to oldies, as mentioned above, they are also fond of going to the karaoke box with their daughters, who thereby become familiar with their *dankai* mothers' repertoire. One informant, thirty-one years old in 2007 (born in 1976, *shinsei dankai* junior), remembered the following episode:

> I know Teresa Teng's songs clearly, although she is not my generation's singer. I never saw her on TV. I feel strange and come to notice that my mother used to listen to Teresa Teng's songs on a cassette tape recorder in the kitchen. My mother sings her songs when we go to karaoke together. That is why I memorize her songs unconsciously.

The late Teresa Teng, a female Taiwanese singer, was popular among the *dankai* generation in Japan. This informant's mother was born in 1950 (*dankai*) and liked her songs too. To my eyes, this is a typical *dankai* family, because they go together as friends to karaoke and other musical activities.

Finally there are the post-*dankai* mothers, who were born in the mid-1950s, and post-*dankai* junior daughters, who were born in the early 1980s. In this combination, for the first time, the daughters' musical identities influence their mothers' musical tastes. While the mothers like the Southern All Stars (an enduringly popular rock band in Japan, like the Rolling Stones in the UK) and the daughters sing their hit song "Tsunami," the mothers listen to their daughters' favorite music, such as *anime* songs, SMAP, TM Revolution (visual J-rock male idol), or Ken Hirai (gospel-type male singer), and perhaps they even go to their concerts together.

THE REPRODUCTION OF MUSICAL IDENTITY FROM FATHERS TO SONS

What about the reproduction of musical cultural capital from fathers to sons? Father-son combinations are also categorized into four types. The first category is fathers born before the war, in about 1920, and *dankai* sons who were born in the late 1940s. Because these fathers, survivors of World War II, sang military songs, *rōkyoku* (a form of recitation born in the nineteenth century in Osaka Town) and *Shōwa kayō* (popular songs in the Shōwa Era, especially in the 1950s and 60s) at home, *dankai* sons are familiar with these old Japanese songs. Radio and television also made a strong impact on *dankai* sons' musical experiences.

The second group comprises the *dankai* fathers who were born around 1950 and their *dankai* junior sons, born in the late 1970s. One of the *dankai* fathers (born in 1949) said, "My son's favorite music is unintelligible." The *dankai* junior group saw its heyday in visual *kei* (rock emphasizing the visual impact, with male members in gaudy costumes and heavy makeup) in the 1990s, and visual J-rock bands were unpopular and even notorious among *dankai* fathers for the female-associated aspects of their appearance. *Dankai* fathers harbor a clandestine interest in what their sons are listening to. One of my *dankai* informants admitted that he secretly borrowed his son's Walkman to listen to Mr. Children, one of the most popular J-pop bands in contemporary Japan, liked by both *dankai* junior and younger generations.

Third, there are the post-*dankai* fathers (born in the mid-1950s) and post-*dankai* junior sons (born in the early 1980s). Post-*dankai* fathers are often fond of British or American classic rock and encourage their sons to play in bands.

Finally, *shin-jinrui* fathers (born between 1958 and 1967) are also pleased to support their Heisei-born (early 1990s) sons. Conversely, one Heisei-born son introduced the ukulele player Jake Shimabukuro (Japanese-American born in Honolulu) to his father, and they went to Jake's gig together. This Heisei-born son recognized that his musical tastes came from the car stereo system on which his father played British rock while driving. His father said that he would not like his son to spend time playing meaningless computer games. Instead, he bought a Fender guitar for his son to experience "real" guitar sounds. It seems that the construction of the musical identity of children through repeated listening to their parents' favorite songs in the family car and living room began in Japan in the mid-1980s. A musical bond between father and son would have been an impossibility before this change of family values from pre-*dankai* to *dankai*.

It is likely that the reproduction of *yōgaku* (Western-European pop/rock) in the family started after the emergence of the *dankai* family. However, if parents born before the war used to listen to *yōgaku* in their youth, their children tended to inherit their musical tastes through the general process of socialization in the family. In the *dankai sedai* childhood, television was more likely to construct the *dankai* musical orientation to *yōgaku* than their parents' musical tastes.

There are gender differences between mother-daughter and father-son relationships. Whereas *dankai* and post-*dankai* mothers do not hesitate to share musical tastes with their daughters, *dankai* and post-*dankai* fathers do not accept their sons' favorite artists, or often secretly listen to their sons' Walkmans to hear new genres of music. It is the *shin-jinrui* father who is willing to share his son's musical tastes.

The inherited capital of the parent is successfully reproduced in the family. It is most effective when there are shared musical practices, such as going to karaoke and concerts together, or musical instruments and equipment, such as a car stereo system and CDs in the living room, or a Fender guitar. While the former corresponds to cultural capital in the embodied state in Bourdieu's term, the latter corresponds to cultural capital in the objectified state (Bourdieu 1986).

This chapter has focused on music-listeners in everyday life rather than on professional performers. However, similar inherited musical capital was found across generations in a study of musicians' families in Britain (Borthwick and Davidson 2002). It would be well worth comparing performers and listeners across generations with reference to the family.

The *dankai* family is a social and cultural outcome of the "roaring sixties" in Japan. The *dankai* father, who had been a Beatles generation lad, played guitar as a hobby in his thirties or forties, and his son has grown up watching and imitating his father. *Dankai* mothers are willing to sing their generation's songs from oldies to *enka* with their daughters. Such new types of relationship between parents and children have changed family values, the meaning of cultural reproduction, and the musical identity of Japanese young people.

Acknowledgment

This chapter grew out of a paper read at the Inter-Asia Popular Music Studies Conference 2008 (Osaka City University July 2008). I give my thanks to conference participants for their comments.

Notes

1. Statistics Bureau, Director-General for Policy Planning (Statistical Standards) & Statistical Research and Training Institute, Ministry of Internal Affairs and Communications (http://www.stat.go.jp/data/jinsui/tsuki/index.htm, accessed 26 September 2009).

2. In the Japanese school system, compulsory education starts with primary school (age six) and finishes at the end of junior high school (age fifteen). After graduation, high school runs from age fifteen to eighteen.

3. Although defining each generation in Japan more precisely is beyond the scope of this investigation, I note here that Iwama (1995) gives us a clear picture of the difference between *dankai, shin-jinrui,* and *dankai* junior.

4. In Japan, the reign of an emperor is designated as an era.

5. Fukuoka city is situated in the Kyushu area of Japan and is a famous birthplace for many folk singers. It is still such a strong focus for local popular music scenes that it is called the Japanese Liverpool. See Masubuchi (2005).

6. See the official site of the *Waterboys* (http://www.altamira.jp/waterboys/music.html, accessed 26 September 2009).

References

Aim Creates. 1996. *Seikimatsu yangu eiji seitai zukan: Taipu-betsu kanzen kaisetsu, dankai junia no sutorīto karuchā (Youth Culture Illustrated: Street Culture of Dankai Junior).* Tokyo: Diamond-sha. (In Japanese.)

Asahi Shimbun (newspaper). 2002. Gagaga SP wa shimittareta mama mae ni susumu [Gagaga SP Goes Ahead Still Being Miserable]. 14 March: 14. (In Japanese.)

Borthwick, Sophia J., and Jane W. Davidson. 2002. Developing a Child's Identity as a Musician: A Family "Script" Perspective. In *Musical Identities*, ed. Raymond A. R. MacDonald, David J. Hargreaves, and Dorothy Miell, 60–77. Oxford: Oxford University Press.

Bourdieu, Pierre. 1984. *Distinction: A Social Critique of the Judgement of Taste*, trans. R. Nice (first published as *La distinction: Critique sociale du jugement*, 1979). London: Sage.

———. 1986. The Forms of Capital. In *Handbook of Theory and Research for the Sociology of Education*, ed. John G. Richardson, 241–258. London: Greenwood Press.

Crafts, Susan D., Daniel Cavicchi, Charles Keil, and the Music in Daily Life Project. 1993. *My Music*. Hanover: Wesleyan University Press.

DeNora, Tia. 2000. *Music in Everyday Life*. Cambridge: Cambridge University Press.

Dentsu Shōhisha Kenkyū Sentā, eds. 2005. *Dankai to dankai junia no kazoku-gaku: Heisei kakudai kazoku* (*A Study on Family of the First and Second Baby Boomers: Heisei Extended Family*). Tokyo: Dentsu. (In Japanese.)

Dibben, Nicola. 2002. Gender Identity and Music. In *Musical Identities*, ed. Raymond A. R. MacDonald, David J. Hargreaves, and Dorothy Miell, 117–133. Oxford: Oxford University Press.

Hall, Stuart. 1990/1997. Cultural Identity and Diaspora. In *Identity and Difference*, ed. Kathryn Woodward, 51–58. London: Sage.

Iwama, Natsuki. 1995. *Sengo sakamono bunka no kōbō* (*A Beam of Light of Youth Culture after World War II*). Tokyo: Nihon Keizai Shimbun-sha. (In Japanese.)

Koizumi, Kyoko. 2002. Popular Music, Gender and High School Pupils in Japan: Personal Music in School and Leisure Sites. *Popular Music* 21 (1): 107–125.

———. 2003. Popular Music in Japanese School and Leisure Sites: Learning Space, Musical Practice and Gender. PhD diss., University of London Institute of Education.

Masubuchi, Toshiyuki. 2005. Kokunai chihou toshi ni okeru ongaku no sangyō-ka katei: Fukuoka-shi no baai (The Industrialization Process of Music in a Local City of Japan: The Case of Fukuoka. *Popyurā ongaku kenkyū* (*Popular Music Studies*) no. 9 (2005): 3–21.

Minamida, Katsuya. 2006. Wakamono no ongaku seikatsu no genzai (Recent Musical Life of Young People). In *Kenshō wakamono no henbō: Ushinawareta 10 nen no nochi-ni* (*Verifying the Metamorphosis of Young People: After the Lost Decade*), ed. Tomohiko Asano, 37–72. Tokyo: Keiso Shobo. (In Japanese.)

Miura, Atsushi. 2007. *Dankai kakusa* (*Disparity among Baby Boomers*). Tokyo: Bungei Shunjū. (In Japanese.)

Yamada, Masahiro. 1999. *Parasaito shinguru no jidai* (The Age of the Parasite Single). Tokyo: Chikuma-shobo. (In Japanese.)

Yomiuri Kōkoku-sha and Hai Raifu Kenkyū-sho, eds. 1999. *Konseputo 2000 dankai kazoku: 20 no kī wādo de yomu dankai to dankai junia* (*Concept 2000 Baby Boomer's Family: Reading the First and Second Baby Boomers by 20 Key Words*). Kyoto: PHP Kenkyū-sho. (In Japanese.)

THREE

From Homeland to Hong Kong

The Dual Musical Experience and Identity of Diasporic Filipino Women

ANNIE ON NEI MOK

How is it that Filipinos are able to sing in spontaneous harmony without notation, I wonder? Hong Kong people are always commenting on how musical the many Filipinos living in that city are, as they have an obvious love of singing and performing. I am constantly amazed by the way so many of them can sing in harmony instantly without referring to a musical score. It seems that music comes into their heads naturally. This is a mystery to me as a music educator and classically trained musician, since I am unable to do it myself, despite my formal education.

I gained some insights into this issue after teaching a music course to a group of Filipino women in Hong Kong. In one lesson I gave them a hymnal and asked them to form into groups to choose a song they liked. I noticed that they tried to harmonize it aurally and orally without the help of a piano and without referring to the written four-part harmony supplied in the hymnal. They accomplished this by a process of trial and error, with feedback and comments also being given by group members. In the end, a number of them were able to sing in two-part harmony simultaneously, quite happily and seemingly without difficulty. I stood beside them to look at the score and was astonished to discover that their harmony was close to the printed one, with only some slight differences. After their performance, I asked them how they had managed to sing the two-part harmony. They simply answered, "Once we have sung a song, we have the harmony in our heads." I was surprised and inspired!

This became the starting point for my research journey, and it is the focus of the present chapter. The main questions I will address are: What kind of musical enculturation had these women experienced? How did they learn to add a harmony line to a song? How had their musical abilities developed once they settled in Hong Kong? What are some of the differences they perceive between learning in the Philippines and in Hong Kong? As a diasporic group, what do the women think of these two kinds of learning experience? Finally, in what ways have their musical enculturation and learning experiences affected their identities? From their accounts of their experiences, I will describe how they acquired and developed their skills using various methods of self-learning both in their early years in the Philippines and later in Hong Kong. I will show how their early musical enculturation gave them a basic love of music that became a significant aspect of their later lives. In particular, the diasporic context in which the women now live revealed some interesting and unexpected findings concerning their views of their music-learning practices and their musical identities.

FILIPINOS IN HONG KONG

A visitor to Hong Kong may be surprised by the number of Filipinos who live in the territory. The local Filipinos are the largest ethnic minority group in Hong Kong, making up 2.1 percent of the total 5.1 percent of the Hong Kong population represented by ethnic minorities in 2001. Since the Filipinos are literate in English, which is taught in schools in the Philippines, they are able to work overseas. As the GDP (gross domestic product) per capita income in the Philippines is US $1,866, compared with US $30,755 in Hong Kong,[1] a number of Filipinos therefore leave their country to work in Hong Kong for financial reasons. Most of the Filipinos in Hong Kong are females who come to work as maids in local families. Yet what they can earn from Hong Kong can support their whole family abundantly in the Philippines. They work for six days and have one day off every week, normally Sunday. On Sundays they usually congregate in some popular gathering spots. While most have a rest and chat with their friends, some may sing and dance informally in public. As more than 90 percent of the population is Christian (of which 80 percent is Roman Catholic), some Filipino maids may choose to attend a Sunday Service in local Filipino churches in Hong Kong.

In order to investigate how they learn their music and to understand their musical enculturation, I interviewed six Filipino maids in depth: Joy, Theresa, Diana, Marilou, Elma, and Mildred (all these names are fictitious). As they came to Hong Kong when they were already adults, they had received their education and early musical enculturation in the Philippines. All six were active music-makers who belonged to church choirs in local Filipino Baptist churches in Hong Kong. I also observed one of their Sunday services. Below are the stories they told concerning their music-learning experiences in the Philippines and in Hong Kong.

MUSICAL ENCULTURATION IN THE PHILIPPINES

Merriam (1964), who followed the lead of Herskovits, explains that enculturation is "the process by which the individual learns his culture, and it must be emphasized that this is a never-ending process continuing throughout the life span of the individual" (Merriam 1964: 146). Green (2004) explains that musical enculturation includes the process of immersion in music and music-making practices of the surrounding community by listening, watching, and imitating. With regard to the settings in which musical enculturation takes place, Campbell (1991) postulates that "it encompasses the varied musical experiences which children have as they grow up within families, neighborhood, schools and various constituent communities" (47). The lifelong process of enculturation can thus take place anywhere, and is not confined to a specific setting.

As children in the Philippines, the Filipino informants who took part in the present study had ample opportunities to listen to their parents' and relatives' live singing performances. They even retained vivid memories of how they sang. Singing at home had no special purpose but was done for enjoyment. Diana said that both her father's and mother's families were musically inclined. Even her great-grandparents were musicians. Her father used to be a lead singer and a keyboard player in a band, with his brothers playing other instruments. All the members of her family were either singers or dancers. When they were together, they would always be singing and playing along with each other. She said that they were all connected in some way with music, that "it's in-born or something that I really like music. Because we were brought up with music."

The families and relatives of Elma and Marilou also loved music and were active performers. Elma started listening to live music performed by her parents when she was small: "I heard her [her mother] singing, actually my family loves music, all of us can sing." Marilou shared a similar musical enculturation experience. Her musical enculturation process started with her immediate family, but she mentioned that other relatives would also play live music to her: "When we were young, my father played the music, my mother sang, and then all my uncles played different kinds of instruments..."

This kind of family influence was also reported by Mildred, Joy, and Theresa. Mildred's father played the guitar in his spare time. Her relatives and the whole family had a band. Theresa's mother would sing around the house, and she also recalled how her aunts sang in harmony. Joy was particularly in awe of the musical devotion of her grandmother, who would get up at four o'clock in the morning to pray and sing. The song "Merciful is God, God is magnificent," sung by her grandmother, came to have a special meaning for her.

FROM HOMELAND TO HONG KONG

SELF-REGULATED LISTENING

Self-regulated listening is a method of learning that can be divided into three levels as suggested by Green (2002): purposive, attentive, and distracted listening. Listening in a purposive way means that the listening has the "particular aim, or purpose, of learning something in order to put it to use in some way after the listening experience is over" (23–24). Attentive listening refers to those listening activities that do not have "any specific aim of learning something in order to be able to play, remember, compare or describe it afterward," even if one listens in as much detail as in purposive listening (24). Therefore, the difference between purposive and attentive listening lies in the intention rather than in the amount of detail in which the music is listened to. The third level is distracted listening, in which a listener listens without any specific aim but purely for enjoyment, entertainment, or as background music.

Bennett (1980), in his discussion of popular music-learning, describes how a musician can learn a song from a recording by sitting in front of a stereo with his/her guitar and playing along with the record over and over again. Learning from the internet has also become an important method of self-regulated learning, not only in Western or developed regions of the world; for example, Mans (2007) has already acknowledged the powerful impact of the electronic media in her study of African musical worlds. Self-regulated listening was found to be one of the learning practices used by the Filipino informants both in their homeland and after they moved to Hong Kong. Below is a description of their use of self-regulated listening as defined by Green.

Joy gave a detailed description of how people learn to sing harmony to a song by means of purposive listening in the Philippines. This sheds light on the way they are able to get the harmony instantly without referring to a musical score:

> We, as Filipinos, have a special talent of doing that; once I hear that, like for example, we will sing, you will sing, the melody, then I just listen [to] it, and then I can catch how can I blend [with] your voices, usually the Filipinos can do it. What we call, just learning from listening. We listen to songs, and then we blend it in our mind, what is . . . the melody of that, and then we can, [fit in] another voice for harmonizing the song, we have a talent in that . . .

Joy learned aurally by simultaneously adding the harmony to a melody sung by others, which is also a type of purposive listening. She would listen and adjust the harmony so that the main melody and the harmony would blend together. This requires listening purposively with a sharp ear.

After moving to Hong Kong, however, all six Filipino informants developed a new habit of listening to recordings, since these are more readily available in Hong Kong than in the Philippines. Diana, Theresa, Marilou, and Mildred are always listening in order to learn music, but this aural method is different from the description given by Joy above. Diana sings in a small ensemble, and sometimes the songs they choose may only be found on a recording, so if she wants to sing the soprano part, she needs to listen intensively in order to learn the melody. Theresa helps the other choir members, in particular with working out the alto part, and copies the harmony entirely by means of purposive listening from recordings. Marilou uses recordings to help her choir members learn their respective vocal parts, which is a common learning method for them. Mildred once memorized a song from a recording by listening repeatedly to the tape.

In summary, when they were in the Philippines they listened to live music for the purpose of self-regulated learning, whereas in Hong Kong they listen to recordings instead of live music.

SELF-LEARNING BY TRIAL AND ERROR

According to Finnegan (2007), self-learning has two major features: The fact that the musician teaches him- or herself and does not receive tuition from another person, and the fact that the learning process takes place "on the job," or in other words, while playing the music. Also included is the fact that self-learning often involves learning how to play without depending on written music.

In the present study, all six Filipinos described their self-learning as a process of trial and error. Mildred emphasized the importance of self-learning and of continuing to practice. When she is listening to a melody, she "hums" another part of her own. When asked about where she learned the skill, she said, "Yeah, I think, self-learning, something like that. Just self-learning." Later she said, "Yeah, just like that, just humming my part and then later on if I keep on practicing and practicing I can go with them . . ." Other comments included: "So usually, when you listen to a song, so then you hum, humming your part."

Marilou started to learn the guitar by observing how her uncle, aunt, and other people played. She then learned to play it herself and also learned plucking techniques and how to tune it. In Hong Kong, Diana learned how to play the drum kit on her own by listening and following the players from her church. Joy did not explicitly mention how she taught herself music. However, she did say that she was willing and eager to learn everything about music. She said she must continue to learn through "trial and error" in order to become proficient. Elma stated that she is able to learn music by herself because she loves music.

Theresa's learning had followed a different path from the others. Un-expectedly, she told me that she had not been able to sing in harmony when she was in the Philippines, but that she could do so now in Hong

Kong, and on further inquiry she confirmed that she had acquired this ability in Hong Kong, not in the Philippines. Although as a child she heard her mother singing around the house, her mother did not encourage her or her siblings to have any interest in music. As she came from a poor family, she described her parents saying to her and her siblings, "Go on whatever skill you can discover of yourself, then just go ahead, as long as there's no money involved. . . ." When she came to Hong Kong, she had more opportunities to listen to music on the radio. She would try to put a harmony part to the music while she listened. Eventually she discovered that she could do it without a score. She explained that while in the Philippines she was unable to concentrate sufficiently to practice this skill because there were always distractions. When I asked her why she had been able to learn the skill in Hong Kong but not in the Philippines, she said:

> Yes, because you see in Hong Kong, I mean, you have no outlet, sometimes when you're in the house of your employers. There are no people you will talk to. While in Philippines there are just a few times you listen to music because you, go and play, you know. You do something a lot in the house, something like that, that's why I discovered when I was in Hong Kong, after listening to the music, I can put [in] the harmony.

In her case, what might be considered a disadvantage had become a blessing. Her solitariness had enabled her to concentrate on music, which eventually led her to discover that she had this aural ability. Now she has become proficient in finding or adding a harmony part to a melody. Also, she said that she did not have much opportunity to do it when she was in the Philippines but that now she can do it every Sunday, and that she has discovered her talent through her service to God.

In conclusion, the Filipinos said that they have "listening ears." They listen to the melody of a song and then they will "experiment" by blending their voices with it. After listening carefully and trying to sing the harmony, by means of a process of trial and error, they will succeed in fitting another voice to it. Joy said that in the Philippines most people can do this but that it takes time and effort to discover and develop the ability. Although it seems that Filipinos have this special talent, their ability to sing in harmony is not acquired without effort, nor is it innate; but it is the result of attentive practice, as well as social interaction and enculturation within specific sociocultural contexts.

A SECOND BREATH: NEW MUSIC-LEARNING EXPERIENCES IN HONG KONG

Once they had settled in Hong Kong, some of the informants had the opportunity to learn to play the piano from a tutor. Learning to play the piano, an experience they were unlikely to have in the Philippines, became an important part of their new musical identity. Mildred enrolled at a private studio but she could only afford to pay for six months' tuition. Theresa and Marilou learned from private piano teachers through the following means. Theresa's piano teacher was a Christian and was willing to accept a reduced "Christian rate" tuition fee, but even so Theresa could only afford to study for a year. Marilou also learned from two private piano teachers. All the above three Filipinos women, together with Elma, continued learning to play the piano in a class at the Baptist Seminary in Hong Kong. This was a three-month course that helped them to acquire some piano techniques so they could serve their church better musically.

Apart from learning the piano as mentioned above, some informants had the opportunity to learn it in a different way. Unlike formal piano lessons, which usually involve direct teaching carried out by a tutor and which follow a systematic, graded curriculum leading to a clear public examination goal and a certificate, two of the Filipinos had learned the piano in an unusual way. Although this learning involved a tutor, the tutor did not directly "teach" them. Instead, they learned to play by means of purposive observations and by listening to the lessons of their employer's son/daughter given by a piano tutor. They also learned from the employers' children when they practiced after the teacher had left. They then copied what the children had been doing and practiced on their own.

For example, Joy mentioned that she learned the piano by listening to her employer's daughter's practice and playing, and Elma said that she learned simply by listening and copying when her employer's son or daughter learned at home.

AM: So, you have the chance to play piano with the little children?

ELMA: Yes, when the teacher comes, I learn it. My ears, I am doing the duties and hear, this is how you play . . .

THEIR VIEWS OF THEIR DUAL
MUSICAL EXPERIENCES

The above account has demonstrated that the Filipino informants received a rich musical enculturation and developed informal learning practices in their homeland, while they had acquired new music-learning experiences since they had been living in Hong Kong. As Campbell (1998) notes, the musical enculturation process continues even when an individual changes cultures and becomes a member of a new sociocultural group. The Filipinos thus became immersed in a new enculturation process after they moved to Hong Kong. They have a "better" living and social environment where they can live in a "proper" house with city electricity and a constant supply of running water. In their hometowns, they may have lived in a remote area in a simple hut with minimal facilities. In Hong Kong, therefore, they have more opportunities to be exposed to a variety of musical genres through listening to CDs, to RTHK 4 (a classical music radio channel), or watching DVDs at home, all of which can broaden their musical horizons. In this way, their new musical enculturation and learning experiences may affect their musical identities. It was therefore interesting to investigate what the informants themselves thought of this dual musical experience. Which experience do they think is better? Which one do they prefer?

From my perspective as a formally trained musician, the Filipinos' ability to spontaneously harmonize, their freely available communal musical activities, and many of their skills, are enviable. I was therefore not quite prepared when, unexpectedly, five of the six Filipinos said they thought that the music-learning environment in Hong Kong was "better" for them than that in the Philippines. Theresa said, "Yes, I am so exposed to music now, not in the Philippines." Diana added: "People in this city [Hong Kong], have a future in music; in the mountains, [in a] remote area [in the Philippines], chances are not so high." Marilou felt that musical life in Hong Kong generally was more balanced than that in the Philippines:

MARILOU: The musical atmosphere in Hong Kong, I think it's balanced, because they have opera, they have, like, love songs, you know, people like love songs, and they have rock songs, they have hip-hop songs, for the teenagers, so I think I can see that it's balanced.

Mildred said that she started to love Western operatic music because her employer often listens to it. Her employer even allows her to take CDs to listen to in her own bedroom. It was quite unexpected that the musical environment and atmosphere in Hong Kong had triggered her emotion about her unfinished business in music. She was the one who had probably the strongest feeling that the musical learning environment in Hong Kong was better. She exclaimed, "Of course here, of course here!" Mildred expressed regret that Filipinos do not have the same opportunities to learn as Hong Kong people. It seems to be her dream to acquire a formal education in music. She said that if she had more money, she would spend more time studying in order to learn more. When I asked her whether, if she had a child, she would like him or her to learn music by ear with friends or to follow a formal learning pattern, she exclaimed,

MILDRED: I wish I could send my children to a music school because I missed that part in my life, you know, to learn more music, in a wide idea of music, you know, because I love music.

Yet she mentioned that her relatives and the whole family had a band. When she visited them, all they did was sing. That was how they used their leisure time. It seems that what she missed was just formal learning in music, not the enjoyment of music in her everyday life.

Four Filipinos emphasized the fact that they could learn more in Hong Kong than in the Philippines, and it seems that they identified with their new musical experiences more than with what they experienced in the Philippines. There were three main reasons for this. First, there is a greater variety of instruments and technology available in Hong Kong, whereas in the Philippines they mainly had just a guitar for accompaniment and it was rare to learn the piano. Elma said that the number of different instruments available in Hong Kong was an eye-opener to her. In the Philippines, however, they explained that only the very rich can afford a piano, although they may not actually be able to play it. Pianos in the houses of rich people are just for display. Second, as already discussed, since all six informants had access to a piano at their employer's home, they had an opportunity to learn that they might never have dreamed of if they had still been in the Philippines. The informants now had the opportunity to watch how their employer's son or daughter learned the piano at home, which had opened them up to a new musical phase in their lives. Third, the advanced technology of Hong Kong had widened their musical horizons. They pointed out that they could access the internet to download music, which allowed them to enter a wider musical world, helping them go beyond the physical boundary of musical experience.

For example, when I asked Marilou whether there was a difference between the Philippines and Hong Kong in terms of opportunities to listen to music, she replied that she had more opportunities in Hong Kong than in the Philippines:

> MARILOU: It's really, really different, it's a big difference, because in the Philippines, I only listen to music during weekends, but, here, where I am working and doing things, I have music on.

Thus, Marilou can listen to music whenever she is working, although she is referring to recorded music. Also, there are two Philippine radio channels set up in Hong Kong that broadcast music and news in their language, Tagalog. Therefore, even though they are in Hong Kong, they can keep up with the latest musical scene in their homeland, as well as listening to Chinese and Western music and the music of other Asian countries. It seems that the prosperity of the city can help promote music. Theresa, Mildred, Marilou, Elma, and Diana therefore concluded that they had much more exposure to music in Hong Kong than in the Philippines.

MATERIALISTIC EXPOSURE OR LIVING MUSICAL EXPERIENCE

The preceding discussion can give rise to the questions: What is a musical experience? What do we mean by exposure to music? From the data, we can see that Filipinos receive a rich musical enculturation in their early years in their home country, which enables them to appreciate and enjoy making music. However, the Filipinos interviewed for this study wanted to go beyond this. It is worth noting that although from my perspective, and no doubt that of many classically trained musicians, they received a more skill-based, and in this sense richer musical enculturation in their homeland than many children in Hong Kong, still they felt they had missed the formal aspect of learning music. Furthermore, although the informants mentioned their greater exposure to music in Hong Kong, what they meant by "exposure to music" is exposure to different kinds of instruments and access to technology, both of which can expand the scope of their musical knowledge. However, this kind of exposure refers mainly to the material side of learning music, whereas the experience they acquired in the Philippines was of living music present in everyday life. Although the importance of the material aspects of learning about music should not be overlooked, it appears that the Filipino informants may not have been aware that their musical culture may have given them a lifelong enjoyment of music and a strong musical identity which, it seems, is unlikely ever to be taken away. Also, it is the consistency of their participation in music-making and their positive attitude toward learning music that makes them musical and gives them such a strong aural ability, as seen in their being able to harmonize a melody by ear alone.

What then are the implications for teachers? Should we, as music educators, first ask ourselves the question: Which do we enjoy more— the material musical advantages offered by a relatively wealthy society such as Hong Kong; or the living musical experience of everyday life? Do we treasure and place a higher value on formal and professional modes of music-making and music-learning than on those used by laymen in informal learning and enculturation?

In summary, it seems that the Filipino informants changed their musical identities as they experienced a new musical environment and new music-learning practices in Hong Kong; yet they are still passionate about music and continued to be active in music-making. We may say that the musical enculturation the informants received in the Philippines had prepared their hearts, while the more opulent environment of Hong Kong was giving them opportunities to grow and expand their musical minds. Both countries have had an effect on the music-learning of the Filipino maids, but in different ways. It may be that these two types of music-enculturation and music-learning can serve to complement each other.

Note

1. Global Property Guide, http://www.globalpropertyguide.com/Asia/Philippines/gdp-per-capita (accessed 25 April 2010).

References

Bennett, H. Stith. 1980. *On Becoming a Rock Musician.* Amherst: University of Massachusetts Press.

Campbell, Patricia Shehan. 1991. *Songs in their Heads.* Oxford: Oxford University Press.

———. 1998. The Musical Cultures of Children. *Research Studies in Music Education* 11: 42–51.

Finnegan, Ruth. 2007. *The Hidden Musicians: Music-Making in an English Town.* Middletown, Conn.: Wesleyan University Press.

Green, L. 2001/2. *How Popular Musicians Learn: A Way Ahead for Music Education.* London: Ashgate.

———. 2004. What Can Music Educators Learn from Popular Musicians? In *Bridging the Gap: Popular Music and Music Education,* ed. C. X. Rodriguez. Reston, Va.: Music Educators' National Conference: The National Association for Music Education.

Mans, Minette. 2007. Learning aesthetic values in African musical worlds. In *International Handbook of Research in Arts Education,* ed. Liora Bresler. Dordrecht: Springer.

Merriam, A. P. 1964. *The Anthropology of Music.* Evanston, Ill.: Northwestern University Press.

FOUR

Village, Province, and Nation

Aspects of Identity in Children's Learning
of Music and Dance in Bali

PETER DUNBAR-HALL

The Indonesian island of Bali, off the eastern tip of Java, is home to a population of approximately three and a half million Balinese. Popular as a tourist destination, Bali's main livelihood is agrarian, with rice as the major crop. Some aspects of Balinese cultural representation are sometimes similar to those of other parts of Indonesia, especially the presence of *gamelans*, ensembles of mostly tuned percussion instruments. However, due to Bali's Hindu religion, which sets Bali off from the majority Muslim population of Indonesia and makes Bali an island in multiple senses of the word, and the ways in which Balinese Hinduism suffuses Balinese performing arts, Balinese music and dance stand apart from pan-Indonesian arts aesthetics. Thus, the study of Balinese music and dance forms a discrete field of research.

One of the main locations that has become popular with researchers and tourists is that around the southern Balinese village of Ubud, where each night performance events are staged for tourists. These events include *kecak* (danced drama accompanied by chanting), *legong* (courtly dance), *musik kontemporer* (contemporary music including jazz and avant-garde styles), *sendratari* (danced drama with *gamelan*), *topeng* (masked dance), and *wayang kulit* (shadow puppet theatre). Although performers in these events receive minimal payment, the presence of an organized, weekly schedule is one aspect of encouraging children to learn to play musical instruments and/or to dance. In some cases, performances are given entirely by children. As the teaching of children often occurs in public spaces, it is common for tourists and researchers to watch children learning to play gamelan instruments and to dance, or to see a rehearsal of a performance intended for inclusion in a temple ceremony, or as an entry in *lomba* (contests) or the annual Bali Arts Festival.

Over a ten-year period, I have observed countless instances of the teaching and learning of Balinese music and dance in Ubud and surrounding regions, and I have discussed teaching and learning with musicians, teachers, and organizers of children's groups, many of whom have become friends and colleagues. These have taken place at lessons and rehearsals, during ceremonies, over meals, and at performances. In many cases, they were not formal interviews—rather, they were friendly interactions, and in some cases were situations in which I was a student.

Music and dance are taught in primary/elementary and secondary schools in Ubud, and the teachers I have interviewed and learned from taught in schools. Music is taught to different levels in different schools and in some cases is an *ad hoc* arrangement. However, despite this formal provision through schools, the main site of teaching and learning for children is in what are known as *sanggar*—Indonesian for "studio" (Echols and Shadily 1997: 480)—privately run organizations that train children in Balinese music and dance. Sometimes instead of *sanggar,* the term *seka*—Balinese for "a villager's" club (Shadeg 2007: 436)—is used, with slightly different connotations, as discussed below. The following mapping of issues surrounding the work of children's *sanggar* and *seka* in the Ubud area is based on my observations of and interviews with people teaching in:

- *Balerung Mandera*—children's dance classes in *Peliatan* (regular public performances on Sundays with the women's gamelan, *Mekar Sari*)
- *Cenik Wayah*—children's dance and gamelan *seka* (regular public performances on Thursdays)
- *Çudamani*—an innovative *sanggar* with international performing and teaching connections
- *Pondok Pekak*—a *sanggar* based in a children's library and learning center (regular public performances on Saturdays [*genggong*] and Sundays [*legong*])

- *Satya Brasta*—children's dance and gamelan group of the Agung Rai Museum of Art, ARMA (regular public performances on Saturdays)
- *Tedung Agung*—a children's *sanggar* in central Ubud with no regular performance commitments.

My observations and discussions have revealed a number of issues relating to individual, group, and Balinese identity at work in children's learning of music and dance. Here I investigate four aspects: the choice of one of the two terms, *sanggar* or *seka*, to name groups; teacher and student identity as vectors of pedagogy; challenges to gender protocols in Balinese music and dance; and sociopolitical implications of encouraging children to learn Balinese performing arts. The ongoing nature of these issues reflects the continually evolving world of Balinese music and dance, where support for the study of traditional styles of music and dance is accompanied by creation of new repertoires and styles, commercial recording of groups, competition between groups, uses of music for economic and political purposes, and interest among musicians in the tunings of Balinese music and their reification in the development of new *gamelan* ensembles and repertoires for them. Teaching and learning music and dance in this part of Bali are not static, but mirror a context of artistic, economic, and sociopolitical flux.

SANGGAR OR SEKA: TERMINOLOGY, GROUP IDENTITY, AND PURPOSES

Collaborative groups underpin Balinese life. Both work commitments and leisure are based around social organizations in which individuals contribute to holistic outcomes (Warren 1993; Hobart et al. 1996). Two main types of groupings are found in relation to the arts: *sanggar* and *seka*. As noted above, a *sanggar* is a group of learners/performers. *Seka* exist wherever group effort is required—for rice farming, for repairing a temple, for organizing a cremation, for performance of music, and such like. Membership in a *seka* is restricted to members of a *banjar* (Balinese for "village subdivision," Echols and Shadily 1997: 50), the important communal identity-creating unit of Balinese daily life. Membership in a *sanggar* is not *banjar*-derived and is open to anyone wishing to participate. Membership in a *banjar* indicates which temples a person attends, and interacts with religious duties expected of all *banjar* members; in this way, Balinese religion is linked inextricably to one form of Balinese identity marker. Use of the term *seka,* with implications of *banjar* exclusivity, to refer to a children's music group appeals to notions of correctness, to *adat* (established village protocols), and to assumptions of how Balinese personal identity is constructed. While use of the term may be perfectly correct (i.e., to refer to children in a performing group who are from one *banjar*), it can also be an appeal to tradition, and in some cases is misleading, as members of some groups are not from the one *banjar.* Use of the term *sanggar* by some groups is more appropriate. The choice of which term to use therefore carries implications about the identity of a group, and how that identity is presented to the Balinese public.

To understand these implications it is worth comparing McPhee's description of a children's gamelan group in the 1930s with today's *sanggar* and *seka.* Canadian composer Colin McPhee (1900–1964) lived in Bali in the 1930s, his *Music in Bali: A Study in Form and Instrumental Organization in Balinese Orchestral Music* eventually appearing after his death (McPhee 1966). One of his projects was setting up a boys' gamelan group, reported in his novella, *A Club of Small Men: A Children's Tale from Bali* (McPhee 1948/2002). McPhee claims that the group he organized was the first children's *gamelan* known. This tallies with other reports: while other writers in Bali in the 1930s, for example Gregory Bateson and Margaret Mead (1942) and Beryl deZoete and Walter Spies (1938), mention how children learned music by imitating adults, the idea of a dedicated children's group was novel to the Balinese but was quite usual to McPhee, with his Canadian/American music education background in which children's ensembles are common.

McPhee's use of the term "club" in the title of his novella is his translation of *seka,* as the following quote from his *Music in Bali* indicates:

> (In Bali) *gamelans* . . . are either village or *banjar* property, or belong to organized clubs. To be a musician or dancer and not to belong to a *seka,* or club, is unthinkable. The club system sets the pattern for all village activities, from road-mending to making music. (McPhee 1966: 6)

That his children's gamelan group was *banjar*-based, and thus a *seka,* is attested to by the fact that when McPhee suggested to its members that children from outside the *banjar* join, the members of the group argued against this as not correct.

In current practice, the distinction between *seka* and *sanggar* is alluded to in an information brochure from Pondok Pekak (as indicated above, a children's library, activity, and resource center):

> The *sanggar* (traditional music and dance studio) portion of Pondok Library and Learning Centre was founded in 1998, originally to provide dance classes for local children who didn't have other opportunities to learn. (Pondok Pekak, undated: 3)

Some of the *sanggar* and *seka* discussed here are integrated into the weekly schedule of performances for tourists in the Ubud area (and in this way generate income), while some are parts of larger organizations or have no regular performance activities. The aims of these groups, however, all coalesce around desires to maintain and further the traditions of Balinese performing arts. For example, Satya Brasta is one application of ARMA's overall aim of preserving and teaching about the "visual, cultural and performing arts of Bali" (ARMA, undated: 1). ARMA's activities include classes on Balinese arts and culture for tourists, internationally touring art displays and performance troupes, a bookshop specializing in Balinese performing arts, and performances of Balinese dance and music (see www.armamuseum.com).

A similar situation exists at Pondok Pekak, where children's learning and performing groups exist alongside a library, a bookshop, a learning center offering classes in Balinese culture, a women's *gamelan* group, and regular dance and music performances by children (including the only local performances of *genggong,* Balinese bamboo mouthharps). Their advertising suggests their goal: "Support literacy and traditional arts by visiting Pondok Pekak Library!" As McIntosh (2006) demonstrates, and advertisements and articles in local newspapers indicate, *sanggar* for children's learning of dance and music also exist in other parts of Bali. These advertisements and articles are explicit about the purposes of children's performing groups. For example, an advertisement for the group Mekar Bhuana, from the village of Sanur, states that the group's aim is "preserving classical *gamelan* and dance" and that "by supporting Mekar Bhuana, you are helping to preserve endangered Balinese art forms." The leader of Mekar Bhuana, Putu Suyadnyani, states that her group exists "to help preserve and conserve rare Balinese performing art forms so that a younger generation of musicians and dancers can learn how to appreciate and perform these gracious old styles" (in Hickey 2007: 26).

Sanggar and *seka,* despite debates over the appropriateness of their use of naming terms, are nonetheless working to maintain Balinese performing arts as a means of preserving Balinese cultural identity.

TEACHER/STUDENT IDENTITY IN PEDAGOGY

Traditionally, and still to a large extent today, the teaching of Balinese music is a role taken up only by men. While I will discuss gender issues below, in the present section I wish to concentrate on issues of identity and pedagogy. Balinese music is of course an aural tradition, and its transmission involves a recognized role occupied by expert musicians. That this situation has existed for some time is indicated by writings from the 1930s, in which teachers working with children are described (Dunbar-Hall 2008). The teaching methods have changed little to the present. A teacher is the embodiment of repertoire, technique, and aesthetic decisions about how a piece of music will be played. Without the teacher, little can be achieved. The teacher works by modeling performance of short segments of a piece of music, playing variously on all the instruments of the gamelan. The children learn by copying the teacher's examples until they have mastered them by rote, as there is no use of notation. Once enough segments of a piece have been memorized, the teacher organizes them into the eventual piece of music being studied.

Experience of this process inculcates those children who will themselves become teachers, continuing a tradition of teaching that relies heavily on the teacher as the carrier of knowledge. Little verbalization by teachers of a pedagogic method occurs. This was often a confounding issue in interviews when teachers were asked about their teaching strategies. Not only did this appear to them as a Western obsession with analysis of practice, it was often met with bemusement that something so obvious and natural needed to be explained. Like Rice's (1994) Bulgarian *gaida* (bagpipe) playing informants, this was a case of teachers not having explicitly learned to teach, but of absorbing teaching practices through their own experiences as students. While this statement might also apply in many other situations, and Western-based studio teaching is an obvious example, in Bali it seems to dominate the ways music is taught.

In this learning situation, and indeed for adult members of a *gamelan* group, a child gives up her/his individual identity to both the instruction of the teacher and the collaborative group effort of learning and performing pieces of music. The term for this socially accepted relegation of individual identity in favor of group identity (as is implied in use of both terms *sanggar* and *seka*) is *gotong royong* (collaborative group contribution). A *gamelan* or dance troupe exemplifies this concept of group identity both in practical terms (through the actions of each member, the use of group uniforms in performance, expectations of helping in moving instruments and setting up equipment, etc.) and in musical ones. The complex structural techniques of Balinese *gamelan* music, in which instrumental parts interlock to produce rhythmically and melodically composite textures, reify the *gotong royong* concept in sound. It is rare to encounter individual musicians practicing their parts alone; rather some form of group effort is expected and generally seen. Likewise, individual lessons between a teacher and one player are rare; learning and rehearsing take place as group undertakings. Individual possession of instruments is also rare, and financially prohibitive for most Balinese musicians. Sets of instruments are owned collectively by a *banjar,* a temple, a *sanggar* or *seka,* or perhaps by a wealthy entrepreneur or a hotel. In these ways, membership in a performing group touches on various levels of identity construction: the embodiment by a teacher of repertoire and style; the yielding of personal interest to a teacher's direction; varying levels of personal identity and group identity; inculcation of teaching methods through which a learner can subsequently develop an identity as a teacher; and musical and logistical reflection of expectations of socially evident group membership and participation. For children learning music and dance, these issues act as a context for becoming performers; they are unstated and at the basis of the activity.

GENDER

As already mentioned, most *gamelan* teachers today tend to be male. In McPhee's "club of small men" it is clear that only boys were allowed, mirroring the practices of the 1930s when gamelans were male-only groups.

Today, women's *gamelans* are regularly seen (Bakan 1997/1998; Susilo 2003; and McGraw 2004), and in some *sanggar,* girls are encouraged to learn to play *gamelan.* Both single gender (i.e., all girls or all boys) *gamelans* exist, as well as ones of mixed gender. However, in my experience, single gender ones predominate. Feminist agendas of women's *gamelans* are made explicit by comments such as the following from the Luh Luwih Foundation, which runs a women's *gamelan:*

> The Luh Luwih Foundation was established . . . as an agency for women in Balinese society—an institution where women's creativity can be developed and expressed. . . . The foundation is meant to give Balinese women an opportunity to perform, be on stage, get outside of the village and be exposed to new ideas. . . . Women in Bali are bound by a myriad of rules and cultural constraints. In the public arena, women have little political or social power. . . . There is very little time for leisure for a Balinese woman. (Luh Luwih Foundation, undated: 1)

Widening of gender roles in music and dance flows down to the level of children's *sanggar,* but not *seka* in the groups discussed here, perhaps a further demonstration that use of the term *seka* invokes a previous period of *gamelan* activity when male groups were the only groups.

For Agung Rai, owner of ARMA, there must be a symbiotic relationship between dance and its accompanying *gamelan* music. Therefore, in Satya Brasta boys learning to play *gamelan* are encouraged to learn to dance so that they will play for dancers with greater understanding; girls who are learning to dance are encouraged to learn to play *gamelan* so that they will interpret the music better (Agung Rai 2007), even though in this group, public performances still tend to present boys as *gamelan* players and dancers of male dances, while girls only perform female dances. At *sanggar* Çudamani, there is a girls' *gamelan* group, perceived in the following ways by ethnomusicologist, dancer, and Associate Director of Çudamani Emiko Susilo, in an e-mail to the author:

> Just as Dewa [the teacher] has the confidence that Çudamani can train exceptional male groups, he has equal confidence that Çudamani will be able to prove that Balinese women are capable of playing music, with technical precision and musicality. There

is not the sense that they are the same as the boys . . . it is a matter of developing musical talent, and each ensemble and musician has a different spirit. Dewa is great in that he puts much thought into selecting repertoire that is challenging and also *cocok* [Indonesian for "suitable," Echols and Shadily 1997, 120] for their spirit at this time in their lives. In a few years, that will be different, just as our *remaja* [Indonesian, young men; Echols and Shadily 1997, 456] group's repertoire has been developed. . . . Dewa and I put a lot of thought into the girls' groups since there is no precedent for training an entire *gamelan* of girls from a young age. . . . The sense of excitement the girls feel when they play great music together is such an important lesson to them about the need to listen to one another, to work together, to appreciate even the player who seems to have the "simplest" job. So, bringing a girls' group to their highest level of musical excellence is a way for us to teach them the value not only of Balinese *gamelan*, but also the value of the little girl sitting beside them, and the young woman blossoming within each of them.

Challenging gender roles through the inclusion of girls (and women) in performance settings that were previously the domain of Balinese men makes Balinese performing arts into a site of contravention of Balinese gender stereotypes and emphasizes the fluidity of Balinese music and dance as symbols of social developments in Bali (and coincidentally the Indonesian Republic).

AJEG BALI: DISCOURSES OF BALINESE IDENTITY

The idea of preservation of Balinese traditional culture, such as children's dance and music that *sanggar* and *seka* promote, has undergone significant impacts in the past few years. These include the effects of two sets of bombings in Balinese tourist precincts (in Jalan Legian, Kuta, on 12 October 2002; at Jimbaran Bay and Kuta, on 1 October 2005), the international economic downturn of 2008/2009, outbreaks of numerous epidemics (including SARS), and a Balinese identity movement known as *Ajeg Bali*.

A major immediate and lasting effect of the Bali bombings, international outbreaks of diseases, and the 2008/2009 economic situation has been a reduction in tourist trade. This affects many Balinese families who had been lured into selling their family lands and training for and seeking employment in the tourist trade while Balinese tourism was vibrant in the decades since the early 1970s. In the opening decade of the twenty-first century, the lack of employment in the tourist industry on which the Balinese economy had come to rely means depressed socioeconomic status for many Balinese people. *"Bangkrut!"* (Indonesian, bankrupt; Echols and Shadily 1976, 53) has become a standard response to the usual greeting of *"Apa kabar?"* ("How are you?") in the streets of Bali. Reasons given for the bombings included those of the terrorists, that tourist venues were an offence to God. Various political commentators interpreted the bombings as intended to unsettle the Indonesian government, as examples of ongoing Bali-Java conflict, or specifically aimed at Australians and/or Americans (Dunbar-Hall 2007). However, to many Balinese the bombings were evidence of divine displeasure at the Balinese allowing tourism to get out of hand, for religious observance being neglected, for *dharma* (righteous living) being ignored. One result of this position has been increased arts activity—the arts in Bali being forms of religious observance and necessary for *dharma* (Harnish 1991). To be an artist (including musician or dancer) is a means to *taksu* (personal and communal spiritual well-being) and a pathway to healing the situation leading to the bombings. This is one reason for increased strength observable in the teaching of dance and music in Ubud since the Bali bombings, and was given as such by many local Balinese people.

Associated with this, and also feeding off post-bombings sentiments, is the movement known as *Ajeg Bali*. *Ajeg* in Indonesian means "stable, constant" (Echols and Shadily 1997: 8). When I asked stall holders in the local market, workers in cafes, drivers, and musicians how they interpret the term and what *Ajeg Bali* means to them, they gave the following comments, sometimes specifically mentioning the need to make sure that Balinese dance and music are taught and kept alive:

- *Bali asli* (*asli*—Indonesian, original; Echols and Shadily 1997: 32)—Balinese people are not to forget to make offerings to the gods and to observe *odalan* (temple events). Balinese people should not let tourism obscure *budaya Bali* (Balinese culture)

- *Bali berdiri* (*berdiri*—Indonesian, independent; Echols and Shadily 1997: 145)—to stay focused on Balinese culture, to teach and learn Balinese language, dance, and music
- *Bali kuat* (*kuat*—Indonesian, strong; Echols and Shadily 1997: 313)—Bali needs to remain strong in itself
- *Bali untuk Bali* (Bali for Bali/the Balinese)—that Bali should remain for Balinese people, not be taken over by property owners from other parts of Indonesia (especially Javanese people).

In an e-mail to a list of scholars interested in *gamelan* in 2007, researcher Elizabeth Rhoads described *Ajeg Bali* as a "discourse on strengthening Balinese identity through promoting and protecting Balinese Hinduism, language and *adat* (custom and customary law)." Specialist on Balinese performing arts Rucina Ballinger commented that there is

> a breaking away from traditional values . . . and Bali is a Hindu island in the midst of a Muslim majority. There's a cultural phenomenon, *Ajeg Bali,* which can mean erect, stand firm when you talk. More practically, however, it means Bali first, Bali pride. It's a very clever way of asserting identity. Very Bali-centric. It's spread like wildfire. The bombs exacerbated things. The Balinese feel threatened. People from the outside are coming in, taking the land, the top positions. And Indonesia could indeed become a Muslim state. There's talk of seceding. They're feeling off-balance. . . . (Quoted in Strachan 2007: 23)

Ajeg Bali appears as the "aim" of study courses for Balinese children, and as the topic of pop songs. The link between the aftermath of the Bali bombings and *Ajeg Bali* is sometimes made explicit. For example, I Nyoman Manda concludes his collection of short stories about the bombings, *Our sorrow in Kuta,* by expressing his hope that "Sang Hyang Widhi Wasa, the One and Only God, always gives his blessing to Bali so it will stay safe, peaceful and steady (*ajeg*) all the time" (Manda 2002: 76).

While Agung Rai, of ARMA, maintained that *Ajeg Bali* did not relate to his programs for teaching Balinese culture to children (as he had been doing this before recent events and has always had a strong commitment to such programs), references to Balinese culture, to language, dance, and music in these explanations of *Ajeg Bali* relate to much of the activity of teaching children dance and music (see also Allen and Palermo 2005; Forbes 2007). What lies behind much of the *Ajeg Bali* discourse is the undertaking to teach Balinese music and dance to children so that Balinese identity (which is Hindu by definition) will remain strong, particularly in the perceived threat of domination of Bali by other parts of the Indonesian Republic (which is Islamic). Through *Ajeg Bali,* teaching and learning music and dance are ways that Balinese people explicitly engender Balinese identity among their children.

Children's *sanggar* and *seka* for the learning of dance and music represent an important aspect of the transmission of music in Bali. They demonstrate ways in which communities and individuals utilize teaching with clear agendas of cultural preservation, local identity construction, elements of Indonesian politics, aspects of local economies, and ways of addressing what community members see as important issues in communal religious lives. The activities of the *sanggar* and *seka* referred to here intersect with movements and concerns on wider levels. They touch, at times, on local pride and competition; as *sanggar* are by definition open to all participants, they explicitly make dance and music available to all children, not only those from families at the higher end of the socioeconomic scale, who tend to favor their children joining what are called *seka;* they proactively challenge gender roles inherited from earlier periods of performance history in Bali, and at times utilize the breakdown of gender stereotypes in music and dance as a pedagogic tool through which better performers can be prepared. In many ways, the teaching of these groups utilizes varying levels of individual, group, and cultural identity as they prepare Balinese children for adult lives.

Acknowledgments

Thanks are due to Agus Teja Sentosa, Agung Rai, Cokorda Ngurah Suyadnya, Cokorda Raka Swastika, Cokorda Sri Agung, I Dewa Berata, Emiko Susilo, I Gusti Ngurah Ardana, I Ketut Cater, Laurie Billington, I Nyoman Parman, and I Wayan Tusti Adnyana.

References

Agung Rai. 2007. Interview with author, 22 May 2007.
Allen, Pamela, and Carmencita Palermo. 2005. *Ajeg Bali:* Multiple Meanings, Diverse Agendas. *Indonesia and the Malay World* 33 (97): 239–255.

ARMA (Agung Rai Museum of Art). Undated. *Cultural Workshop* (museum brochure). No publication data.

Bakan, Michael. 1997/1998. From Oxymoron to Reality: Agendas of Gender and the Rise of Balinese Women's *Gamelan Beleganjur* in Bali, Indonesia. *Asian Music* XXIX-1: 37–86.

Bateson, Gregory, and Margaret Mead. 1942. *Balinese Character: A Photographic Analysis.* New York: New York Academy of Sciences.

deZoete, Beryl, and Walter Spies. 1938. *Dance and Drama in Bali.* London: Faber and Faber.

Dunbar-Hall, Peter. 2007. *Apa salah Baliku?* [What did my Bali do wrong?]: Popular Music and Reactions to the 2002 Bali Bombings. *Popular Music and Society* 30 (4): 533–548.

———. 2008. "Good Legong Dancers Were Given an Arduous Program of Training": Music Education in Bali in the 1930s. *Journal of Historical Research in Music Education* XXX (1): 50–63.

Echols, John, and Hassan Shadily. 1976. *Kamus Inggris Indonesia.* Jakarta: Gramedia.

———. 1997. *Kamus Indonesia Inggris.* Jakarta: Gramedia.

Forbes, Cameron. 2007. *Under the Volcano: The Story of Bali.* Melbourne: Black.

Harnish, David. 1991. Balinese Performance as Temple Offering. *Asian Art* 4 (2): 9–27.

Hickey, Al. 2007. Putu Evie Suradnyani: Dance Teacher and Impresario. *Bali Advertiser,* 26 September–10 October: 26.

Hobart, Angela, Urs Ramseyer, and Albert Leemann. 1996. *The Peoples of Bali.* Oxford: Blackwell Publishers.

Luh Luwih Foundation. Undated. *Luh Luwih Balinese Women's Gamelan and Dancetroupe.* Performance program (12 March 2007, Ubud Kelod). No publication data.

Manda, Nyoman. 2002. *Our Sorrow in Kuta.* No publication data.

McGraw, Andrew. 2004. "Playing like Men": The Cultural Politics of Women's *Gamelan. Latitudes* 47: 12–17.

McIntosh, Jonathan. 2006. How Dancing, Singing and Playing Shape the Ethnographer: Research with Children in a Balinese Dance Studio. *Anthropology Matters* 8 (2). Available at http://www.anthropologymatters.com (accessed 24 October 2006).

McPhee, Colin. 1948/2002. *A Club of Small Men: A Children's Tale from Bali.* Singapore: Periplus.

———. 1966. *Music in Bali: A Study in Form and Instrumental Organization in Balinese Orchestral Music.* New Haven, Conn.: Yale University Press.

Pondok Pekak. Undated. *Pondok pekak.* Performance program (11 March 2007, Ubud Kelod). No publication data.

Rice, Timothy. 1994. *May it Fill Your Soul: Experiencing Bulgarian Music.* Chicago: University of Chicago Press.

Shadeg, Norbert. 2007. *Balinese-English Dictionary.* Tokyo: Tuttle Publishing.

Strachan, Angus. 2007. Dance, Dance, Dance. *The Yak* 14: 23.

Susilo, Emiko. 2003. *Gamelan wanita: A Study of Women's Gamelan in Bali.* South East Asian Papers no. 43. Honolulu: University of Hawaii.

Warren, Carol. 1993. *Adat and dinas: Balinese Communities in the Indonesian state.* Oxford: Oxford University Press.

FIVE

Music for a Postcolonial Child

Theorizing Malaysian Memories

ROE-MIN KOK

I am the native informant. I begin my story with an enduring childhood memory.

I am standing in an air-conditioned waiting area of an expensive hotel in Kuala Lumpur, the capital of Malaysia. My surroundings are meticulously Western in a city and climate unyieldingly tropical. I am seven years old. It is my first piano examination.

There he is. At a desk near the piano. Silver-haired, of regal carriage, replete with the self-confidence and authority of the colonial master. His skin is ruddy, fashionably sun-tanned—a genuine tan acquired in this exotic land. He is attired in white, because white reflects heat rays. It is the color traditionally favored by travelers to hot climes. I have been schooled in the gravity of the situation. I have been trained time and again in simulated settings to be meek and polite, to parrot "Good morning, Sir!" Madams are rare. My piano teacher finds out in advance the gender of the examiner, so that we, her students, can practice the greeting until it is smooth on our young Malaysian tongues. The examiner is all-powerful. Not only can he administer a failing grade to you, thus wasting the previous year's work, time, and money; he can do so at his whim, because nobody else witnesses the examination, held behind closed doors in his hotel room. If this is only a suspicion, it is one born of a colonized mentality that constantly anticipates the white man's displeasure and its consequences—whether it happens in a *ladang getah* (rubber plantation) or in a Western-style hotel. I, the child, have to be respectful at all times and to be careful not to annoy him. My piano teacher's last-minute advice rings in my ears: "Remember to hand him your book of scales and to respond as soon as he asks you to play. Dog-ear the pages so that you can turn them easily. Don't repeat passages in which you make mistakes; cut your fingernails so they don't go 'clack' on the keys—that will irritate him."

In other words, her message to me is: be submissive, play the colo-nizer-colonized scenario, and you will be fine. Subconsciously I super-impose her instructions onto the pieces I play to make up the meaning of what I understand and physically execute as "music." When the time that has been allotted for the examination arrives, my fear has built up to such proportions that I refuse to enter the examiner's room. I can-not remember what to say; I cannot remember how to play. All I see is a towering white man who will speak to me with a strange accent and who will become angry if my fingers slip on the keyboard or my tongue slips in his language. I stand frozen. He comes out of the room, surprised at this disruption of his schedule, and the other waiting children scatter with whispered cries of "The examiner!" As his eyes focus on me, I feel my inadequacies even more and I cannot bridge that gap. I am, at that moment, in my mind, what I am sure he feels me to be: a disobedient little yellow child.

Today I am a scholar of Western classical music, a Malaysian Chinese academic active in North America and Europe.[1] Among other things, I am the product of a colonial music education—a set of policies formu-lated a world apart (literally and figuratively) from that in which it was delivered and received. The policies formed an arc of cultural power that extended from the Associated Board of the Royal Schools of Music in Great Britain to a child in Malaysia, a former British colony and cur-rently an independent, multicultural Muslim nation in Southeast Asia. As a result of ideas about Western classical music transmitted from the former and received by the latter, my cultural identity was aligned over the course of my childhood and early adolescence to identify with colo-nial concepts for the colonized. In this chapter I use postcolonial theory as a mode of cultural analysis wherein musical activity undertaken by a child in a specific time and place is shown to be the result of interconnections between issues of ethnicity, class, nation, and empire.[2] My story intersects with observations made about *fictional* children and imperialism: "There is obviously considerable slippage between constructions of 'the child' and of the native Other under imperialism . . ." (Wallace 1994: 175; cf. Ashcroft *et al.* 1989: 16; Bhabha 1985: 74), but in this case, life events as I experienced them—seen from temporal and geographical distance—form my subject. Theorizing from my personal loci of enunciation,[3] I shall foreground and interrogate forces that have shaped this identity in order to facilitate reconciliation of the fragments created by the dominant discourse of my early musical education. On a broader level, the essay problematizes the process whereby Western classical music was transmitted to non-Western contexts under specific circumstances, addresses issues that underlay its transmission (including the imbalance of economic and political power, the role of national and family histories, and the complicated nature of the colonizer-colonized relationship), and analyzes their impact on the formation of cultural identity among young children in postcolonial settings.[4]

INTERTWINING ETHNICITY, COLONIAL HERITAGE, AND LOCAL HISTORY

The self-evident is often the least examined: how did I come to study Western classical music? I was born to second-generation Chinese immigrants on Muslim soil in a corner of the Asian continent. From birth until my late teens, my existence was thick with Southeast Asian peoples, and Southeast Asian tastes . . . smells . . . and sounds. The British had been in Malaysia for more than a hundred years, but by the time I was born Malaysia had been independent for more than a decade.[5] "Independent," such a deceptive word, for by the time they departed, the British had left their stamp on key aspects of Malaysian life. English was declared the nation's second official language after Malay; we became a parliamentary democracy with a symbolic monarchy; and our legal system and our traffic and driving rules were based on British models. Malaysian high school students sat for British-style "O" and "A" level examinations (*Sijil Pelajaran Malaysia* and *Sijil Tinggi Pelajaran Malaysia*, respectively). Perhaps more disturbingly, we also unconsciously and unquestioningly imbibed and duplicated colonial social practices, for example that of a social-hierarchical system based on ethnicity—an especially problematic legacy for a multiracial society.[6]

Malaysian "understanding" of British cultural practices occurred on a family-by-family basis, depending on ethnicity, income and educational levels, social aspirations, and amount of contact with colonials. My parents, born into large, improvident, Chinese-speaking families, had attended missionary schools in the 1950s and college in the 1960s. All had been staffed by British or British-trained teachers and offered British-based curriculums of study. In these settings, students (including my parents) laboriously polished their command of the English language, a prerequisite for membership in the educated middle classes to which they were taught to aspire. Away from home, in college, students also encountered British-style behavior, talk and dress among peers, teachers, and college staff members.[7] Many of my parents' peers equated "Britishness" with power, with economic and social success. Popular, confident students were not only fluent in the colonial tongue; notwithstanding their Southeast Asian heritages and physiques, they were "British" in as many ways as possible. Most directly copied their teachers' behaviors, thus unwittingly acquiring dated vocabulary, gestures, dress, and tastes (as many of their teachers had left Britain before World War II), an "understanding" of English customs they then transmitted to future generations of Malaysians.

To this day, my parents maintain habits learned as college students: they dunk, eat afternoon tea, enjoy Marmite, digestive biscuits, orange marmalade and lemon curd, and listen to BBC Radio broadcasts in Malaysia. They bought English children's literature for us: I became familiar with Enid Blyton, J. M. Barrie, and Beatrix Potter, and with quintessentially English tales such as *Robin Hood and the Sheriff of Nottingham* and *King Arthur and the Knights of the Round Table*. My sister and I were dressed in Edwardian children's clothing: feminine white blouses with ruffled Peter Pan collars and short puffed sleeves, carefully matched with pleated skirts made of fine, floral-printed cotton—clothing that, as an adult living in North America, I re-encountered with a nostalgic twinge in Laura Ashley stores. These practices were fully integrated into our Malaysian existence, seamlessly lived alongside Sunday morning *dim sum* meals, the ubiquitous Malay language, daily broadcasts of Muslim calls to prayer, strains of Canto-pop and Bollywood, roadside stalls peddling fresh *durian* and star-fruits, sun-drenched beaches, and bustling, humid night markets filled with shiny trinkets from all over Asia. My family was not considered unusual in any way among the people with whom we socialized, as they, too, looked and behaved, thought, dressed, and talked as we did.

WESTERN INSTRUMENTAL MUSIC EDUCATION IN MALAYSIA: BACKGROUND AND STATUS

Middle-class Malaysians saw dazzling social potential in the piano, although after independence in 1957 the national government declared Western classical music a colonial legacy we could do without, and dropped music altogether from the public school curriculum. However, in practice the situation was far from being clear-cut. As G. H. Heath-Gracie, a British musician visiting Malaysia chronicled in 1960:

> Malayanisation is now proceeding apace. The process should be complete by 1962, after which all Ministries . . . will consist wholly of those whose race, outlook and aspirations are specifically Malayan. It must not be imagined however that there is the slightest anti-British feeling which might be stirred up either against Britons as persons or against their institutions. Nevertheless there is a tendency to look away from Britain toward other countries for whatever knowledge and experience Malaya lacks. . . . Of one thing [we] may be certain. Traditional Malayan music, although propagandized by radio all day and every day, is quite incapable of being rebuilt to serve as an element in social or intellectual evolution. Instead of Malayans buying their native instruments their fantastic and ever-continuing increase in individual wealth has boosted the sale of pianofortes on which purely Malayan music is unplayable. These sales are largely to households of Chinese, Indian or Ceylonese extraction which are said to form more than half the population. (1960: 1)

Heath-Gracie's observations reflected a phenomenon rooted in colonial history and local cultural beliefs. In Malaysia, the piano had graced the homes of expatriates and the wealthy since the British arrived.[8] An unmistakable aura surrounded the instrument; it represented, to the

Malaysian mind, qualities associated with the colonizers' lifestyles: "cultured," "wealthy," "powerful," "well-educated," and "refined." Privileged were those who played it. To the Malaysian Chinese community, Western classical music and the piano offered additional attractions. As the piano requires much discipline and time to master, the enterprise of learning the instrument is in line with Confucian teachings, which emphasize among other things continuous, in-depth, and committed efforts in all educational undertakings.[9] Confucius had also taught that cultivation of music would lead to "goodness" of character.[10] Thus a Chinese child's successful mastery of music and the piano would engender satisfaction and guarantee respect for the family from within as well as outside of the Chinese community.

Middle-class Malaysians, especially the Chinese, welcomed the arrival of the Associated Board of the Royal Schools of Music (henceforth ABRSM) in 1948. Established in 1889 as an examining board by London's Royal Academy of Music and Royal College of Music (later joined by the Royal Northern College of Music and the Royal Scottish Academy of Music and Drama), the ABRSM offered to Malaysians by the 1970s and 1980s a system of evaluating skills in Western classical music, organized into eight levels or "grades" that progressed from elementary (grade 1) to advanced (grade 8).[11] Alongside practical skills, the ABRSM evaluated knowledge of music theory and ear-training at every grade, and music history at advanced grades. The system was supported by a range of materials produced by ABRSM Publishing: "examination books" or editions of music preselected by the Board for each grade, instructional manuals covering principles of theory, books of scales and arpeggios for each grade (complete with suitable fingerings), and previous examinations republished for students as practice material.

Quality control was achieved and uniform standards set by a trained corps of "examiners" who traveled to local and regional centers where they heard and judged each candidate's performance on an individual basis. After hearing the candidate's scales, arpeggios, and prepared examination pieces, the examiner administered a sight-reading test and an "aural examination" (ear-training test). The examiner wrote comments about, and assigned marks to, each part of the examination and totaled them up to determine whether the candidate had passed (with "distinction," "merit" or plain "pass") or failed the grade for which the exam was designed. The results were announced and reports sent to candidates a few months after the examination. Passing candidates also received certificates announcing their achievement, printed on heavy paper embossed with the ABRSM seal and signed by its Board of Examiners.

As a concept, the ABRSM was brilliant: with a portable system for the certification of musical skills it became in effect a putative music conservatory for students ranging from the beginner to the preprofessional.[12] Most of those who taught the system in Malaysia had themselves undergone ABRSM examinations. With the ABRSM's forays into the British colonies, beginning with Australia, Tasmania, Gibraltar, and New Zealand in 1897, it became the world's first music conservatory with a distance-learning program abroad.[13] In light of its subsequent activities in the British Empire, it seems significant that the ABRSM was founded only two years after Queen Victoria's Diamond Jubilee in 1887, a time "when imperial consciousness . . . was probably at its zenith" (Cannadine 2001: 181).

The ABRSM could hardly have chosen more fertile ground for its activities than Malaysia, where it arrived in 1948 amid the nation's negotiations for independence, eventually achieved in 1957.[14] Respect for British systems of education remained deeply ingrained among those in my parents' generation—privileged and brilliant Malaysians aspired to Rhodes scholarships at Oxford University or to Cambridge University. The ABRSM's elaborate system and its Commonwealth-wide reputation gained unquestioning respect and approval from Her Majesty's Malaysian subjects from the very beginning. Here was European culture presented by educational experts in a systematic form, within reach of all who could afford to pay for instruments, lessons, books, and examinations. Successful completion of each grade would result in both "international" recognition (since the system was known throughout the Commonwealth) and local respect.[15] The high price tags of lessons and examination fees, the latter converted directly from British pounds, were prohibitive for all but the wealthy or the most committed.[16] Thus the enterprise of taking piano lessons became wreathed in an aura of pride and prestige for its middle-class adherents. For lower-middle-class families such as my own, the piano offered the additional attraction of a long-term investment: music could "round off" the children's education, strengthen their chances for admission to good universities, and provide an alternate means of future income if necessary (a belief held especially true for females in late twentieth-century Hong Kong, Japan, Korea, the People's Republic of China, Singapore, and Taiwan as it had been for females in nineteenth-century Europe and North America). In other words, piano both represented and provided an avenue to upward mobility.

At the age of six, I was aware neither of the historical and social forces described above nor of their imminent impact upon me. A stereotypically obedient Chinese child, I learned, practiced, and absorbed all that my parents and piano teacher taught me about music. My first piano teacher was a young Chinese woman who had decided to teach full-time after completing high school because of the lucrative salary and flexible hours. Her well-educated family included Oxbridge graduates, a fact that boosted her image as a piano teacher in Kuala Lumpur society, although she herself had studied piano for less than a decade before I came under her wing. As a six-year-old, however, I only saw a pretty lady who dressed exquisitely (in lace, frills, and ruffles as the young Lady Diana did), who spoke English and played piano with poise and elegance, and who treated me with affectionate discipline: a veritable fairy-tale princess. Enchanted, I immediately resolved to be just like her.[17]

INSTRUMENTAL INSTRUCTION
AS COLONIZING FORCE

From the beginning, my teacher emphasized that learning to play the piano was a "British" activity, something that children in faraway England did under the supervision of the very same ABRSM system I was learning. Such pronouncements were calculated to reinforce her authority, to reassure my parents that theirs was a wise investment, and to spur me to practice by presenting the piano-playing British child as a role model. To play piano was to be "British," and the better I played, the more "British" I became. I was taught that the mystical, beautiful sounds that could be produced with two hands had been born of "white" history and "white" people, not us. In multicultural Malaysian society, ethnicity has long been a quick, convenient tool of differentiation, so that all Caucasians, whether American, Russian or British, are "white people" to Malaysian eyes—just as to the North American eye Koreans, Japanese, and Chinese are often taken to be "Asians" exactly like one another. Playing Western classical music, I could aspire to become "British"/ "Caucasian." Eventually, surrounded though I was by general cultural impoverishment, I might become civilized. The ABRSM system promised to guide me toward this goal, examination grade by examination grade. To civilize: to "bring out of a barbarous or primitive stage of society; enlighten; refine and educate" (*Oxford English Dictionary*). The elaborate nature of the enterprise seemed to reinforce its quality. How could any mechanism as complicated as this not reflect cultural excellence? The wealth of signs and symbols both intimidated and impressed us; the entire process involved international travel, expensive hotels, embossed certificates and Her Majesty's patronage. Our minds registered the quantitative evaluations as reliable indications of each candidate's worth and degree of "Britishness" in activities ranging from beating time to playing pieces from the Western classical canon.

I was, in short, imbibing postcolonial values alongside note values, chord progressions, melodies, and rhythms prescribed by the ABRSM as suitable for my level of skill. In the wake of independence, as the multicultural population of Malaysia had struggled to define its cultural and political identity, established British models in all arenas beckoned our still-colonized mentalities. Just as the newly minted nation retained its use of British institutional frameworks, segments of its population subconsciously clung to, and thus ultimately perpetuated, the continuity and security they had experienced within British cultural frameworks and values.[18] Such people lived—I lived—in the grip of the colonized imagination, for the "Britain" and "Britishness" we espoused no longer existed. In the hands of institutions such as the ABRSM, however, the colonized imagination could be—and indeed was—transformed into monetary gain. As the ABRSM Honorary Secretary's report from the first foreign tour to Australia in 1897–98 reveals, artistic development and monetary gain were from the outset twin goals: "I recommend the Board to 'go forward' and to carry on this work energetically and without fear of its results. There is I am convinced, a large harvest of useful and artistic work, and also a substantial profit to be reaped therefrom" (Aitken 1897–98: 19–20).

In Malaysia in the 1970s and early 1980s, the ABRSM operated in an arena largely void of other resources for Western classical music: there were few concerts and opportunities for public exhibition of student skills, little air-time on radio and television programs, no music classes in public schools, few if any college-level music courses, and only a handful of music stores in Kuala Lumpur that carried merchandise related to Western classical music (practically all such items were for ABRSM examinations).[19] Undeterred, Malaysians subscribed to the ABRSM in numbers disproportionate to the country's population. Like other Southeast Asian ex-colonies such as Hong Kong and Singapore, Malaysia posted unusually high numbers of examination candidates annually.[20] I was a deeply loyal if equally deeply insecure participant in ABRSM examinations, a blend of the colonized native and compliant Chinese child. From the ages of six to thirteen, I absorbed and trusted wholly in the ABRSM—my only avenue to Western classical music. I believed in the system's infallibility and in its judgment of my skills. In my inexperience and the absence of evidence to the contrary, I thought that the pieces of music prescribed for each grade were the only ones that existed. I did not, indeed could not, have a repertoire other than those pieces, since hardly any other music was sold. I remember playing Bach, Bartok, Beethoven, Chopin, Clementi, Handel, MacDowell, and Mozart over a span of eight years. This limited repertory, hardly representative of music then available in Great Britain, was apparently deemed sufficient for the ABRSM's goals in the colonies and later provided me with the clue that the institution's purpose had been to generate financial gains as well as to educate about music.

Although the ABRSM marketed itself as a prestige-laden private educational enterprise, the depth to which its directors understood the complex cultural situation and music-educational needs of the Malaysian market remains unclear. Had the Board researched Malaysians' attitudes and needs with regard to Western classical music? Did the Board know about the lack of resources Malaysians faced? Was the Board concerned that the ears and brains of those who processed the music it prescribed had otherwise had little exposure to and experience with the cultures of which the music was inextricably part? The ABRSM directors seem to have been contented to transfer its methods, created and practiced in culturally, politically, and economically different Britain, directly into a postcolonial setting, instead of adapting the methods in ways that would have shown sensitivity to the Malaysian context. By selling Malaysians Western classical music under the expired aegis of Empire, the Board joined the multitude of interpellating systems in the colonized imagination and propagated colonial narratives in ex-colonies with vulnerable identities.[21] Catherine Szego has found in her study of a Hawaiian missionary-type school that "[c]olonial education that privileges the learning of a foreign music over indigenous music is an obvious site for exploring power relations" (2002: 716).

FORMING A MUSICAL IDENTITY

As a child, I remember puzzling over the different cultural domains in which I functioned on an everyday basis, albeit at varying levels of immediacy: Chinese-British-Malaysian-Indian. When I engaged in Western classical music activities, however, I underwent what I have come to think of as consistent destabilization of my identity in the encounter between a cultural system perceived as established and hegemonic (European via the British) and one struggling to define itself (Malaysian-minority Chinese). Throughout childhood and into early adolescence my absorbent mind retained messages sent and received in the encounters, and these messages then formed the basis for my later "understanding" of the West, its culture, and its music. My early musical education was a process that did not much foster intellectual curiosity and musical activity, but one in which I was taught to think in terms of cultural, national, ethnic, and economic hierarchies. It is a story of colonial "violence" wrought on young minds and psyches.[22] The "violence" was wrought with a cultural tool—Western classical music—whose much-touted universality supposedly invites and nurtures interaction across time and cultures, geographies, ethnicities, and genders. Yet these very boundaries and limits were constant and often painful components of my early musical education. Motivated by different reasons, all of us—the ABRSM, my parents, my piano teacher, and myself—participated willingly if unwittingly in an ideological process that ultimately reinforced the colonizers' cultural subjugation of the colonized.

Had I, like most of my Malaysian friends, been content to stop my music training at grade 8, I suppose I would not have come to seek full understanding of the circumstances I have described. I derived so much pleasure from playing the piano that by the age of thirteen, as I completed the final grade offered by the ABRSM, I was sure I wanted to become a musician (albeit without knowing what that meant or entailed). Perhaps the decision, born of a colonized imagination, represented a continued yearning to become "British." At this point I began to wonder if one could become a musician simply by passing examinations: where did the process end?

The ABRSM lured children and ambitious parents with certificates and promises of prestige. But when I, a native awkward with youth and an accent, approached ABRSM examiners informally to inquire about pursuing music, I met with discouraging responses: "I don't recommend that you study piano professionally" and "You could sit for our diploma examinations in performance or teaching, and teach piano in Malaysia." Such advice, at once cautionary, well-meaning, and dismissive, may have been considered appropriate in Britain, where "second opinions" could be sought and/or further research conducted with information and opportunities available outside the context of the ABRSM. In post-colonial Malaysia, where the ABRSM was the most respected authority on Western classical music, the words served only to deepen the self-doubt in my colonized psyche. Already fearful and inferior, my adolescent self saw and heard: *We are willing to take you this far—as long as you pay Us—but don't you dare go any further into Our world and Our culture. If you are not one of Us by birth, there is no room for you here. You can dabble in music, yes. But that is Our limit for you, and therefore it should be the limit you set yourself.*

My reaction at that time—surprising as it sounds today—was in fact understandable or even logical in the context of my then limited exposure and training, and my veneration of the ABRSM. Such veneration, the result of colonization processes I describe earlier, decisively colored my interactions and understanding of "white musicians" and "white culture." I began studying Western classical music because it had been held up by my parents, my teachers, my society, and the ABRSM as a way to better myself. I had believed in colonized and colonizer alike. Caught in the web of the colonized imagination, I alternately lost and modified my identity in response to the historical and social forces swirling around and shaping me. Why did that happen? Because I was young and lived in a society where conformity, consensus, and submission are prioritized over criticism and dissent; because at that time I assumed that things had always been that way and would always be so; because I had heard of others who had had similar experiences; because I hadn't been aware that we, colonized and colonizer, had in fact been creating and living together the minutiae and emotional realities of postcolonialism—and thus making postcolonial history.[23]

My early music education under the ABRSM system left lingering effects on my outlook on and approach to Western classical music up until my years of graduate study in the United States, when I immersed myself in critical approaches to knowledge. Before then I did not have the words to describe, or perhaps was not even fully aware of, the subaltern deep within. During my undergraduate studies, my U.S. teachers wondered at my timidity in expressing myself musically and intellectually. I simply thought I was unworthy of judging and voicing my opinions about Western culture (how could I, when I didn't belong culturally?). I did not know what to think or say about music at all. I wanted only to imbibe all that Westerners were willing to teach me, a non-Westerner, and fell silent beside those who were bold, white-skinned, had grown up with abundant opportunities to listen to Western classical music, or had traveled to Europe. I wondered at the casual, friendly terms on which Americans accepted me as a music student, when all Westerners I had come into contact with as a music student in Malaysia had seemed distant to my endeavors. I cringed inwardly at the sound of the British accent, instinctively associating it with unassailable authority and superior knowledge, states I felt I could never achieve. I worried about discussing Western music as a non-Westerner to a roomful of Western faces. I mistrusted my multicultural identity, irreconcilably hybridized and fragmented with relativistic planes of understanding and inferior, I thought, to what I saw as the "white" world's privileging of factory-like uniformity, linearity, and efficiency of feeling and thought. At every turn, my colonial-style early music education functioned as a cultural cue *cum* social reference point for the process I underwent: surprise and shock, followed by a growing awareness of its long-term effects on me, and finally a struggle to realign the parameters of my identity and understanding of "white people" and their music.[24]

I have submitted to analytical scrutiny here what I remember of the inevitably unstructured and subjective impressions and feelings that made up my private childhood experiences of learning Western classical piano music in Malaysia. Looking back on the experiences as an adult scholar, I realize that like much childhood knowledge they were at once opaque and perspicacious, limiting and broadening, fiction and fact, past and present.

Unlike other types of childhood knowledge, however, the colonial presence I already sensed in my youth had been a constant and mysterious enough source of ambivalence that I eventually sought its identity and its name. In finding both, I have finally found part of myself.

Acknowledgments

This chapter was first published in Susan Boynton and Roe-Min Kok, eds., 2006, *Musical Childhoods and the Cultures of Youth*, Middletown, Conn.: Wesleyan University Press, 89–104. Its republication in the present volume was made possible with the support of the British Academy and the Institute of Musical Research, University of London, UK.

Notes

1. This chapter explores the formation of my musical identity primarily from the ages of six to thirteen (late 1970s–mid-1980s). I left Malaysia to pursue undergraduate and graduate studies in music in the United States. The ideas in this essay were initially developed in a graduate seminar on literary theory at Duke University in spring 1995, team-taught by James Rolleston, Walter Mignolo, Frederic Jameson, and Barbara Herrnstein Smith.

2. On the history of the term "postcolonial," see Mishra and Hodge (1991).

3. Mignolo argues for the importance of "postcolonial loci of enunciation as an emerging discursive formation and as a form of articulation of subaltern rationality" (2000: 88). By "subaltern forms of rationality," Mignolo means "not only that subalternity is a social class phenomenon and an object of study but that subalternity is characteristically theorized by those who are implicated in the very forms of subalternity they are theorizing" (ibid.: 86). Such work "attempt[s] to incorporate knowledge of the personal and social body, to restore the body to reason, and to reason from the subaltern (social and personal) body" (ibid.).

4. Few music scholars have explored the application of postcolonial theory in their work; a thought-provoking and valuable exception is Agawu (2003). Agawu begins by highlighting postcolonial theory's "potentially fruitful and ethical ways of making sense of the (musical) world," and identifies scholarship that is "postcolonial in spirit" (ibid.: xviii). Like postcolonial theorists Gayatri Spivak, Edward Said, and Homi Bhabha, Agawu brings perspectives born of his status as both (African) native insider and (Western) scholar outsider to critique what he sees as problematic aspects of African music scholarship, ranging from ideologies of representation to issues of notation and ethics.

Perhaps in keeping with Agawu's goal to de-exoticize contemporary Africa in the eyes of the West, he describes but does not problematize Ghanaian students' participation in Western classical music activities at Achimota School (ibid.: 13–15). The activities seem to have been a well-established tradition by the time he attended the school in the 1970s. In my essay I problematize my experience of learning the Western classical piano tradition at a time when the tradition was still a novelty to Malaysians.

5. The British gained Penang Island in 1786 and by the final decades of the nineteenth century had established control over West Malaya and East Malaya. Independence was achieved in 1957. For a history of Malaysia see Andaya and Andaya (1982).

N.B. "Malaysia" was coined in 1961, before which the country was known as "Malaya." For convenience, I use "Malaysia" throughout the essay.

6. On British-created class hierarchies in the colonies, see Cannadine (2001).

7. Edward Said has described a comparable situation in a British-run educational institution in Cairo, Egypt, around 1949–51. At Victoria College, "the Eton of the Middle East," students were "schooled in the ways of a British imperialism that had already expired . . ." (2000: 185–186).

8. Leppert (1995: 116–117) describes the cultural significance of the piano in eighteenth- and nineteenth-century India. The situation seems to have paralleled that in pre- and post-independence Malaysia. Leppert focuses on the musical activities of colonials ("Anglo-Indians") and does not deal with Indian reception of the piano and Western classical music.

9. As illustrated in, for example, Confucius's teaching of the Way and in Ssu-ma Ch'ien's account about Confucius tenaciously practicing a *ch'in* piece until he could sense the character of, and accurately identify, the composer. See Lin (1943: 67–68).

10. "If a man is not good, what has he to do with the rules of propriety? If he is not good, what has he to do with music?" (Confucius 1998 *Analects* 3, p. 3). Endnotes 9 and 10 may be examples of what Agawu calls "convergence at the level of background of ostensibly different cultural systems" (2003: 168).

11. [Editor's note:] This refers to the Board's examination system as the author remembers it from the late 1970s to the mid-1980s. The system practiced today remains similar, with the addition of a range of further exams including group tests and new practical musicianship tests. However, Grades 1 to 8 continue to be the mainstay of the system. See www.abrsm.ac.uk.

12. Although the ABRSM is not a "music conservatory" in the traditional sense of the term (it is not a physically centralized institution, nor does it employ a stable corps of music teachers), it offers systematic music education via a standardized set of examinations which certifies the accomplishment of certain musical skills. The music requirements appear to have been partially based upon Felix Mendelssohn's curriculum model at the Leipzig Conservatory (1843), popular in Europe since the nineteenth century, wherein training in harmony, theory, and musicianship was emphasized alongside applied skills. See Parakilas (1999: 154–155).

13. Agawu (2003: 14) mentions in passing the ABRSM's activities in Ghana, Sierra Leone, South Africa, and Nigeria in the 1970s. See also Kwami (1994 and 1989).

The British-based Royal Academy of Dance (RAD), established in 1920, offers a similar worldwide system of evaluation for dance. In Canada, the Royal Conservatory of Music (established 1886) began offering music examinations at the elementary and intermediate levels in 1935 and may have been adapted from the ABRSM system. The Canadian system of music examinations is available throughout North America (as compared to the international reach of its British counterpart). I thank Elizabeth Day for information about the RCM.

14. See *The Associated Board . . . Annual Report . . . 1948.* Also corroborated by an agenda item: "3. Malaya. Mr. Macklin reported that the Board had been in correspondence with the education authorities and it was hoped to hold Practical Examinations in Malaya in 1948." *Draft Minutes . . . 1947.* I am especially grateful to Mr. Richard Morrison, Dr. Nigel Scaife, and Ms. Sarah Levin for allowing me access to primary sources in the Board's archives in London.

15. For example, by 1948 the ABRSM was conducting examinations in Australia, Canada, New Zealand, India, Ceylon (now Sri Lanka), Malta, Jamaica, Trinidad, Ber-

muda, Barbados, Antigua, British Guiana, Malaya (now Malaysia), and Singapore. See *The Associated Board ... Annual Report ... 1948.*

16. The exchange rate of the Malaysian ringgit (MR) to British pounds (BP) in the late 1970s and early 1980s fluctuated between 7–8 MR to 1 BP.

17. My reaction speaks of the esteem in which teachers are traditionally held in Asian societies, a theme that has been explored by ethnomusicologists with reference to indigenous musical traditions. See, for example, Wong (2001).

18. Historically, the minority Chinese and South Asian communities of Malaysia were more pro-British than were the native Malays. Most members of the Chinese and South Asian communities had immigrated to Malaysia at the end of the nineteenth century, fleeing economic difficulty and famine in their homelands. Welcomed by the British as much-needed labor for the rubber and tin mining industries in Malaya, both ethnic groups flourished economically and professionally under colonial rule. Post-independence, my Chinese parents may well have felt for their pre-independence educational experiences in British-run institutions something Svetlana Boym describes as "restorative nostalgia ... [which] attempts a transhistorical reconstruction of the lost home ... [and] does not think of itself as nostalgia, but rather as truth and tradition" (2001: xviii).

19. Chopyak (1987) has documented the Malaysian government's efforts, presumably in the 1980s, to establish a musical culture that would promote national unity. As he explains, however, "There is currently [i.e., 1980s] a shortage of qualified music teachers in Malaysia.... there is often a great disparity between what appears in the music syllabus and what is actually taught in the [public] schools. In a number of schools observed by this writer music classes were simply singing sessions in which everyone sang songs (in Malay or English) to a piano or guitar accompaniment. Efforts are being made to train more music teachers within Malaysia itself ... a few potential teachers are also sent to the United States to study music education" (ibid.: 434). Chopyak does not specify the schools he visited, but they were probably located in urban areas; in addition, the *Kurikulum Baru Sekolah Rendah p. Buku Panduan Khas Muzik, Tahun Satu (The New Elementary School Curriculum p. Special Guidebook for Music, First Year)* was published relatively late, in 1983 (ibid: 453). In the late 1970s to early 1980s I attended public elementary schools in rural areas (*Sekolah Rendah Kebangsaan Kem Terendak* in Malacca, and *Sekolah Rendah Kebangsaan Our Lady's Convent* in Sitiawan, Perak), both of which featured little music in their curriculums.

Other than Western classical piano music, I sporadically came into contact with Canto-pop and Bollywood movie music on radio and television; American popular music of the 1940s–1960s (through American television shows and my father's LP collection); and American popular music of the 1980s (through my sister's tape collection). In my mid- and late teens (i.e., a period that falls outside the years I discuss in this essay), I attended a high school that had originally been an Anglican missionary school. My headmistress organized a school choir (it was not part of the school curriculum) that performed Christian-inspired choral music at annual school concerts. I served as rehearsal pianist and accompanist of this choir for three years.

20. For example, out of a total of 78,317 candidates outside Great Britain in 1977, Singapore entered 15,159 candidates; Hong Kong, 11,850; and Malaysia (including East Malaysia, or Sabah and Sarawak), 17,806; as compared to New Zealand, 12,152; Trinidad, 882; Guyana, 627; India, 566; and Belgium, 186 (*The Associated Board ... Annual Report ... 1977*). In 1980, of a total of 104,150 entries outside Great Britain, Singapore entered 19,792 candidates; Hong Kong, 17,858; and Malaysia (including East Malaysia, or Sabah and Sarawak), 28,956. See *The Associated Board ... Annual Report ... 1980.*

21. I use "interpellating" in the Althusserian sense. In "Ideology and ideologized state apparatuses" (1993) Althusser argues that subjects are ideologically produced to perform roles they are allocated in the social division of labor. Considered in this light, the ABRSM was one of several ideological systems that conditioned me into the role of the colonized. Reports from ABRSM examiners, for example that by Heath-Gracie quoted above, provide evidence that they often gained partial understanding of local economic, social, and cultural conditions and limitations during their tours. Research on institutional response to these reports is part of my ongoing project on the history of the ABRSM's international activities. Historically, colonization has been attributed to diverse motivations, including capitalistic exploitation, the desire on the part of the colonizer to "civilize" native populations, and the desire to remake colonized societies outside of Britain in the image of British society. See, for example, Howe (2002: 76–87), Said (1978), and Cannadine (2001).

22. This discussion relates to Pierre Bourdieu's notion of "symbolic violence" (2003: 122–128).

23. Readers have asked whether Malaysians considered setting up an alternative system of musical education. I emphasize that as far as I could tell, all who subscribed to the ABRSM, including my family, did so out of a respect for and belief in the system. In other words, we were happy with the ABRSM and saw no reason (again, as far as I could tell) to think about devising an alternative. This attitude in itself speaks of many things, including the quality of the ABRSM system, Malaysian subscribers' judgment of the same, the deep inroads colonization had made on this aspect of Malaysian life—in short, the complicated and compromised nature of the colonizer-colonized relationship.

24. See Mueller (2002) for an overview of research on music and identity among youth.

References

Agawu, Kofi. 2003. *Representing African Music: Postcolonial Notes, Queries, Positions*. New York: Routledge.

Andaya, Barbara Watson, and Leonard Y. Andaya. 1982. *A History of Malaysia*. London: Macmillan.

Ashcroft, Bill, Gareth Griffiths, and Helen Tiffin, eds. 1989. *The Empire Writes Back: Theory and Practice in Postcolonial Literatures*. London: Routledge.

Bhabha, Homi. 1985. "Sly Civility," *October* 34: 71–80.

Bourdieu, Pierre. 2003. *The Logic of Practice*. Stanford, Calif.: Stanford University Press.

Boym, Svetlana. 2001. *The Future of Nostalgia*. New York: Basic.

Cannadine, David. 2001. *Ornamentalism: How the British Saw their Empire*. Oxford: Oxford University Press.

Chopyak, James D. 1987. "The Role of Music in Mass Media, Public Education and the Formation of a Malaysian National Culture." *Ethnomusicology* 31 (3) 431–454.

Confucius. 1998. *The Original Analects: Sayings of Confucius and his Successors* [Lun yu]. A new translation with commentary by E. Bruce Brooks and A. Taeko Brooks. New York: Columbia University Press.

Everett, Yayoi Uno, and Frederick Lau, eds. 2004. *Locating East Asia in Western Art Music*. Middletown, Conn.: Wesleyan University Press.

Howe, Stephen. 2002. *Empire: A Very Short Introduction*. Oxford: Oxford University Press.

Kwami, Robert M. 1994. "Music Education in Ghana and Nigeria: A Brief Summary." *Africa* 64: 544–560.

———. 1989. African Music Education and the School Curriculum. PhD diss., University of London Institute of Education.

Leppert, Richard. 1995. "Music, Domesticity, and Cultural Imperialism." In *The Sight of Sound: Music, Representation, and the History of the Body*, 90–117. Berkeley: University of California Press.

Lin, Yutang, ed. and trans. 1943. *The Wisdom of Confucius.* New York: Random House.

Mignolo, Walter D. 2000. "(Post)Occidentalism, (Post)coloniality, and (Post)Subaltern Rationality." In *The Pre-Occupation of Postcolonial Studies*, ed. Fawzia Afzal-Khan and Kalpana Seshadri-Crooks, 86–118. Durham, N.C.: Duke University Press.

Mishra, Vijay, and Bob Hodge. 1991. "What is Post(-)Colonialism?" *Textual Practice* 5 (3): 399–414.

Mueller, Renate. 2002. "Perspectives from the Sociology of Music." In *The New Handbook of Research on Music Teaching and Learning: A Project of the Music Educators National Conference*, ed. Richard Colwell and Carol Richardson, 584–603. New York: Oxford University Press.

Parakilas, James, ed. 1999. *Piano Roles: Three Hundred Years of the Piano.* New Haven, Conn.: Yale University Press.

Said, Edward. 2000. *Out of Place: A Memoir.* New York: Vintage.

———. 1978. *Orientalism.* New York: Pantheon.

Szego, C. K. 2002. "Music Transmission and Learning: A Conspectus of Ethnographic Research in Ethnomusicology and Music Education." In *The New Handbook of Research on Music Teaching and Learning: A Project of the Music Educators National Conference*, ed. Richard Colwell and Carol Richardson, 707–729. New York: Oxford University Press.

———. 1999. *Musical Meaning-Making in an Intercultural Environment: The Case of Kamehameha Schools.* PhD diss., University of Washington, Seattle.

Wallace, Jo-Ann. 1994. "De-Scribing *The Water Babies:* 'The Child' in Postcolonial Theory." In *De-Scribing Empire: Postcolonialism and Textuality*, ed. Chris Tiffin and Alan Lawson, 171–184. London: Routledge.

Wong, Deborah. 2001. *Sounding the Center: History and Aesthetics in Thai Buddhist Performance.* Chicago: University of Chicago Press.

PRIMARY SOURCES: LONDON, ENGLAND: ARCHIVES OF THE
ASSOCIATED BOARD OF THE ROYAL SCHOOLS OF MUSIC.

Aitken, Samuel. 1897–98. *Mr. S. Aitken's Report on his Tour in Australasia & Canada 1897–1898.*

Draft Minutes of the 27th Meeting of the Joint Committee for Music . . . held at 14 Bedford Square, London, W.C.1., on Saturday, 15 February 1947, at 11 AM

Heath-Gracie, G. H. 1960. *Mr. G. H. Heath-Gracie's Report, Malaya Tour 1960.*

The Associated Board of the Royal Schools of Music: Summary of the Ninety-Second Annual Report of the Board for the Year 1980.

The Associated Board of the Royal Schools of Music: Summary of the Eighty-Ninth Annual Report of the Board for the Year 1977.

The Associated Board of the Royal Schools of Music: Sixtieth Annual Report of the Board for the Year 1948.

SIX

Continuity and Change

The *Guru-Shishya* Relationship in Karnatic Classical Music Training

SOPHIE GRIMMER

Described by the Indian scholar T. G. Vaidyanathan as the "master paradigm that runs like a leitmotif through India's checkered history" (1989: 148), the bond between a master (*guru*) and a disciple (*shishya*) is particularly significant in the training of the arts in India. Underpinning both of India's classical music traditions for centuries, *guru-shishya-parampara* has enabled the intricacies of both the Hindustani and Karnatic forms to be passed orally from teacher to student for generations. The latter component of this tripartite term, *parampara*, referring to the mode of music transmission that occurs within a *guru-shishya* relationship, literally means "an uninterrupted row or series, a succession" (Monier-Williams 1899: 587).

Traditionally, in a system known as *gurukulavasam* (ibid.: 359), the *shishya* becomes a member of the *guru's* household. Regarded as part of the family, provided with food and clothing, the *shishya* is assimilated into the *guru's* schedule. Ranked higher than biological parent, a metaphysical entity representing God and both parents, the *guru* assumes ultimate authority, in part predicated upon the *shishya's* devotion and total obedience. As the *guru* "lives, eats, breathes and sleeps music" (Neuman 1990: 54), so the *shishya* imbibes the atmosphere of the art, inadvertently internalizing both musical knowledge and a broader foundation of contextual information. With "no separation between a 'teacher' and a 'curriculum' to be taught" (Weidman 2006: 276), the *shishya* learns by emulating the *guru*, "by becoming absorbed in him or her." Naresh, a young Karnatic singer interviewed for research that forms the basis of this chapter, describes this traditional musical embodiment:

> The *guru* never used to tell the *shishya*, "I'll teach you." Never.... You live with the music, and after a point, you literally *live* the music.

With no distinction made between "life" and "music," the traditional *gurukulavasam* provides a social context for two modes of transmission, cognitive and cultural (Booth 1996), in which behaviors and customs necessary for oral/aural learning processes are supported and validated.

At the beginning of the twentieth century, keen to emphasize the commensurability of Indian and Western classical music but also wanting to distinguish that which set the Indian tradition apart from its Western counterpart, a South Indian elite chose to highlight both the primacy of the voice and the oral/aural nature of musical transmission. Against this background, in a post-colonial discourse dominated by concerns of authenticity and fidelity to "tradition," heightened by a perceived threat of new technologies (Weidman 2003), *guru-shishya-parampara* remains a potent contemporary issue for Indian musicians and for their *rasikas* (discerning listeners, connoisseurs of music). According to Ranade, "GSP [*guru-shishya-parampara*] . . . has become a charged entity, providing a sure sign of its cultural status. . . . Indians have a psychological complex about it!" (1998: 39).

Inevitably, the processes of training in Indian classical traditions have undergone significant modifications in response to dramatic societal changes in modern India and to influences from the diverse pedagogic approaches of a global diasporic community. The *shishya* living in India today, unless brought up by professional musicians, is unlikely to experience the total learning environment of *gurukulavasam*. Nevertheless, just as Neuman (1990) discovered from Hindustani musicians in Delhi in the late 1960's, contemporary classical artists continue to revere aspects of the apprenticeship model. Arts training institutions, both independent and state-sponsored, attempt to incorporate elements of *guru-shishya-parampara* into their curricula, making changes to Western education methodologies inherited under British rule (Alter 1994; Prickett 2007). Musicians, for their part, still believe that working independently within the *guru-shishya* relationship is critical to success as a performer. The special contact between *guru* and *shishya* is considered fundamental to the development of musical expertise, to becoming "a genuinely learned musician" (Neuman 1990: 209). Even where conditions militate against supporting traditional aspects of the relationship, fundamental principles would seem to be kept alive in spirit, if not in practice, through various strategies adapted to contemporary circumstances.

Much insight into Indian classical music pedagogy, particularly the *guru-shishya* relationship, comes from ethnomusicological studies. Investigating the music itself, from the "inside" (Baily 2001: 94), researchers often become "participant observers" in the field. In the process of developing musical skill, usually under the guidance of one *guru* over an extended period, not only is the structure of the music "apprehended operationally" (ibid.), but researchers become attuned to the sociocultural context of learning and performing. Ethnomusicological research of this nature concerning Indian classical music has tended to focus on instrumental rather than vocal music, most particularly from the Hindustani tradition of North India (e.g., Sorrell 1980; Kippen 1988). Far fewer studies focus on Karnatic music (e.g., Brown 1965; Higgins 1994). Alongside other education-focused research employing ethnomusicological methodologies (Booth 1986), this study focuses primarily on the *guru-shishya* relationship itself. Rather than drawing on data collected from direct experience of a single teaching and learning context, the approach aims to facilitate a broader understanding of several *guru-shishya* environments within the Karnatic tradition where singing is the primary focus. While the two classical musics of India share essential elements, including certain *ragas*, Karnatic music is strikingly different from its Hindustani counterpart: the textual content is predominantly religious; ornamental material is given greater emphasis; and improvisatory boundaries are determined more profoundly by the rendition of compositions. In addition, the sociocultural history of each canonical style has given rise to different pedagogies and associated social networks.

This chapter investigates contemporary perceptions of the *guru-shishya* relationship among advanced vocal students (*shishyas*) and their teachers (*gurus*) within the Karnatic tradition. How is the relationship experienced by these *shishyas* and *gurus*? How does it influence their understanding of the teaching and learning processes? In what ways does it forge their relationships and roles as students, teachers, musicians, and participants within a larger and long-standing cultural tradition?

Fieldwork took place between 2006 and 2008 in South Indian urban centers including Mysore, Bangalore, and Chennai. I conducted in-depth interviews with nine *gurus* (six men and three women), on several occasions spanning a period of twelve months. I also observed these *gurus* in two contexts: as they taught advanced *shishyas* and in the company of those same *shishyas* outside the lesson environment. Fifteen *shishyas* (six men and nine women) involved in the observed lessons also gave interviews. All participants were encouraged to reflect on the development of their musicianship with reference to the contexts of their teaching and learning, both formal and informal.

Because I came to the field with extensive experience of Western classical singing as a solo performer and singing teacher, as a cultural outsider to the Karnatic tradition yet aware of the complexities of developing expertise with a "hidden" instrument, I was fascinated to examine the teaching and learning processes employed by Karnatic musicians for the development of an equally sophisticated yet utterly different vocal style. I was provoked by a desire to question certain aspects of Western classic singing training; consequently, exposure to such profoundly different pedagogical approaches, and to such extraordinarily different perspectives *upon* those processes, helped to facilitate a reexamination of my own cultural context. While the data here originate in a larger research project concerning singing pedagogy, specifically the transmission and development of vocal skill for solo performance within the Karnatic tradition, the focus of this chapter is the pivotal *guru-shishya* relationship.

LEARNING MUSIC "PROPERLY"

NARESH (SHISHYA): I needed to start learning vocal music *properly* under a guru.

Many *shishyas* remember a particularly pivotal stage in their musical development when they decided to turn to a *guru* for training, either exclusively or in conjunction with more formal institutional approaches. Usually having experienced group music classes prior to this critical moment, *shishyas* seem to associate the *guru-shishya* relationship, for several reasons, with a "proper" kind of teaching.

SURRENDER TO A SINGLE BANI EXPONENT

RAJANI (SHISHYA): Ultimately you need to fall into a school [*bani*], because otherwise you will be rudderless. . . . You'll just be lost. You won't know what to do or how to do it. . . . It's just a question of finding a path of your own, finding a path which is comfortable for you as an individual, as a musician, and which fits into your capabilities.

While finding a unique voice is central to the expression of Karnatic classical music, with its unusual combination of compositions (*kalpita sangita*) and improvisatory possibilities (*manodharma sangita*), the early stages of a *shishya*'s training with a single *guru* concern the comprehensive establishment of a musical foundation. A *shishya* embodies the music of a particular *bani* (school, style or lineage) through blind imitation of the *guru*'s music over an extended period. The intricate *gamakas* (ornaments) that intertwine with a predominantly devotional *sahitya* (lyrics), so prominent a feature of Karnatic music, receive special attention and play a significant part in distinguishing one musician's rendition from another. Accumulating an armory of musical knowledge within a particular stylistic paradigm, participants explain that the *guru* provides a "groove," a direction for this process.

The decision to commit to this kind of training with the exponent of a particular *bani,* a significant moment for any aspiring musician, is often provoked by an intense first encounter. Within this study, both *shishyas* and *gurus* when recollecting their experiences as *shishyas* describe how they were seduced by the intoxicating qualities of their *guru*'s music—sometimes to the point of obsession (note that the possessive adjective is always applied in this context):

RISHU (GURU): I heard my master teach. I was attracted by his style of singing and I became mad.

RAJANI (SHISHYA): I used, like a madman, you've seen the Chennai traffic, you've seen the Chennai by-lanes, you've seen the Chennai temples and temple streets [laughs], like a madman, I used to open *The Hindu* [Chennai newspaper] and see where he is singing today and it would be a place far off from where I was living. I mean I used to take three buses up, three buses down, skip my breaks, skip my dinner, do all sorts of weird things, but I used to end up listening to him. It was a kind of a madness which enveloped me.

Having chosen a *guru*, a *shishya* is expected to follow the musical "path" associated with that particular *guru*. Traditionally, commitment to the "path" is considered synonymous with commitment to the *guru*. According to (*shishya*) Shyam, *shishyas* who do not trust their *guru* implicitly and wholeheartedly are rendered "directionless":

> If there is a negative feeling in me that somebody is not capable of teaching me or I am not capable of learning from them, how will music flourish?

Considering it critical to give in completely to the experience of learning, with total dedication, Rajani (*shishya*) embraces the necessity for "absolute surrender" in the relationship. Reflecting something of the etymological roots of *guru* as spiritual preceptor, he explains that "sometimes you just need to follow with blind faith."

Stipulating a ten-year commitment at a school combined with family living, Jaya asks her *shishyas* to inhabit the extreme end of this "surrender" continuum. She believes the quality of their commitment, even more than their natural musical ability, determines success. Jaya explains that *shishyas* with the courage to trust her, who can follow her instructions without questioning the process too much, are more likely to develop into great singers. During one interview she cited a particularly extreme example of *shishya* courage. An advanced musician who had worked extensively with a previous *guru* on a *sruti* (drone pitch) "not suited to her natural voice" arrived at the school in significant vocal difficulty. Requesting that this *shishya* start her training all over again, in a sense, Jaya imposed an extraordinary ban:

> So for one year I told her to stop singing. You will not sing at all. You will only sit here [at the school] and listen, listen, listen. You will stop the use of your voice for music. But one thing, she [the *shishya*] agreed. She kept quiet.

Naresh is unique among the *shishyas* in learning from two *gurus* simultaneously. Apparently compromising the traditional "surrender" to a single *bani* exponent, Naresh explains that such an arrangement would not have been appropriate earlier on in his training. With permission sought from both parties, having already established a solid foundation with a single *guru* as a younger *shishya*, Naresh is now capitalizing on an opportunity to develop his own unique style from dual absorption, combining the masculine and feminine qualities of two schools.

DISCIPLINE

Many *shishyas* long for the discipline associated with *guru-shishya-parampara*—discipline both in delivery of the music itself and during the learning process, particularly in relation to a dedicated practice regime:

> **HARSHAD (*SHISHYA*):** He [my *guru*] is a very sincere disciple, a very strict teacher that I should have, because my music is not so strict. It is not so perfect.

> **SHYAM (*SHISHYA*):** Perfectionist in whatever you do. That was the mental make-up. With that sort of a background, he used to train us.

> **RAJANI (*SHISHYA*):** It inculcates or imbibes in you a desire to be perfect. Because you see perfection, you say, so this is the attention to detail you need to have.

Even if the demands made upon a *shishya* result in nights of sobbing over personal practice, high expectations and a meticulous attention to musical detail are considered part of proper teaching: proof of a *guru*'s stature. According to Rajani, once a commitment is made to the *guru,* creativity becomes a "very serious matter":

> **RAJANI (SHISHYA):** I have to live up to my guru's name, to my guru's reputation. I better deliver. You become more professional, you become more focused in your approach. The casual approach, the casual attitude is cast away and that's very important. You have to be professional when you perform. It's serious work.... A performance has to be a carefully thought out, carefully organized, meticulously planned exercise. You cannot take it lightly. And being from, if you are the *shishya* of a good, a great guru, the responsibility is that much greater.

And this responsibility to maintain the *guru*'s reputation, providing a disciplinary teaching tool in itself, establishes in the *shishya* a high benchmark of expectation for development; an expectation that can be overwhelming sometimes:

RAJANI (SHISHYA): Oh, it's a burden sometimes, of course. The first thing is that your standards are way too high. So ten years ago if I were to sing a concert, at the end of it, I would think, OK, I was OK, I was pretty good. But today when I sing a concert, because my standards have increased so much, because of my *guru*, I'll probably say, hmm [outward sigh]. And that concert would have been a hundred times better than the concert I did ten years ago. My response would be less.

EMOTIONAL ATTACHMENT: "FEELING PART OF THE GURU"

Often distinguishing it from the unidimensional teacher-student relationship, participants describe the bond between *guru* and *shishya* as multifaceted and all-encompassing. While a *shishya* might learn to execute musical details from a teacher, the totality of the experience of a *guru-shishya* relationship is thought to facilitate a more profound embodiment of the esoteric, elusive dimensions of the musical tradition. Beyond learning technique, it can support musical absorption "in a deeper way" (Harshad, *shishya*). Development of a close personal relationship over time, the nurturing of a mutual emotional attachment, is thought to play a fundamental role in facilitating a gradual percolation to the unconscious of the intangible musical touches considered so critical for powerful performance—touches that highlight the *bhakti* (spirit) and *bhava* (emotion) within the music:

RAJANI (SHISHYA): It's [bhakti] palpable but it's very difficult to put words to it. You can almost feel it when he is singing. I can touch this raga. Deep within you, you can say, I can feel this raga inside me, and that aspect is really important. That, the intensity.... If you are putting your heart and soul in and tell yourself that, at this point in my life, this is the only thing I have to live for, which is how he [my guru] sings, then that is music. Anything else would be gimmicks.

NARESH (SHISHYA): It is so difficult to put into words [*bhakti/bhava*]. As far as the philosophical content of music, the spiritual content of music, the power of music [is concerned].... It's a very vital aspect ... that devotion, that deep spiritual yearning.

Commonly employing familial terminology to help convey something of the intense feelings of love that can develop within the relationship, *shishyas* describe their sense of belonging to the *guru:*

> NARESH (*SHISHYA*): The relationship is one of belonging to the fam-
> ily. That sense of belonging is there. It is a very strong sense that it is
> *always* there. . . . He [my *guru*] is a father, son, friend, brother. He is
> various things at various times.

> RAJANI (*SHISHYA*): And when the guru-shishya relationship grows, as
> it grows and it matures, you begin to feel a part of the guru. . . . You
> feel you belong to the guru, and that's very fulfilling.

And such a close relationship also enables the *guru* to gain a detailed
picture of individual *shishyas;* their vocal idiosyncrasies, personal traits,
musical capabilities and sensibilities. At later stages of the training, when
the *shishya* is essentially on an autonomous journey, gradually bringing a
unique stamp to the *bani,* the *guru* is then better positioned to offer specific, personalized, and particularly useful advice. When practicing improvisation in call-and-response exchanges during a lesson, for example,
Rajani (*shishya*) relishes hearing any musical suggestions from his *guru,*
usually relayed vocally. Coming from someone who has intimate knowledge of him, both personally and musically, such suggestions appear to
Rajani a precious contribution to the development of his own individual
voice, as do other *shishyas:*

> YASH (*SHISHYA*): The most important thing from a guru is, he should
> be a tailor. He should measure you, he should make things just enough
> for you, not too big, not too large, and he should be able to change his
> measurement as time goes by.

> NANDI (*GURU*): I have to re-create the same information in a differ-
> ent package for both of them [shishyas], understanding how *they*
> understood it.

CULTURAL CAPITAL: BELONGING TO A
REPUTABLE MUSICAL LINEAGE

While dialogue during the lessons is essentially sung, often a fluid uninterrupted exchange of melodic material between *guru* and *shishya,* any

extensive verbal communication between the two parties often occurs outside the lesson environment, in less formal social contexts. Usually initiating conversation, the *guru* might tell stories or relay anecdotes that relate specifically to aspects of Karnatic music. Particularly nostalgic in flavor are those reflections that concern the *gurus'* own *guru/s:*

> YASH (SHISHYA): He [my guru] talks about his [own] guru at length. That is a great education for me. He doesn't talk about himself, but he talks about his *guru* in a very detailed way. I think those are the moments that I really like.... You can't stop him when he talks about his guru because ... for him he is part of his guru even now.

Due to the changing landscape of modern India, few *shishyas* are able to replicate the duration and intensity of training that many of their *gurus* experienced from a very young age as *shishyas.* Nevertheless, as the *gurus* recollect and describe their own processes of learning, so the spirit of the historical *guru-shishya* relationship would seem to be kept alive in the present. The contemporary *shishya* is encouraged to feel part of an ongoing history of teaching and learning; to feel pivotal within the broader cultural picture of an oral tradition. What's more, anecdotes relayed by the *guru* that extol the virtues of present musicians from the same *bani,* that describe extraordinary performances by musicians of the past whose lineage can be traced back to the same *bani,* would seem to further embed in the *shishya* a sense of pride in being part of a musical heritage—of being let in on the secrets of a particular stylistic school:

> SHIV (SHISHYA): It is doubtless to say, he comes from the *guru-shishya-parampara* of Tyagaraja himself [one of the much-revered Trinity of Karnatic composers]. I take pride in saying that I am the sixth generation coming down, seventh generation of the great Tyagaraja.

A contemporary musician's identity within the Karnatic tradition continues to be significantly shaped by this genealogical heritage. Within the power structures of different stylistic schools, working within a particular *bani* can bring with it significant "cultural capital" (Bourdieu 1986), providing professional opportunities as a result of the *guru's* historical pedigree and musical reputation.

NEO-*GURUKULAVASAM*

For most contemporary *shishyas,* the experience of training in a total learning environment akin to the traditional *gurukulavasam* is a vicarious one, relayed indirectly through stories told by older musicians or described in historical texts. Few live permanently with a *guru* or experience, by that association, direct contact with music and music-related activities day and night. Nevertheless, the *gurus* and *shishyas* of this study continually adapt their teaching and learning processes to accommodate aspects of *gurukulavasam* considered critical for genuine musical development, while also embracing the new demands of modern life (see, e.g., Sangeet Research Academy 1998: 4–32 and 47–54). As practical conditions and behavioral patterns are continually negotiated, so new pedagogies would seem to be emerging out of an accommodation of two worlds: a neo-*gurukulavasam* comprising inevitable variations on the "traditional" model.

BEHAVIORAL PATTERNS IN THE RELATIONSHIP: "THE BEAUTY OF THE BOUNDARY"

Asked to reflect upon their own learning as young *shishyas, gurus* commonly describe a formal atmosphere within the *guru-shishya* relationship in which certain hierarchical behavioral patterns were assumed. Demonstration of respect for the *guru* was paramount. *Shishyas* would rarely ask questions or talk freely in their *guru's* presence. Some had to adhere to particular physical codes of conduct: prostrating at the *guru's* feet (still a common practice today) or standing with arms folded throughout a lesson. With a learning process entirely controlled by the *guru, shishyas* would have to seek permission from the *guru* to take part in any performance, to attend concerts by other *vidvans* (master musicians), or to work with another *guru.* Yatin, for example, having to leave his *guru's* hometown for financial reasons, was asked by his *guru* never to train with another master, in order that the *parampara* be protected from outside influences.

With inevitably less tolerance among *shishyas* for such serfdom in modern times, and with *gurus* reflecting on the negative impact of certain aspects of their own training, the gap between *guru* and *shishya* would seem to be closing:

YATIN (GURU): In those days we were not that free with our teachers. There was always a distance between the teacher and the taught. Now it's more personal, more intimate. And the eye contact, the body language, everything is there now.

Having worked with several *gurus* at different stages of his training, one *shishya* in the study seems to have experienced both ends of this distance spectrum. Accused of not demonstrating the appropriate humility or "vibrations" of a *shishya,* Naresh struggled over many years to adhere to the devotional demands made upon him by his octogenarian *guru.* Now Naresh is working with a rather younger master, and he feels an "immense comfort" in the process of learning. In light of unpleasant experiences as a *shishya* himself, Naresh's *guru* (Rishi) positively encourages questions from his *shishyas,* consciously aiming to create an atmosphere in which knowledge is felt to be shared.

But whatever form these shifts in the *guru-shishya* dynamic take, a sense of duty, reverence and respect towards the *guru* still prevails among contemporary *shishyas* and manifests itself in many different behaviors. Though many state that the debt of gratitude can never be repaid, *shishyas,* as in the past, find ways to honor their *guru's* contribution to their musical development. These include running errands for the *guru's* family; lending money to the *guru;* crediting the *guru* at concerts; never performing the *guru's* trademark intonations or signature *sangatis* (ornaments); singing "two notches" below the guru in any improvisatory exchange; and maintaining formal codes of conduct during lessons, even when the atmosphere beyond that arena is more informal. Rajani (*shishya*) believes that upholding certain boundaries between the *guru* and *shishya* optimizes the learning, providing an invaluable structure, both musical and social, for the process:

RAJANI (SHISHYA): We share a very interesting relationship because age-wise, he is two years elder to me . . . so if he was not my guru, I would be putting my arms around him and saying let's go for a drink. But inside the music room . . . the relationship begins with the *guru-shishya* boundaries that say he is my guru, I am his *shishya,* and that is a very nice beautiful boundary within which we can work.

INSPIRATION IN THE *GURU'S* COMPANY

While the one-to-one lesson would seem to be the principal arena of learning for the *shishyas,* many engage in other activities, often informal in nature, that provide a complementary layer of information transmission relating to Karnatic music. I observed many *shishyas* spending considerable time with their *guru* in different professional and private contexts: helping the *guru* to prepare thematic presentations or concerts; sitting with the *guru* on stage during a performance; sharing post-performance reflections with the *guru;* and attending the concerts of other *vidvans* in the *guru's* company—and this despite significant time restrictions and the financial pressures of modern life, with some *shishyas* sustaining two careers in parallel. All the *shishyas* had performed with their *guru* in concert, either accompanying on the *tambura* (fretless lute providing a drone with multiple harmonics) or support-singing on a reduced-volume microphone. This provided a powerful resource for gaining insight into issues of performance practice:

> **VINATA (SHISHYA):** I'd go to all the concerts. You learn how he does things, how he behaves, how he takes care of the different situations. When we sit in the concert, we sit behind him, getting to know the interaction between everybody on stage and how it's different on stage, everything. You get to experience that.

Believing that mere association with the *guru* is critical to an authentic development, a notion stemming from the historical ideal, the *shishyas* I observed also spent time in the *guru's* company in more relaxed surroundings: at the family home sharing a meal, talking on the telephone, or sharing ideas via video-conferencing on the computer. The *guru* is thought to provide a role model for living, as a musician, as a professional negotiating a music career, but also as a human being living according to a particular philosophy. *Shishyas* describe how they are inspired musically but also "in life." Rajiv tries to emulate the honesty of his *guru's* "childlike" personality; Naresh admires his *guru's sadhana* (spiritual practice for self-realization) as a devotee of Tyagaraja; while Rajani has reassessed his own approach to life on a number of occasions, both practically and psychologically, having observed the extraordinary extent to which his *guru* is disciplined and dedicated as a teacher and performer:

RAJANI (SHISHYA): You need a certain positive approach to work with music, because there will be times when you are practicing and you just don't get anything right. You know creativity is always like that. There are days when you start singing and you see a black box in front of you [outward sigh]. Give me a break! And he's always there, even if he's not physically around sometimes, like if I'm in Bangalore and he's in Chennai, right, his positivity, his approach to music, his approach to life, keeps us going. . . . You begin to feel that whatever the guru does, something in you can also do it.

SHISHYA NETWORKS

In traditional *gurukulavasam, shishyas* learned from observations of the *guru* but also from regular contact with fellow *shishyas,* or "siblings" from the same familial musical household. In Jaya's school, an extensive amount of informal learning occurs among her *shishyas,* echoing the peer-directed learning practices of Western popular musicians (Green 2001: 76–83). In a lesson environment, *shishyas* observe their peers being taught. In the *guru*'s absence, they learn from one another, encouraged "to criticize in a healthy way" (Jaya, *guru*). Forming mixed ability groups with *shishyas* of different ages, they practice together or help to teach one another:

SHILPA (SHISHYA): There is so much give and take within us. . . . [We get] more than learning individually. I think this group, our team effort, has done [to] each one of us great things, because we are able to practice together, we are able to learn from each other. I take a lot of good qualities from them. Each of us observes the other person and what they are good at.

Other *shishyas,* without the luxury of such an established *shishya* community, arrange jam sessions with fellow *shishyas,* picking up new ideas through call-and-response exchanges of *manodharma* (improvised) material. Naresh (*shishya*) arranges regular informal *shishya* concerts that evolve out of such exploratory sessions, but also attends a weekly online meeting where Karnatic musicians from all over the world discuss particular areas of interest, often sharing recordings or providing live sung examples.

THE MULTIPLE VOICES OF A TECHNO-*GURU*

In stark contrast to an older generation of musicians who listened almost exclusively to live performance during their training, either in concert or via All India Radio broadcasts, the contemporary *shishya* has extraordinary access to all kinds of music, to multiple voices. With half a terabyte of Karnatic music downloaded onto his computer, a year's worth of listening, Naresh (*shishya*) found it impossible to adhere to a request from his former "task-master" *guru* that he restrict his listening to the music of certain performers:

> He wants that kind of dedication. [It's] so difficult in today's world. I mean you are surrounded by so many distractions and you have so many avenues to listen to music now. You can't say, "No I won't listen."

Despite Naresh's experience, *gurus* generally accept that their *shishyas* are exposed to countless recordings of numerous artists via new technologies. The broader listening palette is generally considered a powerful teaching resource, but *only* in conjunction with a *guru* training. Unless *shishyas* comprehensively establish the bedrock of a *bani* with a *guru*, developing "intelligent listening" in the process, they cannot draw the best out of other music to improve their own. Jaya actually restricts the listening of her inexperienced junior *shishyas* to avoid confusion in this regard. The more embedded the *bani*, the more a *shishya* is likely to be attracted to musical ideas from "outside" that perfectly reflect both that *bani* and their own musical personality. From within the *bani* boundary, the singer then draws on a memory bank of these remembered repertoires in the moment of performance (Neuman 1990: 22).

Insisting that immediate live correction from a *guru* is critical when a new composition is being learned, all the *gurus* caution their *shishyas* against using recordings for that purpose. Not only is it hard for *shishyas* to deduce the accuracy of their "reproduction" without external guidance, because of the internalized nature of their instrument, but they may often unintentionally ignore or incorrectly absorb significant melodic details. Similarly, if a concert recording is the template for learning, they may unwittingly imbibe mistakes that occurred in the flow of performance. Just as notation should only serve as a memorandum *after* appropriate absorption by ear, similarly recordings should only be used once a composition has been thoroughly learned via the *guru* "by impregnation, mimetism, memory and improvisation" (SRA/Tournier 1998: 53).

Gurus also treat the use of recording equipment as a teaching aid with some caution. Before such facilities were available, when a lesson was one of the only opportunities to hear the *guru's* music comprehensively, a *shishya* needed to focus acutely in the moment. *Gurus* perceive that *shishyas* today, safe in the knowledge that a lesson can be recorded and then played back repeatedly, are inclined to be more complacent in their listening, less attuned to the subtle yet essential musical details.

PEDAGOGICAL SHIFTS AND THEIR IMPACT ON THE FUTURE OF KARNATIC MUSIC

While the *guru-shishya* relationship continually adapts to the changing political and social climate of modern India, the perennial issue of authenticity remains prominent in the discourse among Karnatic musicians and their *rasikas*. Pedagogical shifts arising out of the increased availability of advanced listening and recording technologies are of particular concern to many of the *gurus* involved in this research. They fear that inexperienced musicians, the teachers of the future, exposed to a multitude of musical styles via a technological neo-*guru,* are more likely to learn and pass on confused misrepresentations of the *bani. Shishyas* identifying with a multitude of crossover styles, under pressure to succeed and with minimal experience of training under a *guru,* might even unwittingly contribute to a distortion of the classical boundary itself. In addition, as musicians refer to recordings as a reminder and rely less on their memories to recall repertoire, *gurus* perceive that Karnatic music is likely to become more "fixed." Nandi (*guru*) sees music as perpetual motion, with subtle changes occurring as a consequence of musical exchange from one person to another and with the fallibility of human memory and the individuality of each voice playing its part in the music's continual development and enrichment. Without this dynamic interchange, a certain stagnation might occur:

> **NANDI (GURU):** My proposition is that music is going to change less now because of recordings. Say I want to know how Todi sounds, how raga Todi is sung. I have a hundred recordings, so how will Todi

change? It has changed over two hundred years because everybody worked on their memory and each musician gave their own twist and turn to it.... If I'm proved wrong, I'm happy, honestly, but my belief is [that] in a hundred years from now, most musical forms won't have changed as much ... because we have tools that will constantly remind us of how they sounded a hundred years ago.... I don't believe it's good for any music because it leads to a stagnation of sorts. What is really beautiful about tradition is that a big thread or a root is kept constant, while the bulb around it is always changing.

A similar viewpoint, expressed slightly differently:

The major risk of working too much on fixed images of ragas and not on perpetual motion ones, as is the case during regular successive courses of a traditional teaching, is that it becomes more difficult to part from the memorised fixed image and slips oneself away from the musician improviser. (SRA/Tournier 1998: 53)

This chapter has focused on the *guru-shishya* relationship within the Karnatic singing tradition, revealing the extent to which it has historically been, and continues to be, a vital part of classical music training in South India. Not addressed here, but contributing to the pedagogical dilemmas facing *gurus* and *shishyas* in contemporary India, are issues such as ethnic identity in the context of increased globalization; the increased atomization of a traditionally holistic model of oral/aural training; the impact of other world music pedagogies; the intellectual and analytical influences of a postcolonial "middle classization" in Karnatic training; the changing role of women in Karnatic performance and training; and the conflicting imperatives of devotion and virtuosity within the tradition.

References

Alter, A. 1994. Gurus, Shishyas and Educators: Adaptive Strategies in Post-Colonial North Indian Music Institutions. In *Music Cultures in Contact*, ed. M. Kartomi and S. Blum, 158–168. Basle: Gordon and Breach.

Baily, John. 2001. Learning to Perform as a Research Technique in Ethnomusicology. *British Journal of Ethnomusicology* 10 (2): 85–98.

Booth, Gregory D. 1986. The Oral Tradition in Transition: Implications for Music Education from a Study of North Indian Tabla Transmission. PhD diss., Kent State University.

————. 1996 Cognition and Culture: Systems of Music and Music Education in India and the "West." In *Indian Music and the West,* ed. A. Parikh. Bombay: Sangeet Research Academy.

Bourdieu, P. 1984. *Distinction: A Social Critique of the Judgement of Taste.* Cambridge: Harvard University Press.

Brown, Robert. 1965. *The Mrdanga: A Study of Drumming in South India.* PhD diss., University of California, Los Angeles.

Green, Lucy. 2001. *How Popular Musicians Learn: A Way Ahead For Music Education.* London: Ashgate.

Higgins, Jon. B. 1994. *The Music of Bharata Natyam.* Sittingbourne, Kent: Asia Publishers.

Kippen, J. 1988. *The Tabla of Lucknow: A Cultural Analysis of a Musical Tradition.* Cambridge: Cambridge University Press.

Monier-Williams, Monier. 1899. *A Sanskrit-English Dictionary.* Oxford: Oxford University Press. 2008. Revised version at http://www.sanskrit-lexicon.uni-koeln.de/monier/ (accessed 5 December 2009).

Neuman, Daniel M. 1990. *The Life of Music in North India: The Organization of an Artistic Tradition.* Chicago: University of Chicago Press.

Prickett, S. 2007. Guru or Teacher? Shishya or Student? Pedagogic Shifts in South Asian Dance Training in India and Britain. In *South Asia Research* 27 (1), 25–41.

Ranade, Ashok D. 1998. The Guru-Shishya Parampara: A Broader View. *Sangeet Natak* 129–130: 39–54.

Sangeet Research Academy/SRA. 1998. Teaching of Indian Music. Seminar papers. Ed. A. Parikh. Mumbai: Sangeet Academy.

Sorrell, Neil and Ram Narayan. 1980. *Indian Music Performance: A Practical Introduction.* Manchester: Manchester University Press.

Vaidyanathan, T. G. 1989. Authority and Identity in India. *Daedalus* 118 (4): 147–169.

Weidman, Amanda J. 2003. Guru and Gramophone: Fantasies of Fidelity and Modern Technologies. *Public Culture* 15 (3): 453–476.

Weidman, Amanda J. 2006. *Singing the Classical, Voicing the Modern.* London: Duke University Press.

SEVEN

"Music Is in Our Blood"

Gujarati Muslim Musicians in the UK

JOHN BAILY

In many parts of the Muslim world there is a strong link between the professions of barber and musician. The connection has been most thoroughly explored by ethnomusicologists in Afghanistan, where two important instruments of rural music, the *sorna* (shawm) and the *dohol* (double-headed frame drum) are played exclusively by men who are themselves barbers or at least from barber families (Sakata 1983: 78–83; Baily 1988: 102–103). The barber-musicians Sakata and I worked with in western Afghanistan come from a low-ranking endogamous ethnic group which calls itself Gharibzadeh, a word literally meaning "born of the poor," and more generally could be translated as "foreigner." This gives a good idea of the low place of such musicians in the larger society (Baghban 1977). Sakata has discussed in detail why these two occupations, barber and musician, are connected. According to her analysis, the answer is that both occupations are seen as polluting. "Perhaps it is the magical and powerful by-products associated with musicians and barbers that relegates their handling to a certain class of people" (Sakata 1983, 80).

Ethnomusicologist Alan Merriam long ago identified the ambiguous place the musician occupies in many societies: providing a service of high importance (e.g., music for rites of passage such as weddings), being of low rank, and having a "license to deviate" (Merriam 1964, 123–144). While

Merriam's characterization is over-generalized and takes no account of the possibility of the high-status musician in a number of societies (especially Western ones), it does seem to apply quite broadly. It is especially relevant when applied to musicians in Muslim societies because of the long-standing debate about music and religion, and the frequently voiced assertion that music is *haram,* forbidden within Islam. While it may be a ritual necessity (especially for weddings), those who provide music are stigmatized and often recruited from low-ranking ethnic minorities. The condemnation of music has most recently been a significant part of Taliban ideology in Afghanistan, where all musical instruments were banned in the areas under their control (Baily 2001). According to the Taliban, "Those who listen to music and songs in this world, on the Day of Judgment molten lead will be poured into their ears."[1]

Khalifa is the name of a small Muslim community settled in the UK, one of a number of Muslim castes or sub-castes from the predominantly Hindu state of Gujarat in northwest India. In Gujarat two "traditional" ascribed Khalifa caste occupations are barber and musician. Members of this community migrated to the UK in the late 1960s, and today a significant number work in the hairdressing business and as professional and semiprofessional musicians. The purpose of this chapter is to examine the musician role performed by these migrants in the UK context. This inevitably involves a consideration of the discourse within the Khalifa community about their connection with these formerly low-status occupations.[2]

KHALIFAS IN INDIA—PLAYERS
OF *SHAHNAI* AND *NAQQARA*

The Arabic word *khalifa* has a variety of meanings and usages and is connected with the word "Caliph." Opinions differ as to how this lowly community in Gujarat acquired its name. It certainly fits a wide pattern of "Ashrafization," that is, a tendency for Indian Muslims to claim descent from Arabian ancestors, and the adoption by them of Arabic caste or family names such as Qureshi, Shaikh, or Khalifa.

Khalifas in Gujarat live in a large number of villages in Valsad District, to the south of the city of Surat. My knowledge of Khalifa life in India comes largely from Maulana Osman. He studied for nine years at a *madressa* near Surat before resuming residence in Britain, where he works as a social worker in a community center in Coventry and fulfills an important role in the Khalifa community as an elder and religious leader.[3] According to his very detailed account, until recently a few Khalifa families would live in each village in this area, where they provided the basic service of barber to the predominantly Hindu population, usually visiting the houses of their patrons to perform their services. They were of low caste, though not untouchable. Maulana Osman spoke sympathetically about the Khalifas' subordinate position in Gujarati society and of the "inferiority complex" (his term) that can develop in the psyche of the low-caste individual. Recent intercommunal violence in Gujarat has shown just how precarious is the situation of its Muslim minority.[4]

Their work involved handling polluting substances, hair and nail parings, and their women were in some cases midwives. Certain barbers also carried out circumcisions, and barbers were much involved in match-making, an activity facilitated by the access they enjoyed to the homes of their patrons. They carried out various duties in the context of Hindu weddings, including the performance of processional music on *shahnai* (shawm) and *naqqara* (small kettle drum pair). They also played other instruments. According to Maulana Osman, Khalifas did not necessarily take much pride in being musicians:

> He'd be either playing the drums or the *shahnai*, and . . . they start off being not very professional in their playing, not very skilled, but because he has to do it he gradually improves, and as time goes on he becomes a master of whatever he is doing. So then you have barbers who are noted for their *shahnai*, or for their *dholak* [double-headed barrel drum] or *tabla* [drum pair] or whatever, and if someone rich is getting married and he's willing to pay something extra, he would pay his village barber and say, "Look, I'm not asking for your services, now here's your due, you've got to help with the wedding arrangements and all that," so he's happy. "I hear so-and-so from your clan is quite good in *shahnai*, why don't you ask him to play at our wedding." So he's instrumental in getting someone else . . . that's how the various *tabla, dholak, shahnai* . . . flourished within the caste, because it became part of the occupation's duties, not just cutting hair.

Performing music was not, then, a matter of being an "artist," but of providing the right kind of ritual sounds on the appropriate occasions. In recent years Khalifas in Gujarat have moved into a wider range of higher ranking professions that are not inherently caste ascribed. And those who work as barbers nowadays operate in barbershops and less in the homes of their patrons. When one of my musician friends returned from several months' visit to his ancestral village in 1993 he showed me some of the many hours of video he had shot, including footage from each of the seven barbershops in the local bazaar, all the barbers there being his close relatives.

In the 1940s many Khalifas migrated to Kenya, Uganda, and Tanzania, places offering opportunities for barbers because of the presence of other South Asian migrant communities who needed servicing. There was also a special connection with British armed forces in East Africa. They were probably what Cohen would call an "auxiliary diaspora," "ethnically different camp-followers of military conquests or minorities permitted or encouraged by the colonial regimes" (Cohen 1997, 84). In East Africa new opportunities arose for them to improve their position in the social hierarchy. They were now in the middle stratum of a society that had Europeans at the top and Africans at the bottom. They had access to European-style education, and the possibility of improving the status of their traditional connection with the barbering trade through modern hairdressing salons that catered to Europeans as well as Asians. From East Africa they came to the UK as forced migrants in the late 1960s, faced by problems of citizenship in the newly independent countries with their policies of "Africanization."

THE KHALIFA JAMAT IN THE UK IN THE 1990s

The Khalifa Jamat (Community)[5] in the UK numbers about 5,000–6,000 people and is located in a number of industrial cities in the midlands and north of England. When they came to the UK they settled in what were still essentially mill towns, where low-paid jobs were readily available. Khalifas in Britain show a high degree of social cohesion. They have a well-organized network of local Khalifa Societies (also called Jamat), with their committees, officers, and duties. Membership, usually about £10–£15 per year per household, is carefully monitored. Only male members of the community are entitled to membership in the local Society. The local Societies are in turn affiliated to the Federation of the Gujarati Muslim Khalifa Societies of the UK, whose constitution deals with matters such as engagement, marriage, divorce, and the settlement of disputes. The community is very largely endogamous, and women who marry outside the Khalifa community are usually denied full membership in the local Society.

A good picture of the ideals of Khalifa community life is found in the Aims and Objects of the Federation of the Gujarati Muslim Khalifa Societies of the UK. Here are some of the points made in the constitution published in 1982.

- To take desirable steps for the general betterment of the members of the Khalifa Community residing in the United Kingdom.
- To increase unity with love among the members of the Community.
- To attempt to make positive progress in religious, social and economic spheres for the Community.
- To maintain good and amicable relations with other Islamic Organisations.
- To propagate Islamic and secular knowledge among the members.

The slogan of the Khalifas, as illustrated in several of their own documents, is Unity and Brotherhood. Each local Khalifa Society helps its members deal with two major rites of passage, marriage and death. Wedding engagements are registered with the local Society and documents drawn up with details of date, number of guests, dowry, etc. Khalifa community life in the UK involves frequent gatherings of large numbers of people. Wedding celebrations often entail inviting 500–1,000 guests, requiring the mobilization of considerable labor resources from within the local community to prepare and serve food for so many people. Burials and memorials (*fateh*), also organized by the local Society, likewise bring together many people. Members of the Khalifa Jamat of the UK are much concerned with self-improvement through education, and proud of those who have become accountants, dentists, solicitors, school teachers, and social workers. They are an example of a successful South Asian community which through hard work and coordinated action has been able to improve its place in society. They are also concerned with improving the lot of their relatives in India, especially through funding educational scholarships.

The Khalifa Jamat of the UK, then, forms a tightly bound and well-organized community with clear rules of membership. The local Societies provide a strong, perhaps overwhelming, sense of group identity, where the individual feels part of one huge extended family. In the process they have become a rather "exclusive" community. As one man put it, referring to his own local Society:

> The various communities can get together in the mosque, but this is a special community, the Khalifa community, which is only for the Khalifas themselves. People from outside, even though they are Muslim, cannot join the Khalifa community. This community is meant for the Khalifas only [so that] outsiders cannot interfere in the welfare [of the Khalifas]. I'll give you one example. We've got our own *madressa*, religious classes, which are run there. And the Pakistani community, which is also Muslim, they wanted to join us, they wanted to join with our community, they said, "Oh, we want to be a member, whatever the fee is, we'll pay." But the rules and regulations and objectives is for the Khalifa community only. . . . The other Muslims cannot join it. Otherwise there will be too much interference culture-wise, their culture will be different. The social work of their individuals will be different, and they will interfere in the Khalifa culture and welfare. Khalifa culture includes the Gujarati language. We are from Gujarat, this is our mother tongue. These other communities, Muslim as well, like Pakistanis, they speak Urdu language, some others the Kutchi language, so it would be very difficult, you see, to intermingle as well.

There is a certain irony in all this; the formerly stigmatized, polluted, low-status social group becomes in this new environment a well-organized community that is successful in orchestrating communal endeavor such as setting up *madressas* and community centers. They create organizations that others outside would like to join, and they refuse those outsiders membership because of the "cultural pollution" they would introduce (Harrison 1999, 10).

KHALIFAS AS HAIRDRESSERS

Despite their attempts to get into other kinds of work through training in higher status professions, the Khalifas' connection with hairdressing remains strong among the community in Britain.[6] Some own or work in hairdressing salons, others do their haircutting in the front rooms of their houses or may visit clients to give them haircuts at their homes, just as they used to do in the villages of lower Gujarat. According to one Khalifa community leader:

> We've got advocates, we've got school masters, we've got dentists, especially in the UK, because of the education. When we came in this country we were able to get better education, and grants to support higher education. But our initial trade is the haircutting, you see.

Some Khalifas feel the community should give up its connection with hairdressing. One said,

> The youngsters, they don't tend to take up the hairdressing business. Our forefathers don't want us to become hairdressers. They wanted us to become better educated people. They've seen the lifestyle they've taken, they don't want us to follow in their footsteps. That's why people have started to become either lawyers, teachers, engineers, doctors, and things like that.

I asked another source whether the relatively better status of the hairdresser in the UK made any difference.

> Well, I think so, there was a lot of people who knew how to do barbering. Then they started working in a factory. Now a few of them are very interested in hairdressing. They're saying, "This is a good job, you can make good money like this." So a few of them are coming back into barbering now. They're making good hair styles now, they're learning all the while, and they're coming back into that job now. They used to work in factories, and then they probably thought that barbering is better than doing a factory job.

Many Khalifa men know how to use "scissors and machine," as they sometimes put it, even if only on a casual basis. As one man told me when I asked him if he knew how to cut hair:

Yeah, I learned it here, in Batley [a northern English town]. My dad
had a shop here and I used to come from school, he made me learn
this. . . . Today, you know, it's really worth it, because where I work,
I work for Leicester County Council, for the mentally handicapped,
I'm one of the ambulance drivers, so I give them a free haircut. I know
the basics but I don't know the styles like my brother does. I can give
you a haircut from the 1960s, you know the way they used to do it, I
can give you that one.

I was curious to find out what Maulana Osman would have to say
about the future of hairdressing as a suitable occupation for Khalifas.
After all, it was precisely this occupation that had so stigmatized the
Khalifas as a lowly and humble community in Hindu-dominated Gujarat, and he had had ample opportunity to observe the role of the barber
in Gujarati society during his many years of theological study. I asked
Maulana Osman whether the Khalifas were trying to create a new identity for themselves that would help them get away from the low-caste
stereotype of the Gujarati village barber. His answer surprised me, for
he did not mention the fact that in the UK there is nothing particularly
low status about hairdressing, and indeed hairdressers, under the guise
of being "hair stylists," can become rich and famous, as did Vidal Sassoon
and Mr. Teasy-Weasy. His reply was couched in the rhetoric of black pride
and self-esteem:

> I don't think it's [a matter of] a new identity, I think it's about being
> positive about one's identity and doing away with the negative aspects
> of it, and as a human being, being proud of being what you are, and
> where you come from, and being clear about where you want to go,
> and not hinder your progress . . . by looking back and being worried
> that maybe if I try to sort of move forward the things from my past
> will catch up on me and hinder that progress. So it's not doing away
> with your past, it's learning to accept the past, and being positive
> about yourself, and of being proud of what you are. . . . I think what
> needs to be done is for them to be given the support and encourage-
> ment, moral support as well as financial support, to educate them,
> still maintain links with their origin, with their caste occupation, but
> do it not with an inferiority complex. But be proud that they have a

skill which other people haven't got. Be proud that whether he's the king or the chimney sweep, he has to bend his head in front of the barber. Right, do it with that pride! . . . and if someone says you happen to be Khalifa you say, "Yes, I'm proud to be from that stock." And, you know, be positive about it.

KHALIFAS AS MUSIC-MAKERS

Khalifas form a significant proportion of South Asian Muslim musicians in the UK. In the mid-1990s I knew of about thirty musicians in this community, and there were undoubtedly more. Of these, five were full-time professionals, working as performers and/or music teachers. Some were semiprofessional, having another fulltime job (such as bank clerk, schoolteacher, factory worker, ambulance driver), but making some extra money from playing. And some were casual, participating in bands because they enjoyed it and saw this as a way to improve their performance skills.

I knew of four predominantly Khalifa bands, and these showed a remarkable long-term stability, having been in existence for ten years or more. Their names are of interest: *Saz aur Awaz* (Music and Song), *Naya Saz* (New Music), *Diwana Arts* (Crazy Arts), and *Khilona Arts* (Toy Arts). A number of other Asian music groups playing in the UK had Khalifa members. In such bands Khalifas played with Hindu, Sikh, and white English musicians. Overall, as *Muslim* musicians, Khalifas had and continue to have a high profile in the UK Asian music scene.

Whatever the instruments they played in the past, principally *shahnai* and *naqqara,* once in the UK Khalifa musicians gradually took up the modern style of popular South Asian music-making, vocal accompanied by keyboard, electric guitar, bass guitar, trap drum set, drum pads, etc. The only traditional Indian instrument may be the *dholak,* the double-headed barrel drum common in India and Pakistan. There is a strong emphasis on percussion, especially Latin percussion, with congas, bongos, and various types of rattle. Khalifa interest in percussion was probably bolstered by their sojourn in Africa, where they sometimes witnessed African drumming. A group usually has several singers to cover different languages, including Hindi, Urdu, Punjabi, and Gujarati. There are songs for men and songs for women to sing. Some songs are duets, or even trios, as sung in the movies, and these should be re-created in performance as duets or trios. The Asian women who sing in Khalifa groups are usually Hindu or Christian South Asians, and work freelance, performing with a number of groups. They are much in demand. Khalifa women are not supposed to sing in public, although in exceptional circumstances it may happen.

Such bands perform mostly *filmi* songs from what are now known as Bollywood movies, old and new. They do not play much Gujarati material, even for Gujarati audiences, apart from the dances that Gujarati Hindu women perform at the time of the religious festival of *Nowratri* (*ras* and *garba*). If traditional items such as *ghazal* or *qawwali*, or dance numbers like "twist" or "rock and roll," or a "happy birthday" song are performed, they are also derived from films, which have presented a great variety of musical genres over the years. Khalifa musicians have little or no interest in composing new music; they stick to a standard repertory of well-known film songs. I know of only one Khalifa with a keen interest in composition, who several years ago recorded a CD of new songs that he coauthored. The band he regularly works with expressed no interest in learning and performing these songs, probably because they were not going to be familiar to their Bollywood-conditioned audiences and for that reason would not be appreciated or requested.

Khalifa bands like *Naya Saz, Diwana Arts*, and *Khilona Arts* provide music for a wide variety of South Asian communities in the UK, Muslim, Hindu, and Sikh. The general term these musicians use for an engagement is "gig." They perform what they call a "stage show," on a stage if there is one, or at one end of the hall or function room if there is not. They use powerful amplification equipment, with someone to do the mixing, and they usually wear band uniforms. They play for wedding celebrations; dinner-dances for charity, or at the time of Christmas, New Year's Eve, and St. Valentine's Day; private parties celebrating birthdays or sporting victories or the like; religious festivals such as *Nowratri*; and the opening of new business enterprises. They play concerts, college "Asian Nights," summer fairs (*melas*), and competitions, and occasionally they appear on radio and television. At many of these events their main role is to provide music for Asian style social dancing, at least during the later part of the event. The style of dancing is much influenced by that seen in Bollywood movies.

KHALIFA CONCEPTS ABOUT
THEIR OWN MUSICALITY

Many Khalifas think of themselves as constituting a "musical community," often saying they are "born in music" and that they have "music in
the blood." Proof of their musicality is provided, they believe, by the fact
that they do not need to be taught to play but can learn informally, by ear.[7]
They say you can tell someone is a Khalifa by the way he taps his fingers on
listening to the sound of music. This tapping is no ordinary tapping, but
a fast alternation between the first and other fingers, as though one were
playing on a drum head. The master-disciple relationship, about which so
much has been made in studies of classical musicians in India, has no relevance for them. Thus, Khalifas are not usually in receipt of *talim,* musical
teaching couched in terms of music theory and oral and written notation.
They know little about Indian music theory, about *rags* and *tals.* They do
not learn by "A B C D" as one musician put it, meaning in a systematic
manner, from first principles. In their own much-used phrase, they just
"pick it up." And there is a certain pride in being self-taught, which they
regard as a sign of their inherent musicality. In fact, my research indicates
that they learn through processes of imitation, watching others and trying
things out for themselves later, a mode of learning noted for boys and girls
in hereditary musician families in Afghanistan (Doubleday and Baily
1995). Musical performance is learned but not taught, through a process
of self-paced self-instruction.

Only Khalifa men play music. The sole musical performative role
normally available to Khalifa women is singing certain special songs in
conjunction with wedding celebrations, when they also accompany themselves with the *dholak* (double-headed barrel drum). But Khalifa men like
to claim that their women have a keen ear for music and will readily point
out any mistakes in a performance. Thus the claim to be "born in music"
extends to women as well.

KHALIFAS AND THE RELIGIOUS
DEBATE ABOUT MUSIC

One aspect of deliberate self-improvement in the Khalifa community is
an increasing commitment to religious education. This Muslim community, low-ranking in the caste system of Gujarat, was not expected, espe-

cially by members of higher ranking Gujarati Muslim castes like Tais and Worras, to produce educated mullahs.[8] Members of the community in the UK are rightly proud of the achievement of people like Maulana Osman in having reached a very high level of religious education, equivalent to a PhD. There are also a number of Khalifa men who have gained the title of *Hafiz,* having memorized the Holy Koran in its entirety. One result of this greater commitment to religious education in the UK is a rejection of the Khalifa connection with music, which is an embarrassment, especially in maintaining status vis-à-vis other Muslim communities, which look down on music-making as a questionable activity. As a result there is a lively ongoing debate within the UK Khalifa community about music and its performance, even though music commands respect in the UK and has an important place in the school system, a strong "indicator of esteem." Musicians in the UK can attain the highest rank, as Sir Yehudi Menuhin and Sir Paul McCartney have shown.

I have heard at length from both sides of the argument. From Maulana Osman I heard a moderate and cautious condemnation of music. On one hand, he invoked a *hadith,* a "Tradition of the Prophet," that clearly condemns music:

> If you look at the sayings of the Prophet, there is specific mention of Him saying, "I have been sent down to do away with musical instruments, to destroy musical instruments." And the words there are quite explicit.

He was not able to remember the source for this *hadith,* which is certainly not cited in the usual literature concerning the lawfulness of music. On the other hand, he cited some well-known *hadith* that contradicted this outright condemnation.

> I think it was on the occasion of the Prophet coming to Medina from Mecca, after migration [*hijra*], and there were young girls, children, and they were singing "A new moon has appeared to us from a certain direction, and therefore it's compulsory for us to thank God for this blessing." They were referring to the Prophet's arrival from Mecca to Medina, and the girls were singing with a duff, which is an instrument like a tambourine, without the metal bits, a one-sided drum. There is another incident, when the girls are playing a *duff* at some other

ceremony, on the occasion of 'eid or something, and Al-Abu Bakr, knowing the Prophet's displeasure about music and instruments, reprimands the girls and says, "Stop it!" and the Prophet is resting, and He turns round and says, "No, leave them! Leave them to enjoy themselves as they are!" The instrument the girls were using was just a *duff*. From that the scholars have said that a *duff* is permissible as an aid to singing. Others have used that incident, that narration, to say that it does not relate [only] to this instrument, but to any musical instrument, and that is the difficulty when theologians discuss and debate this. . . . So, to be on the safe side, what many scholars have said is that if it is a *duff*, and no other instrument, that is acceptable. Again, that is the instrument used by a lot of the African Muslims as part of their religious festivals at shrines. They would not use the tabla or any other instrument, but they would use that *duff* because it has a place in Islamic history at a time of celebration.[9] My attitude is that *Al-halal*, whatever is permissible, is clear-cut, whatever is *haram* is clear-cut, and in between there is a grey area. . . . It's best to avoid the grey area.

From musicians and others I heard various views expressed. In general, they accepted that music is "un-Islamic," but they did not consider they were doing anything really wrong by listening to or playing music. As one put it: "As far as religion is concerned, the musical thing is against the law of Islam. We should not play, we should not sin." But in the next breath he told me:

In Egypt they play wonderful music. If you go to Cairo, the way they play, most of the music is also copied in India from there. From Cairo, the instruments they use, it's so melodious, if you listen to that. I'm very much interested in music, really. And I go to every function. The Muslim religion does say [it is unlawful], I agree, I have read it with my own eyes. That is the problem.

The musicians' viewpoint was expressed most eloquently to me in the following terms by a singer who specialized in *qawwali*, the religious music associated with Sufism and Sufi shrines in India and Pakistan:

According to our religion music is not allowed. I know, because I am a Muslim, and music is not allowed in Islam, no matter whether it is dance music or classical music or light-classical music. But from my point of view if you do it respectfully it's okay. We take our Holy Prophets' names, we keep remembering them, that they worked a very good job for our Muslims. And they are very very near to God, and if you pray to them [through singing *qawwali*] God can listen to them very easily. You can go all over the world, to any corner of the world, and you will find music, either in Muslim countries or anywhere else. I don't do anything wrong with music. I always sing respectfully *ghazals* and *na'ts* [songs specifically about Prophet Muhammad] and *qawwalis*. I have no reply if religious people tell me it is wrong. But I do it and I am going to carry on doing it.

Certainly Khalifa musicians report incidents when others, both Khalifas and non-Khalifa Muslims, have brought pressure on them to give up playing. But I have not heard that disagreements about music have been the cause of deep divisions in the community in the way that some other issues have. Those with a strong interest in music and those with a strong commitment to religion and religious education live side by side without rancor. However, it does seem that the religious faction is gaining the upper hand. In 1997 the Federation issued a statement calling on Khalifa community leaders to eliminate the playing of music at Khalifa weddings, describing music as an anti-Islamic practice. This was a significant step because in the past Khalifa musicians often provided this service on a voluntary basis, celebrating their own musicality in the process.

The question of the possible role of music in providing a sense of identity for the Khalifa community presents the ethnomusicologist with some unusual data to reflect upon. For example, there is no specific Khalifa music, and Khalifa musicians seem to have little interest in the music of Gujarat, the area of India from which they come and where their close relatives still live. They perform mainly Bollywood film songs, a highly eclectic popular music genre. The lack of interest in Gujarati music may stem in part from the fact that the Gujarati film industry is small and few Gujarati films achieve great fame. One could argue that Bollywood *filmi* music provides the connection with "home." But I do not see the music played by Khalifas in the UK as looking back to the past—rather to the future, to a music relevant to British Asians in the twenty-first century. It is not a question of reviving something from Gujarat, but of contributing to the very positive role that new music can have for the British Asian audience. Khalifas may not be interested in composing new songs, but they are much concerned with innovation, in processes of modernization (adopting electric and electronic instruments) and Westernization (the harmonization of formerly monophonic music).

More interesting is the way that many Khalifas think of themselves as constituting a "musical community." They are "born in music," they have "music in the blood," they do not need to be taught to play but can "just pick it up." It is this musicality that in my analysis is a marker of Khalifa identity, rather than allegiance to a putative traditional music. However, Maulana Osman did not accept my contention that musicality was a factor in Khalifa self-identity. He told me I was wrong to think of the Khalifas as being generally involved with music-making; this activity was confined to a few families, he said. He spoke of the reaction of some members of the community to the creation and organization of Khalifa bands as one of out-rage, and said that a lot of people still see it in those terms. He went on:

> I think because music hasn't been the main part of their life, it's not something that I think people would attribute to their culture, to their identity. Cutting hair has been the main thrust of their activity. ... This [music-making] is a side thing, and again, within only a few families, not across the board.
>
> I think where people have started to become more religious, cer-tain families, although they were sort of playing music at weddings and whatever, they've given it up and they said, "Well, I don't play music any more, I've left the old ways." And they gave music up, not just because of music, but everything else that was associated with it, drinking and other social ills. People changed their ways, mended their ways, as they say, and therefore music, along with the various other things that went with it, you know, were left, and only a few families practiced just music ... So people don't look back with pride at the contribution of music, but rather they look for figures within their forefathers, or within the community as a whole, that have had contribution in other walks of life.

His claim that only certain Khalifas are involved with music is in-teresting, quite understandable from the moderately anti-music position he advocates, and is in some ways perfectly correct. An analysis of the recruitment of musicians shows that musicianship does run in families. The explanation for this, in my opinion, has nothing to do with genetics, and everything to do with the child being brought up in a supportive and loving family environment in which music-making is the norm and where musical instruments are accessible in the home (Doubleday and Baily 1995, Sloboda et al. 1994).

From these considerations it does seem that musicality is not "officially" invoked by Khalifas as one of the important things for them to uphold, in the way that Osman Sheikh maintained should be the case for barbering. In that sense it is *not* a symbol of their identity, at least not at a conscious level. But if you think of yourself as being "born in music," as having "music in the blood," then surely that must be part of your feelings about who and what you are. That points to an "unofficial" identity, one not paraded by the powers who represent the community at formal and official levels, but one that is recognized by ordinary Khalifa people.

This chapter concerns a small community that is a disadvantaged minority in its place of origin—Gujarat State in India. Their migration has been complex, and in two stages. In the first stage, from India to East Africa, they were mainly economic migrants exploiting a niche market opened up by the migration of other South Asian communities. In East Africa new opportunities arose for them to improve their position in the social hierarchy, with more access to education and improvements in the status of their traditional connection with the hairdressing business. In the second stage they were forced migrants faced with discrimination and possible persecution in newly independent African states. In moving to the UK they found themselves in a milieu very different from both India and East Africa, and one in which no special stigma was attached to their traditional occupations of barber and musician.

As music-makers in the UK Khalifas did not seek to maintain their cultural identity through adherence to a traditional music. Instead, there is a strongly ingrained sense of themselves as being highly musical. There is no identifiable Khalifa music, and Khalifas, perhaps not surprisingly, do not feel sentimental about the music of Gujarat. In the UK they have followed the path of many other migrant communities in the West, the invention of new hybrid forms of music which entail the Westernization and modernization of an older repertoire, in this case Indian film music, which is a Pan–South Asian popular repertoire rather than an "ethnic music." There is a notable lack of composition of new songs, and a recycling of old material in new performance styles. They have not created a Gujarati equivalent to *bhangra* [a form of hybrid popular music developed in the UK and originating from the Punjab area of India and Pakistan], which was a possible outcome.

To some extent Khalifas use music in an inward-looking manner, performing at their own social gatherings in a way that celebrates their sense of themselves as inherently musical. In the wider context, when they perform for other British South Asians' festivities, their performances are not expressly intended to flag their identity to others. Their propensity to music-making within their own communities, in connection with weddings or other events, can have both cohesive and divisive outcomes, for the very act of making music is open to condemnation by the more religious among them. Their own authorities have attempted to restrict their music-making, yet there are limits to the effectiveness of such censorship in a Britain that regards music as normative, healthy, and a sign of civil society. Music may yet be an issue that ends up dividing rather than uniting members of the Gujarati Khalifa Jamat of the UK.

Acknowledgments

This chapter was first published in the *Journal of Ethnic and Migration Studies* 32 (2) (March 2006): 257–270, and is republished with their kind permission.

Notes

1. My source is the Herati newspaper *Itafaq-e Islam* for 10 December 1998, in an account of the public burning of musical instruments in the local sports stadium. The "molten lead" *hadith* is found in the writings of the sixteenth-century jurist Ibn Hajar Haytami of Egypt (d. 1567 CE). I am grateful to Dr. Katharine Brown for this information. The *hadith* seems to have common currency in Pakistan—where no doubt the Taliban heard it—but it is not generally accepted as authentic.

2. My work with the Khalifa Jamat began in 1986, when I researched and directed the film *Lessons from Gulam: Asian Music in Bradford* (Baily 1986). My research with the community resumed in 1992 and lasted intermittently until 1996, with a small research grant from Goldsmiths University of London. My work concentrated on attending and videoing music performances and cricket matches, and conducting extensive recorded

interviews with eleven musicians and two community leaders, one of them a Maulana. All were Khalifas, male, mainly of the middle generation, born in Africa but brought up and educated in the UK. All interviews were conducted in English. In this chapter I write mostly in the present tense even though the research was conducted some years ago.

3. A Maulana holds the equivalent to a doctorate in Islamic theology.

4. The many Muslim communities living in India have been absorbed into the Hindu caste system over the centuries. Khalifas are not the only Muslim caste or sub-caste in Gujarat. There are, for example, Tais and Worras, but they have no connection with hairdressing. Khalifas would seem to be the lowest ranking Muslim caste (or sub-caste) in Gujarat.

5. The word *Jamat* is used extensively in Khalifa discourse in English, and is often used interchangeably with the word "community." Many of the local Khalifa Societies have the word *Jamat* in their official names. Thus the term *Khalifa Jamat* can refer to a) the total Khalifa population in India, East Africa, Fiji, the UK, and anywhere else the Khalifa transnational community is located, b) the Khalifa community in the UK, or c) members of a particular local Khalifa Society.

6. The terms "barber" and "hairdresser" are used interchangeably here, although strictly speaking they are rather different. A barber's work includes the shaving of whiskers and facial massage, which a hairdresser does not do. Hairdressing implies a rather more artistic approach to the hair on the head.

7. The term "musicality" is used here to mean an innate, inborn predilection for music, a potential to acquire musical ability through a learning process. There are good reasons to believe that musicality is a human universal; see Blacking (1973), Sloboda et al. (1994).

8. It is an interesting question as to whether Osman could have studied for the qualification of Maulana if he had not been a UK citizen. As a "visiting migrant," a "temporary returnee" from a wealthy country he was afforded a special status, and that included the right to study subjects (such as advanced religious studies) that might otherwise had been unofficially reserved for higher castes. This, of course, encroaches on the fascinating question of how the returned migrant is treated by those who remained "at home."

9. It is noteworthy that the frame drum (*duff, daireh*) was the one instrument not banned by the Taliban in Afghanistan.

References

Baghban, H. 1977. *The Context and Concept of Humor in Magadi Theatre.* PhD diss., University of Indiana.

Baily, J. 1986. *Lessons from Gulam: Asian Music in Bradford.* 16mm film, VHS video. London: Royal Anthropological Institute. With accompanying 38-page study guide.

———. 1990. Traditional Music in the Muslim Communities: Qawwali in Bradford. In *Black Music in Britain,* ed. P. Oliver, 156–169. Milton Keynes: Open University Press.

———. 1995. The Role of Music in Three British Muslim Communities. *Diaspora* 4 (1): 77–88.

———. 2001 *"Can You Stop the Birds Singing?" The Censorship of Music in Afghanistan.* Copenhagen: Freemuse. With accompanying CD.

Blacking, J. 1973. *How Musical is Man?* Seattle: University of Washington Press.

Cohen, R. 1997. *Global Diasporas.* London: University College of London Press.

Doubleday, V., and J. Baily. 1995. Patterns of Musical Development among Children in Afghanistan. In *Children in the Muslim Middle East Today,* ed. E. W. Fernea, 431–446. Austin: Texas University Press.

Harrison, S. 1999. Cultural Boundaries. *Anthropology Today* 15 (5): 10–13.

Merriam, A. P. 1964. *The Anthropology of Music.* Evanston, Ill.: Northwestern University Press.

Sakata, H. L. 1983. *Music in the Mind: The Concepts of Music and Musician in Afghanistan.* Kent, Ohio: Kent State University Press. With two accompanying audio cassettes.

Sloboda, J. A., et al. 1994. Is Everyone Musical? *The Psychologist* 7 (8): 349–354.

EIGHT

Greek Popular Music and the Construction of Musical Identities by Greek-Cypriot School Children

AVRA PIERIDOU-SKOUTELLA

I like dancing *tsiftetéli*[1] and *zeïbékiko*.[2] I like *laïka* and traditional songs. They make me feel very different. I don't like the songs of modern Greek singers. They sound foreign, not ours. My cousin from Nicosia says they are modern, so they are better. She tells me that I am *píso pou ton kósmo* (behind the world) and *chórkatos* (peasant). When she comes to a village wedding she dances Greek *laïka* but she goes back to Nicosia and makes fun of them saying they are Arabic. (Kiriaki, age eleven, from a rural school in Cyprus)

Elements of "Greek-ness" in Greek-Cypriot children's constructions of their musical identities are expressed through their talk and musical behaviors. The complexity and diversity of children's musical identity construction is marked by their relations to different musical styles within Greek popular music in the Greek-Cypriot context of the Republic of Cyprus. Musical manifestations of neo-Hellenic identities were particularly interesting around the critical historical moment in May 2004 when Cyprus joined the European Union, and thereby finally "arrived" at its long-awaited destination—Europe, modernity, and the "West." More generally, processes of Westernization, modernization, and globalization in relation to Cypriot reality are common to various countries around the Mediterranean rim, as well as to those in many other parts of the world, where there are efforts to "modernize" or "Westernize" their ethnic and cultural identities (see Pieridou 2006 for further discussion).

There is a continuum in Greek popular music with local musical characteristics at one end—where Byzantine music, Greek folk/traditional songs, rembétika and laïka songs occupy a place—and global characteristics that absorb Anglo-American popular music at the other, where Greek language remains the crucial signifier of Greek national identity. Somewhere in the middle there are many styles, such as elafro (light), pop-laïko, elafro-laïko, that are all hybrids of local musical elements and global sounds (Dawe 2003). Cyprus has no local music industry or CD production facilities. Greek major private radio and TV stations have transplanted local ones in the country, and these only broadcast Greek and Anglo-American popular music. Musical identity construction in the lives of Greek-Cypriot children has enormous potential for illuminating our understanding of the construction and articulation of collective and individual musical identities in childhood. Musical identities are "mobile, a process not a thing, a becoming not a being, best understood as an experience of the self-in-process when the subjective and collective sides of musical identity are inseparable" (Frith 1996: 110). This chapter thinks of children's music-making as human action in culture (Blacking 1967), and of musical experience as being central to the shaping of individual and group musical identity. It focuses on children as agents and participants in the construction of musical knowledge and daily musical experience, through their dialectical interactions with the agents of enculturation.

The discussion represents part of a broader ethnographic project undertaken in urban and rural areas of the Republic of Cyprus during 2003 and 2004 among fifty-five nine- to twelve-year-old children (Pieridou 2006), and then extended in 2007 to include twelve five- to eight-year-old children (Pieridou-Skoutella 2008). The fieldwork was carried out on two sites: an urban one in the city of Nicosia, and a rural one in a region known as Red Villages on the east coast of the island. The data collection used three qualitative methods. First, it involved participant and non-participant observations in settings where children's musical identities acquire significance. In school playgrounds, school bus trips, at excursion sites, afternoon clubs, homes, local parks, and neighborhoods, children determine and control their own participation in musical process. The second method involved tape-recorded, in-depth interviews and informal discussions; and the third involved collection of musical products. Data was also collected during social events in which children take part in musical practices in the presence of knowledgeable adults, such as at weddings and family gatherings.

I will first situate this study of musical identity construction in its historical and national context.

HISTORICAL AND NATIONAL CONTEXT

Cyprus's geographical position and small size hold the key to its turbulent history as well as to its "vulnerability" to worldwide economic, social, and cultural changes. Due to the island's strategic position on the periphery of Europe at the southeastern fault line of the Mediterranean Sea, Cyprus has been colonized by numerous nations since 1050 BC, when it was settled by ancient Greeks. Consequently, Cypriot identity is highly complex, fluid, and contested. Cyprus first came under self-rule in 1960, but the new republic proved to be unworkable. There were constitutional problems followed by intercommunal conflict, a coup, a Turkish invasion (1974), and the occupation of 37 percent of the country's territory by Turkey. Since then the two major ethnic communities living in Cyprus—the Greek-Cypriot majority (80 percent) and the Turkish Cypriot minority (18 percent, the latter having grown during the Ottoman rule)—have lived apart; and until 2003, they were unable to cross the border between their lands, despite ongoing negotiations. They developed distinct cultural elements and two strong separate national cultures attached to Greece and Turkey, respectively.

Ethnic identity in Greek Cyprus is highly contested between two ideological sides: the nationalist Hellenocentric identity, which emphasizes the Republic's Greek-ness, and the Cypriocentric one, which points to their Cypriot-ness. Official state ideology, although acknowledging the political independence of Cyprus, considers Greek-Cypriots to be members of the Greek nation. Cyprus has always shared an ideology of racial supremacy with mainland Greece due to its mutually assumed common ancestry and ancient past (Argyrou 1996), while the Orthodox Church of Cyprus, along with the educated elite, has fervently supported Greek nationalism on the island by emphasizing the historic, religious, and cultural links between Cyprus and Greece.

In its efforts to distinguish itself from its threatening and "inferior" middle-eastern neighbors, the Greek-Cypriot state and society have identified with Europe as the basis of their cultural practices (Argyrou 1996). Consequently, Westernization, modernization, and globalization processes have deeply influenced social, cultural, and political practices. In my earlier research I found that Greek-Cypriots construct a Greek, European, "modern" musical identity (Pieridou 2006, 2007) not only for showing off to foreigners but also to distinguish among themselves in terms of high versus low social classes and rural versus urban cultural contexts, with direct consequences for the social status of musical practices. The child's words quoted above are indicative of this.

In the process of constructing a national culture through the formal music education system, I found that the Cypriot and Greek local and traditional musical traditions have been standardized and decontextualized, implicitly sending the message that Hellenism is a unified cultural and national entity, ignoring any unwanted cultural interaction and influence. National public school events aim to reinforce a sense of Greek national identity and a need to liberate the occupied territories. Standardized Greek and Cypriot traditional, patriotic, and fighting songs, representing honorable struggles and a heroic common past, are performed. At the end of all national celebrations the children sing the national anthem, which, being shared by Greece and Cyprus, demonstrates the unity of Hellenism. Musical elements that point to the European character of Greek music are embraced as "proper" Greek music for learning, while others, such as laïko, are marginalized.

In the light of the above-mentioned contexts and ideologies, it is fruitful to ask in what ways and in which contexts a Cypriot child chooses to adopt or reject a particular Greek musical identity outside school.

BEING "MORE-THAN-ONCE" GREEK

BYZANTINE MUSIC IN CHILDREN'S MUSICAL ENCULTURATION

The term "Byzantine music" denotes the Greek Orthodox ecclesiastical music, presently experienced only during the church liturgy, which few contemporary Cypriots attend. It has always been thought of as representing the Greek roots of indigenous Cypriot musical cultures, and as the origins of Cypriot folk music.

Urban children's musical enculturation provides less familiarity with this style; in my interviews and observations, the majority of children expressed unfamiliarity with it and alienation from it. Some of them explained that they rarely go to church with members of their families except for the major liturgies of Christmas and Easter, and that even then most of them stay outside to play with their friends. All of them referred to liturgy attendance with the school. However, as Stelios (age eleven) said, "When we go to church with our school they want us to stand still and we can't do it for a long time. We start talking, laughing."

Another small group, comprising mostly rural children and a few urban children, discussed richer experiences. For instance, Antri (age eleven) goes to church every Sunday:

> I wake up at 7:00 o'clock in the morning and I go by foot. It takes me twenty minutes. I like going to the church. I listen to the Bible. I don't like chanting. I prefer listening to chants. The priests have nice voices and they sing softly and slowly. It makes me feel different.

Anastasis (age eleven) helps the priest at the altar:

> Sometimes when I don't sleep late on Sundays I go earlier than my mother and grandmother. I go from 7:30 to help the priest. I enjoy doing this a lot. I also try to chant with the chanters.

For these mainly rural children the church context is a familiar one that they appropriate according to their needs, selecting different participatory roles.

> KATERINA (TEN): My grandfather is a chanter and when I go to his house I hear him chanting Byzantine music, and many times when he comes to pick me up from school he chants in the car. Sometimes when I go to the *psaltíri* (choristers' stand) I chant the psalms I know.

Katerina's learning experience is perhaps enhanced because a beloved member of her family, and a role model for her, is a knowledgeable adult who has introduced aspects of this music at home.

All the children in the study referred to this music according to its setting, sound, and function: "Music in church is religious and it reminds us of Christ's life"; "Byzantine music is the music sung only in the church and it tells us the life of Christ, and what he did with the Apostles, so it is very important. It is very ancient music." However, because it was unfamiliar to them, the majority had difficulty in relating to it. As George (eleven) explained:

> It isn't only difficult to understand the words, which are old and ancient, but also it's difficult to understand the melody too. One word might last for a long time, with many notes, and then you lose the word. You just don't understand where the melody goes.

Due to its highly melismatic chanting, Kipros (eleven) does not perceive it as music, because "priests seem to read a poem rather than singing one. They only keep their voices longer on certain words going up and down," while, as Thomas (ten) said, "There aren't any instruments. So I don't call it music. Besides you find it only in church." He summarized:

> I don't understand it so I don't stay in the church for long unless we are with the school. Then you aren't allowed to leave, but we get bored and we start talking. How can you like something if you don't understand it? I don't like this music. We only know *Páter Imón* ["Our father"] and *Pistévo* ["I believe"] because we learn them at school.

In Green's terms (1988/2008), being "aggravated" by this music's inherent or intra-musical meanings, they reject it. However, they express respect toward its delineations, or social connotations, and acknowledge its importance in Greek Orthodox religious practices. As Miranda (ten) declared: "We must listen and learn this music because it's holy music for us, the Greeks, and we must respect what it represents, which is God and His worship." However, some children did respect its intra-musical meanings due to "affirmative" experiences (Green ibid.) with intimate knowledgeable adults, as mentioned above. Sofiana (ten) said:

> I think it is beautiful music. But you need to pay a lot of attention to understand it. I like listening to it and I try to chant myself. My grandmother helps me with that.

THE MODERN GREEK MUSICAL SELF

Greek popular musical styles have deeply penetrated children's musical worlds, particularly urban ones. Children have access to them on their radios, through the internet, on television, in talent shows, in toy shops, on CDs, and in concerts by famous Greek singers. The songs' Greek language means that children can understand and learn the lyrics; and the mixing of local with global musical elements facilitates their learning and reproduction. Children consider these musical styles to be *their music,* their "audible badge of identity" (Blacking 1967: 29), and opposed to the music of their parents and other adults. As such, these styles occupy a high-status position in their lives and support a wide range of both private and social functions (see Pieridou 2006).

Their likings, though, are more than a matter of preference. The children in this study *identified themselves* with these musical styles, sounds, and artists because they consider them to represent what they feel and who they would like to be. Furthermore, they identify with the concept of "modern" as an acceptable way to be Greek. For example:

> Greek modern music is modern music sung in Greek.
>
> Greek modern dance is the kind of dance that keeps the beat, and you learn certain dance moves for. Only modern songs hold the beat. You can learn these dances from songs' video clips.
>
> If you want to be modern then this is the music you should listen to.
>
> We listen to these singers because their songs are modern.

Children appear overwhelmed by the prestige these styles carry. Their cultural environment, which is dominated by the media, perpetuates ideologies that place high cultural status on imported musical products. Media presentations of musical images and global sounds, even provision of information about Greek popular singers' personal lives, accentuate songs' delineations, which children consume and reproduce.

> CHRYSANTHOS (NINE): Singing on television, the whole world is watching you. It's a big thing. So these people and their songs are important songs. When you appear on television you have to be good. Imagine the foreign artists . . . the whole world knows them. So these

singers are good singers. Did you know that Sákis (Greek male singer) has a girlfriend?

Children try to assert and project such musical identities by rejecting other local Greek styles as "inferior," thereby defining by default the sonic spaces of their daily lives. Urban children in particular value the possession of CDs, which aid significantly in the construction of their modern identities. Their CD collections, which are gender- and age-specific, point to a particular musical identity since they articulate "a number of highly idiosyncratic sets of places and boundaries" (Stokes 1994: 4). Urban children have created local sound spaces within the realm of modern popular music—global and Greek—thus setting boundaries against all other styles. On the contrary, as the next section discusses, many rural children present more diversified social and private musical preferences.

While boys in general do not dance modern dances, girls reproduce choreographed performances of their favorite songs on the playground, aiming at close imitation of them. However, the majority remain at the periphery as watchers and are consequently left out from these other girls' "modern" musical community. As a result they inhibit their own musical practices: the majority remain observers who, according to their own words, are embarrassed by their inability to express themselves in front of, or even alongside their classmates.

> STAVROULLA (TEN): They know how to dance. We [other girls] don't. They go to dance lessons, watch the video clips, copy the movements, and they can do it. I try these movements at home, alone or with my sister. But I can't dance well, so I prefer to watch.

The ideological voices of modernization, coupled with the society's Eurocentric ideology, dominate these children's perceptions and their constructions of a "proper" Greek musical identity. These voices suggest to children that only very few of them can dance adequately or in professional ways, purchase up-to-date CDs, buy radio equipment, and attend dance, electric guitar, or voice lessons.

> ARETI (ELEVEN): We don't know how to sing. I mean we sing but it isn't real singing. Singing is when Álkisti Protopsálti sings. I will start voice lessons because I want to sing modern songs and right now I can't.

Sometimes children, though they are often unaware of it, consume and reproduce Greek local musical elements that they have otherwise rejected. During an urban school excursion Julie (nine) was dancing on the table in a *tsiftetéli* rhythm to a rap song with Greek lyrics. Its underlying rhythm pointed to this oriental dance. She explained:

> *Tsiftetéli* is *laïko* dance which is *chorkatiko* (peasant) and old but when the song is modern then the dance becomes modern too. Songs like *Síko chórepse kouklí mou* are *tsiftetéli* songs and they are old, not good for us. So the *tsiftetéli* is not modern. But with our songs it becomes modern.

Julie seemed aware of such transformations of local Greek and oriental music into "acceptable" Greek music, and accepts the ideological subordination of local Greek music to global sounds as an appropriate way to celebrate contemporary Greek-ness. Even if they participate in such local events, children treat them as "other" to their modern Greek identity, as the quote at the beginning of the chapter indicates.

GREEK *LAÏKO* SONG IN CHILDREN'S LIVES

From among the different Greek musical styles, special reference should be made to Greek *laïko* song. *Laïko* emerged from *rembétika* in the 1960s and continues to express the culture of the urban lower class. It uses *zeïbékiko, hasápiko* (2/4 and 4/4 dances typical of *rembétika*) and *tsiftetéli* rhythms with strong oriental influences, and has a range of sub-styles. As a result of globalization processes, I found that Greek *laïko* has to a great extent replaced and marginalized Cypriot traditional music's functions in familial and societal events in the rural areas of Cyprus.

THE "INFERIOR" MUSICAL STYLE

Most urban children appeared to be less familiar with this type of music. They identified Greek *laïko* as an old, rural, and in their view inferior musical style. As Alina (nine) explained:

> *Laïka* songs are the village songs we listen to when we go to *kéntra* [huge restaurants] in villages or other places outside Nicosia for a wedding or christening.

They relate these songs with adults' musical preferences, from which they have purposefully distanced themselves.

> **ANNA (ELEVEN):** . . . *laïka* songs are songs of the old times. My parents sing them, thank God not very often. They know them from their times and they like them.

> **ALEXIA (ELEVEN):** Sometimes singers translate Turkish songs. Or they compose new songs which are similar to Turkish songs. We don't like this. They are not suitable for us.

The children also referred to some new and contemporary types of *laïka* (see Dawe 2003 for a description of these) in a similar manner, especially those that include strong Middle Eastern elements. These styles serve the needs of rural, low-class, and "culturally inferior" society, and are thus deemed inappropriate for modern urban children.

> **NICHOLAS (TEN):** *Laïka* is oriental music.
> **STELIOS (TEN):** Oh my God! They shake their bellies! Arabic stuff!

While Cypriot society has been assumed to be the last bastion of European civilization, their culture reminds Cypriots of the consequences of orientalization (Herzfeld 1987) during the Ottoman era, and of the threatening oriental "other" that inhabits part of their land.

Rural children also seemed to have internalized this ideology of local cultural inferiority. Although they enjoy, participate in, and celebrate *laïka* songs among themselves and with their families, they feel highly embarrassed by their tastes and hide them in front of foreigners, and from their local modern peers, in favor of a more "proper" musical identity. However, I found that children with a stable Cypriot musical identity openly admit their preferences toward this style, regardless of their peers' reactions.

LAÏKO MUSICAL IDENTITY

Rural children discussed *laïka* in relation to christenings, engagements, weddings, and other family gatherings. In such contexts children have the freedom to enjoy themselves in close connection with familiar knowledgeable adults. Nicoletta (eleven) explained:

When I'm with my friends we don't put on *laïka*. Also I don't put on *laïka* when I clean my room. I like *laïka* in weddings and when we go to family dinners. If I know the song then I sing and dance too.

Certain urban children, whose musical enculturation facilitated experiences of Greek *laïko* because of intimate adults, or through close participation in rural social events, provided similar responses. Children contextualize this music in relation to adult social musical practices, emphasizing that these songs have been an important part of their enculturation.

YIORGOS (ELEVEN, RURAL): When I was little I used to listen to my mother singing these songs. So I put all these songs and all these sounds in my memory and I distinguish them when I hear them. In weddings I dance *varetó* [*zeïbékiko*].

NICOLETTA (ELEVEN, RURAL): When we go for dinner to our relatives' houses, they don't play modern songs, they put on *laïka* and they sing. When most of the guests leave and the closest members of the family stay, then they get up and dance, others clap or sing. Everybody dances *varetó* [she gets up to dance it], men, women, children . . . I also like *Moustafá* [Turkish song].

Knowledge of these songs, rhythms, and dances was considered to be a "social necessity" (Blacking 1995: 31) at such events. Local private dance schools teach these dances in a systematic way, primarily to girls from the age of six. In addition, Cypriot children learn these songs and dances—and not necessarily the easier ones—by imitating adult relatives or close friends. Kiriakos reported that his grandfather puts on a radio program that broadcasts *laïka* songs:

Sometimes he stands up and he dances *zeïbékiko*. He tries to show me how to do it.

During wedding celebrations I documented several episodes when fathers on the dance floor were trying to show their five- or six-year-old sons *zeïbékiko* movements. Greek *laïko* dances provide a rare opportunity for Cypriot males, regardless of age, to present masculine virtuoso skills. Some boys openly expressed their pride in performing them, even those who prefer modern songs:

LEFTERIS (ELEVEN): I prefer to be modern and to listen to modern songs, but I don't dance modern dances. I only dance *zeïbékiko* in weddings.

In my study, many children appeared to perform a wide and demanding repertoire of *laïka* songs and dances with astounding melodic and rhythmic precision. Often they combined their singing performances with dancing, because "you have to dance these songs. If you only sing them then you have to clap your hands." Being able to perform appropriately in the style signifies both belonging and social identity, "because performance competence is both a sign and simultaneously a product of shared musical knowledge and experience" (Turino 2008: 43). Anastasis (age eleven) brought his bouzouki to the interview. "I always carry my bouzouki with me, and if someone wants me to play I play." Rural boys of all ages identify with *laïko* musical culture in certain contexts. But while eleven- and ten-year-old girls expressed interest in dancing and singing it, nine-year old girls seemed to be more interested in modern popular music.

CONTESTED GREEK MUSICAL IDENTITY

In accordance with the demands of different national and cultural ideologies, Greek-Cypriot children competently celebrate diverse forms of Greek-ness in their daily social musical practices. Children use this music to play the role not only of themselves, but also of who they would like to be. Their construction of Greek musical identities is contextual, highly contested and multiply articulated. In particular, differences between urban and rural children are notable.

Urban children construct modern Greek musical identities through their appreciation of and identification with those Greek popular musical styles that connect with Western and global music, rather than with other styles that denote a "purer" local Greek sound. But these boundaries are fluid, since these children do often "visit the other side," not least because most of their families originally came from rural areas. Although rural children consume and reproduce ideologies of local cultural inferiority, they express much richer musical understanding, due to local affirmative enculturation experiences.

KATERINA: I think that every song is important and different. In modern songs you sing and dance modern dances and you have fun; in Greek and Cypriot traditional songs you dance traditional dances and you get to know old times in Cyprus. You dance traditional dances in weddings too. And with *laïka* you learn *laïka* dances to dance in weddings. So you end up with a collection of dances that you can dance when needed.

Similarly, many rural children's collections of CDs and tapes include a wider spectrum of popular songs, including *laïko* songs and sometimes some from Cypriot tradition. These collections were longer lived than the urban ones.

Certain urban children listen to particular musical styles, seeking localized personal meaning. For example, some boys select Greek rock music:

MIHALIS (ELEVEN): Modern Greek music is made out of Western and musical elements, such as electric guitars, computers, of everything. The lyrics many times don't make sense, they are stupid. I can't describe these songs. We respect the artists of Greek rock. The lyrics of their songs talk about feelings in a serious way. We like the Greek rock style, their melodies and the voices. This is our music!

GEORGE (ELEVEN): I truly enjoy when I go to concerts to listen to my music. When I'm sad I listen to these songs. Some songs give me courage. As long as I like this music I don't mind if it isn't that modern.

These children resist the dominant invasion of modern delineations. Instead they interpret and reinterpret the received messages in their own terms.

The Cypriot primary music education system, which is dominated by nationalist ideologies, is disconnected from children's daily musical experiences. This chapter suggests that there is an urgent need for a redefinition of Greek national and musical identity in the light of contemporary Greek-Cypriot children's musical enculturation. In particular, more investigation from sociologists of music, music educationalists, and ethnomusicologists is needed into Greek popular musical styles in Cyprus, and appropriate teaching materials need to be developed. I would suggest that more locally connected music education practices, embracing the diversity of Greek popular music and taking its delineations seriously, are more likely to lead to musical understanding and positive musical experiences of such music both in and out of school.

Notes

1. Dance from Asia Minor related to "oriental" or "belly" dancing.
2. Nine-beat rhythm dance of Turkish origins that is associated primarily with *rembétika* and *laïka*.

References

Argyrou, Vasos. 1996. *Tradition and Modernity in the Mediterranean: The Wedding as a Symbolic Struggle.* Cambridge: Cambridge University Press.

Blacking, John. 1967. *Venda Children's Songs.* Chicago: University of Chicago Press.

Dawe, Kevin. 2003. Between East and West: Contemporary Grooves in Greek Popular Music (ca. 1990–2000). In *Mediterranean Mosaics: Popular Music and Global Sounds,* ed. G. Plastino. New York: Routledge.

Frith, Simon. 1996. Music and Identity. In *Questions of Cultural Identity,* ed. S. Hall and P. Du Gay. London: Sage Publications.

Green, Lucy. 1988/2008. *Music on Deaf Ears: Musical Meaning, Ideology and Education.* 1st ed. (1988) Manchester: Manchester University Press; 2nd ed. (2008) Norwich: Arima Publishing.

———. 2002. *How Popular Musicians Learn: A Way Ahead for Music Education.* First pub. 2001. Aldershot, UK: Ashgate.

Herzfeld, Michael. 1982 (1986). *Ours Once More: Folklore, Ideology, and the Making of Modern Greece.* New York: Pella.

Pieridou, Avra. 2006. *The Construction of Musical Identities by Greek Cypriot School Children.* PhD diss., Institute of Education, University of London.

Pieridou-Skoutella, Avra. 2007. The Construction of National Musical Identities by Greek Cypriot Primary School Children: Implications for the Cyprus Music Education System. *British Journal of Music Education* 24 (3): 251–266.

Pieridou-Skoutella, A. 2008. Small Musical Worlds: In Touch with Young Greek Cypriot Children's Musical Lives. In the Proceedings of ECME 13th International Seminar *Music in the Early Years: Research, Theory and Practice.* Frascati, Italy: International Society for Music Education.

Stokes, Martin. 1994. Introduction: Ethnicity, Identity and Music. In *Ethnicity, Identity and Music: The Musical Construction of Place,* ed. Martin Stokes. Oxford: Berg Publishers.

Turino, Thomas. 2008. *Music as Social Life.* Chicago: Chicago Studies in Ethnomusicology, University of Chicago Press.

NINE

Music-Learning and the Formation of Local Identity through the Philharmonic Society Wind Bands of Corfu

ZOE DIONYSSIOU

Corfu is an island of 108,000 people, the largest of the seven Ionian Islands, located in western Greece. The island was occupied successively by the Venetians (1386–1797), the French (1797–1799 and 1807–1814) and the Russians (1799–1807). It became the capital of the nineteenth-century independent state named Ionian State (*Ionion Kratos*) (1816–1864), which was under British protection until 1864, when the Ionian islands were affiliated to Greece. Italian culture and music were the main influences on musical life in the island (Leotsakos 1980). Its geographical position, its close political and cultural ties with Italy and the Italian Renaissance, and the fact that Corfu was never under the Ottoman occupation all gave the island and its people a very different cultural identity from that in the rest of Greece. "Art," "serious," or "classical" music in Greece (*Éntechni Neoellinikí* or *Ellinikí Musikí*) was first developed in the Ionian Islands, which in the eighteenth and nineteenth centuries put on important operatic and orchestral performances (Motsenigos 1958). Yet, from the foundation of the Greek State in 1928, Ionian music was systematically boycotted by the mainly German-educated composers and musicians of Athens and the mainland and was only recognized much later, toward the end of the twentieth century (Leotsakos 2001a).

Today Corfu still reveals signs of its strong cultural and musical past. This includes what are known as Philharmonic Societies, which mark many of the Ionian islands and which number eighteen in Corfu alone, where they enjoy great popularity among the Corfiotes. Membership in the Philharmonic Societies is freely available to anyone who wishes to join them, and they include both adults and children. An important part of the Philharmonic Societies are the wind bands, which constitute the oldest systematic music education centers in Greece. The term "band" in the present chapter refers to groups of musicians playing combinations of brass, woodwind, and percussion instruments following the pattern of the symphonic band, where groups of instruments serve in sections analogous to those in symphony orchestras. Bands have been present in Europe since the thirteenth century, but they became widely known from the seventeenth century in three roles: as *military* bands; as *harmonie* bands, both for military purposes and outdoor festivals; and thirdly, as *civic and church* bands, for public music services, playing in churches, public and private balls, parties, and concerts. After the beginning of the nineteenth century their military function became limited and their role was extended to more general uses (Polk et al. 2001). The first wind band on the island of Corfu was the marching band of the British army, when the island was under British protection. Since then wind bands in Corfu and later in the rest of Greece have followed the principles of the post–French Revolution military bands of nineteenth-century Europe.

The main scope of the Philharmonic Societies in Corfu was, and remains, the teaching of music for free to anybody interested. The first Philharmonic Society, named the Corfu Philharmonic Society (*Philharmoniki Etairía Kekríras*)—today known as the Old Philharmonic Society (*Paliá Philharmoniki*)—was founded in 1840.[1] Nikolaos Halkiopoulos Mantzaros (1795–1872), the composer of the national anthem of Greece, played a key role in its foundation and served as artistic director and teacher, providing music studies of a very high standard (Leotsakos 2001b). During the nineteenth century and the beginning of the twentieth century the Corfu Philharmonic Society formed many active musical ensembles, with the wind band being just one of them. The second society was the Mantzaros Philharmonic Society, founded in 1890, and since then Philharmonic Societies have been founded in many villages of Corfu, reaching the current total of eighteen.

From the second half of the twentieth century on, the expansion of Philharmonic Societies on the island resulted in a change of focus: they cannot be regarded as music academies any longer, as the music education provided in them is confined to the teaching and learning of wind instruments in order to satisfy the needs of their wind bands only. Although administrative committees would prefer them to be regarded as more formal institutions, they are quite far from that. Many musicians who have followed a more specific musical career (usually at the university level) and participated in the sample of this study considered them institutions of low musical and educational standards, in which there is "no serious music education" and "music of no particular value" is performed. The bands still follow many militaristic principals in their organization, hierarchy, presentation, repertoire, and most importantly in the education of students. This shift in the level of music education provided demonstrates the lack of focus that some musicians in the bands are not happy with today. Yet wind bands are still regarded as second nature by Corfiotes, characterizing the musical identity of the locals and raising the status of everyone who participates in them.

This chapter examines some aspects of music teaching and learning that take place in the Philharmonic Societies of Corfu. It emphasizes conceptions and memories of present and past musicians about the music education they received in the bands, examining how they experienced music-learning in the wind bands and what they believe this type of learning offered them in their lives. The chapter aims to show that music education in the bands interrelates considerably with local identity. The research is based on a series of ten semi-structured interviews and at least twenty informal discussions, with a snowball sample of the same number of participants (students, musicians, teachers, and conductors in bands of the island). During the last few years I also attended approximately ten instrumental lessons and rehearsals as a non-participant observer, as well as several concerts and other festivities of the bands on the island. Data described below derive from a qualitative analysis of the ten semi-structured interviews, informal discussions, and observations. Many musicians who decide to study music at greater depth enroll at the university for a degree in music and can participate in both institutions, since taking part in the band is a part-time activity. Hence, my connection with the university made it easier for me to approach university students who have or had some connection with the bands. While this had the disadvantages associated with subjective involvement, it also had the advantages associated with "insider research," enabling me to access the wind band's world through a group that was close to me. The names of the participants have been altered to maintain their anonymity.

JUST JOIN AND PLAY

Music education that is offered in the Philharmonic Societies of the island is confined to the teaching and learning of instruments used in the wind bands; very few societies offer lessons in other instruments. Therefore, the name "bands" was often used by my informants and local people in general to indicate the Philharmonic Societies. Interestingly enough for music educators, while the education offered in the Philharmonic Societies is often conservative and out of date by contemporary scientific standards, and while formal teaching in the wind bands is often described as old-fashioned and unadventurous, band musicians usually learn to perform simply by seeing others playing, by playing along and imitating them. They are also motivated by their wish to perform in public as soon as possible. This self-education gives those who follow professional musical careers later in life a range of skills which they regard as highly advantageous.

WHY DO PEOPLE JOIN A BAND?

Corfiote children who want to study music usually join a Philharmonic Society at a young age and borrow an instrument from the band for free, keeping it for as long as they remain active members in the band. Among the musicians who participated in this study, those who started to study music early (around seven to nine years old) usually did not show a particular interest in joining the wind band, but their parents insisted and motivated them to register. Those who started after the age of ten or twelve seemed to have been more conscious about their desire to play music. Most musicians of the first category (those who started at a young age) stated that it was a norm for a child in the 1980s to go to a band, as they might go to an afternoon school for learning foreign languages or playing sports.

> COSTAS: All the children here (in Corfu), we grew up with the band. We all had the image of the wind band in our minds. At home parents were telling us "you must go to music."

PATROCLOS: My father wanted me to go (to the band). I wanted to join a football team, but my father insisted to learn to play music because he didn't learn it himself. In the beginning I didn't want to go. I cried. For a year and a half I cried at home asking my parents not to make me go. They gave me an instrument that I didn't like: euphonium. I wanted to play the trumpet.

Most participants of the sample, especially those who joined the band at a younger age, did not seem to have enjoyed the lessons at first; yet they started to appreciate them some years later.

HOW DOES MUSIC-LEARNING TAKE PLACE?

Participating in a band is a demanding task, since children must go and study on the premises of the society sometimes every evening or at least two or three evenings a week. A young woman, twenty years of age, recalls her involvement in the band and how difficult it was for her to follow its heavy program in her teenage years:

ZD: What memories can you recall from your participation in the band?

MARIA: I remember I was passionate about learning music, I loved music! Despite the fact that I had to participate in the rehearsals almost every evening—because we had many festivities and concerts—I loved it. Yet I gave trouble to my parents who had to drive me to the band and take me back home, I lived far away, the rehearsals went on until very late, I was young. The conditions were difficult and tiring. The everyday basis of rehearsals was very tiring. It didn't help the mind to rest and recover. My lips and my jaws hurt from playing. My back hurt from sitting on the chair for so long! And the conductor only cared for our appearance to the public, how many of us would march outdoors!

Similar conditions exist even when children grow up and, as adult members of the band, have to participate at least two times a week in the rehearsals. Most of my informants agreed that despite the many hours of practicing there, they received a very basic, poor quality music education.

The informants of this study fall into two categories according to how they experienced music-learning: those who are pleased with the basic education provided in the bands and believe that what they have learned is everything a band player needs to know; and those who consider there are insufficiencies in their music training and try to pursue further studies in a conservatory, at the university, or privately. People in the second category recall their music education to have been problematic. They all talk about non-systematic teaching, where a lot of children played music simultaneously in one room and the teacher passed by and listened to each one. According to them, nobody showed them the technical requirements of their instrument, how to breathe, how to produce various sounds, and in most cases nobody even showed them how to play at a basic level. They consider that they learned subconsciously, as the extracts below reveal:

> COSTAS: We learned how to breathe by accident. We asked here and there. I remember we knew a guy who studied trumpet in Athens, and one summer we asked him: "Hey, how are you doing this?" and he explained it to us. We did not learn anything technically in the band.

> HARRY: They [music teachers] don't care about teaching children to play technically; they only care about them learning the repertory, so that they can join in [the wind band in outdoor performances and marches] as soon as possible.

Patroclos, as the extract below shows, had to cope with the insufficient music teaching and with the fact that he was given an instrument he did not like.

> PATROCLOS: I was given an instrument and nobody told me how to play it. For three months I was carrying it between home and the band just looking at it. No playing. The teacher told me: "The other children of your class can play, why don't you play?"
> ZD: Why didn't he show you?
> PATROCLOS: He didn't know how to show me. He was a practical [self-taught] player himself. Most people here [in the band] play accidentally or by instinct. If someone asks them how they play, they cannot tell. They play accidentally, but they play well. I learned that the lips vibrate in order to produce sound on a brass instrument at the university!

Many band musicians play by ear. Most musicians after many years of practice learn to sight-read, but they are not fluent in it and are good at keeping the rhythm, so they keep scores in front of them but know the pieces mostly by ear. Maria, the young woman who is quoted below and commenced her musical education in a band when she was twelve years old, describes the essence of music education in the wind bands as social learning.

> MARIA: I learned many things subconsciously, not because someone showed me.
> ZD: What do you mean by subconsciously; didn't your teachers show you how to play?
> MARIA: They were telling me few things, but in the rehearsal the conductor doesn't tell us how to interpret each phrase and whether we need to play it piano or forte or whatever, but inside us we knew how we should play it. After all the long rehearsals we had listened to the same piece so many times that we instinctively knew it, and I would say to myself, "Hmm, I will play this so and so." In other words, we understood things that were not written on the paper and that nobody—teacher or conductor—told us anything about.

This seems to be how learning takes place in the bands. Students learn something simply by seeing and hearing other musicians doing it. This is clearly a type of informal learning or "learning by osmosis," which has been strongly associated with popular, traditional and folk musics (Green 2002). However, as Green mentions (2002: 6), brass bands in the UK, as well as many other community music ventures, also adopt various types of informal learning. Furthermore, although the bands include many approaches that fall under the category of "informal," they are of course heavily teacher-directed, or conductor-directed, and in this sense their approaches are closer to those that have come to be known as "nonformal," that is, somewhere between the formal and the informal. My interviewees and informants indicated that informal and nonformal approaches seem to be the main learning pathways in the wind bands of Corfu.

Another young woman, recalling her memories, found her participation in a band a totally unmusical experience, as her main task was to play loudly.

ELLI: I couldn't play the modulations and the dynamics, because everything was so loud! They only cared about how many of us would go marching outdoors. My only task was to play loud, totally unmusical.

The above interviewee had originally studied her instrument at the university, and she joined the band later. As she seemed well tuned into formal teaching and learning of music, she possibly did not appreciate the approaches to informal or nonformal learning in the band. This might mean that informal learning may not engender the same enthusiasm in adults who are already accustomed to formal learning approaches as in those who have always learned informally.

After some basic training, the young children band members engage in the band's repertory straight away. The repertory consists of overtures and extracts from operas, extracts from classical pieces, contemporary composed pieces adapted for woodwind and brass bands, and less often jazz, Latin music, and Greek traditional Corfiote folk songs. This repertory is regarded as traditional music associated with Corfiote local identity, carries notions of authenticity, and is regarded as repertory worth preserving. Most Philharmonic Societies play the same marching repertory for many decades, which some of my informants interpreted as a sign of stability and conservatism.

Most participants in this research agreed that music education in the bands is limited to enabling children to perform the repertory, not training them to grow musically and to become gradually able to play a wider repertory. The older the children become, the less they like the repertory. Adult musicians of the sample stated that they find the music they play rather dull and unimaginative and that they would prefer to play different and more modern styles, including more jazz and Latin music. It seems that, despite aspects that are informal in some respects, the learning is nonetheless teacher-directed, and it therefore lacks a playful approach to music-making as well as experiences of flow and imagination (Green 2008: 59). Yet there was plenty of enthusiasm when young members participated in the band outdoors, which made them feel like "proper musicians." This enthusiasm remains even with experienced and professional musicians. Yiannis, a musician of the sample who commenced his training in the band but followed an international career in addition to positions in well-known symphonic orchestras, remains an active band member. He reported, "I cannot grasp that it's Easter time unless I play with the band!"

Many students of the sample reported that when they were younger they had difficulty cooperating with teachers who are aural musicians, which resulted in a low quality music-making. This gradually seems to be changing in our time. While in the past there were many aural musicians and teachers in the bands, nowadays more of the teachers have studied music in a conservatory or in a university music department. These are usually the younger generation of music teachers, who make use of techniques associated with formal music education (such as warm-up, technical exercises, breathing exercises, tuning, virtuosity exercises, etc.). Still, the overall informal or nonformal character of the music education provided in the bands has not been altered, because internal social structures and hierarchies in the bands prevent any real changes.

SOCIAL STRUCTURE AND HIERARCHIES

Philharmonic societies take steps to preserve the hierarchical social structures of their bands. Participation in a wind band has become something of a family matter for locals. Some musicians count their participation in a band by how many of their family members have participated in it, or by how many generations of musicians their family goes back. For example, "I have been playing in this band for three generations," said Spiros, a middle-aged male informant, meaning that he has the right to speak over young musicians. However, especially the young people with whom I spoke for the purpose of this research were not happy with this type of oligarchy. They spoke about often experiencing isolation in the band. They confessed that what counted most was not skill, but length of time participating. The hierarchy in the band, they said, reminded them of the army. Those problems in social structure and hierarchies seem to weaken both the bands' educational role and the quality of music-making.

> ELLI: There is hierarchy in the band not according to how a musician plays but according to how many years he or she plays.

> MARIA: I feel like a soldier when I play in the band. Sometimes they speak to us abruptly and underestimate us. I don't want to feel like

soldier. I am a girl who likes music, and I may play better than some teachers there.

HARRY: The band followed the structure of the army, the old guy versus the young guy. For example, the elder people kept the new instruments and we played the old and damaged instruments.

Participation in a band is a matter of pride for Corfiotes. It raises people's status, independently from their profession. This was especially true in the past, but remains so to a large extent today. "Most people join the wind band because they are Corfiotes," as Costas said. This means that it is a highly significant event for them to participate actively in local music-making. The pleasure, enjoyment, and affirmation they receive from their participation in this local symbol, the band, is a declaration of their local identity. Hence, the vast majority of the people I interviewed or spoke with who did not have university music training play in the band to support the "musicality of the island," provided of course that they enjoy it. They did not seem to be ready to work hard for real artistic improvements in the band or for their own musical effectiveness.

The administrative committees of most Philharmonic Societies consist of the elder generation, whose main priority is to keep the tradition as it was and to promote their band over other bands of the island. This attitude reveals their need to preserve the past and their unwillingness to update the band's approaches and repertory to reflect contemporary educational and musicological debates.

HARRY: Their [the administrative committee members'] first goal is to promote their wind band, not to make art, although they want us to believe that this is art and wind band is maybe the best music ensemble ever. Of course, as soon as people grow and think more broadly, they understand the fallacy. Wind bands today lack quality! People celebrate it because it is part of their culture, not because of its good quality.

The administrative committees, through newsletters, local newspapers, and various meetings reported by the local media and press, often admit that the societies have serious financial problems that lead to poor allocation of buildings and difficulties in appointing musically educated staff. They also often complain of weak financial support from the Ministry of Culture and the local authorities. On the other hand, some of the younger generation of music teachers—the musically educated ones—often protest that this is only one side of the coin, and in fact the administrative committees are pulling the wool over the eyes of the public. In reality, they argue, the committees could make a lot of improvements but are reluctant to take on big changes, because "it will stir up the dirty waters," as Harry put it. In general it was evident in my sample (especially among those who have graduated from the university) that musicians do not always approve of the work of the administrative committees and rather think that they bring stability and conservatism to the wind bands at the expense of improvements in musical or pedagogic matters. Humphreys et al. (1992) acknowledge that in many wind bands they have witnessed a similar lack of educational and musical focus.

WHAT DO MUSICIANS FEEL THEY GAIN FROM PARTICIPATION IN THE BAND?

Most of my informants agreed that the most important positive effects of the wind bands in the development of young musicians are socialization and discipline. Many recall how important their participation in the band was for their own personal musical development; for establishing communication with other members of the band; and for sharing their local cultural identity. The older my informants were, the more they valued the opportunity that the wind bands offered them to play together in such a demanding and challenging way that they could not have met anywhere else. Despite their shortcomings, participation in the bands also gives children the opportunity to receive basic music education for free, and to discover whether they like music and whether they are good enough at it to continue studies in a conservatory (an extracurricular organization of music studies for children and adults) or later at a university—all without having to buy an instrument or pay for lessons. It also brings them into contact with a repertory they wouldn't get to know in a conservatory easily.

> COSTAS: The band is everything! We learned things that we couldn't learn in the conservatories. We learned how to work and remain strong in a group. Socialization through music!

PATROCLOS: Yet many talented musicians have grown out of this experience. In Thessaloniki when I was telling people that I come from Corfu, they were going, "Hmm, you must play well then." They didn't need to listen to me playing.

It has become a norm in most symphonic orchestras throughout Greece that the best brass players are Corfiotes. One of my informants, a professional tuba player, reported that playing in a band gave him a vast experience in cooperating with other musicians in a music ensemble that he would not get in any conservatory:

> **ZD:** How did your participation in the band help you later in performing in the orchestra?
>
> **YIANNIS:** The band taught me how to participate in a music ensemble; it taught me how to keep discipline in the group. I have seen many musicians who graduated from a conservatory—especially string players—and it takes them much more time to adjust to the orchestra, because they don't have the experience of group playing. Corfiotes adjust easily, but we need work to improve in other ways.
>
> **ANDREAS:** In symphonic orchestras everywhere in Greece, most brass players are Corfiotes. We have to be fair: Corfiotes adapt themselves easily to all circumstances, because they have a vast experience in group playing under difficult conditions. But they have bad sound and inadequate technique.

This chapter has examined some perspectives on, and experiences in, the learning of music in the wind bands of Corfu, looking at parameters such as reasons for joining a band, how music-learning takes place, social structures and hierarchies, and benefits from participating in the bands. I tried to show some differences among various groups involved: musicians seem to enjoy the role of the bands as community music centers, while some people—mostly musicians of the older generation or members of administrative committees—would prefer them to be regarded as more formal institutions.

For my informants, studying music in wind bands was a community activity, a cultural practice, and by participating in this practice they learned the practice (Folkestad 2006: 138). As mentioned earlier, the type of music-learning analyzed above can be described as nonformal learning, which is associated with learning that takes place in community centers as well as brass bands in many countries, in schools and other educational contexts (LaBelle 1982; Green 2002; Dionyssiou 2002). Even when music is taught systematically, because bands function as community centers, music teaching is perceived as nonformal or informal education. In any case, in most learning situations formal and informal learning interact and need not to be seen as a dichotomy, but rather as two poles of a continuum (Folkestad 2006). This means that although some formal educational practices may appear in teaching and learning situations, the overall educational character of the band remains strongly nonformal or informal.

Music teaching and learning in wind bands play a vital role in the formation of the Corfiote musical identity and works interchangeably with it, the two reinforcing each other. Hence, the band tradition reinforces the formation of personal and local identity (Fornäs 1995); and conversely, the way bands function in society enables social, nonformal or informal learning. In that sense it seems important for wind bands to maintain their community character and at the same time to improve the education they offer.

Music education research acknowledges the shift of focus from teaching to learning, from the teacher to the student, from formal to informal and nonformal learning situations. Even if music teachers in the wind bands do not realize it yet, the attitudes of their students are slowly changing toward a more liberal music education, a type of education in which the teacher facilitates and supervises learning, and students pick up more information and practices from their peers and other band musicians. As Green (2008: 24–25) puts it, the teacher in informal learning situations becomes more of a facilitator and sharer of students' knowledge. Yet the teacher needs to possess good subject knowledge and subject-specific skills, to be able to link informal or nonformal strategies to more formal situations, and to be able to work with pupils as "diagnosers," guides, and musical models (Green 2009).

This chapter has suggested that in the wind bands of Corfu music teaching, learning, and identity interact in many ways, and music education needs to be informed and empowered by the way music functions in the community. Music education can gain considerably when it acts in parity and interchangeably with local musical traditions and practices. This seems to be the way to place music education in culture. More research is needed to develop practices for music teachers to enable informal and nonformal learning in the bands in ways that help students to get the most out of them. Another area of interest would be to examine what informal and nonformal leaning offers to different types of students, and how community music education can advance students' learning musically and musicologically while remaining true to its community character.

Note

1. A possible reason for its foundation that appears in some written and oral sources is that the wind band of the British army declined participating in the litanies of the Greek Orthodox Church for the local saint, St. Spyridon (Motsenigos 1958). However, this claim has not been confirmed by reliable historical data.

References

Dionyssiou, Zoe. 2002. *Use and Function of Greek Traditional Music in Music Schools of Greece.* PhD diss., Institute of Education, University of London.

Folkestad, Goran. 2006. Formal and Informal Learning Situations or Practices vs. Formal and Informal Ways of Learning. *British Journal of Music Education* 23 (2): 135–145.

Fornäs, Johan. 1995. *In Garageland: Rock, Youth and Modernity.* London: Routledge.

Green, Lucy. 2001/02. *How Popular Musicians Learn: A Way Ahead for Music Education.* First published 2001. Aldershot, UK: Ashgate.

———. 2008. *Music, Informal Learning and the School: A New Classroom Pedagogy.* Aldershot, UK: Ashgate.

———. 2009. Response to Panel. *Beyond Lucy Green: Operationalizing Theories of Informal Music-Learning,* AERA Conference 2008, New York. http://www-usr.rider.edu/~vrme/v12n1/vision/Green%20Response.pdf (accessed 1 August 2009).

Humphreys, J. T., W. V. May, and D. J. Nelson. (1992) "Research on Music Ensembles." In *Handbook of Research on Music Teaching and Learning,* ed. Richard Colwell, 651–668. New York: Schirmer Books.

La Belle, Thomas J. 1982. Formal, Nonformal and Informal Education: A Holistic Perspective on Lifelong Learning. *International Review of Education* 28: 159–175.

Leotsakos, George. 1980. Greece, III: After 1830. In *New Grove Dictionary of Music and Musicians,* ed. S. Sadie, vol. 7: 672–675. New York: Macmillan.

———. 2001a. Corfu. In *New Grove Dictionary of Music and Musicians,* ed. S. Sadie and J. Tyrrell, vol. 6: 464–465. London: Macmillan.

———. 2001b. Mantzaros [Halkiopoulos], Nikolaos. In *New Grove Dictionary of Music and Musicians,* ed. S. Sadie and J. Tyrrell, vol. 15: 787–788. London: Macmillan.

Motsenigos, Spyridon G. 1958. *Neohelleniki Musiki: Simvoli es tin Historia tis [Neohellenic Music: Contribution to its history].* Athens.

Polk, Keith, Janet K. Page, Stephen J. Weston, Armin Suppan, Wolfgang Suppan, and Raoul F. Camus. 2001. "Band." In *New Grove Dictionary of Music and Musicians,* ed. S. Sadie and J. Tyrrell, vol. 2: 622–651. London: Macmillan.

TEN

Playing with Barbie

Exploring South African Township Children's Musical Games as Resources for Pedagogy

SUSAN HARROP-ALLIN

On any day in a primary school playground in a South African urban township, children are engaged in varied musical-dance play and performances. Their myriad forms of "musicking" (Small 1998) manifest their musical and social identities, communication, and interactions. On the same day in the same township school in the Arts and Culture classroom, one may also discover children sitting at desks learning staff notation and writing down facts about music, with little active music-making taking place.

This is likely to be the scenario in an average South African government school. The situation is very different in what are known as re-sourced schools, particularly private institutions where there are trained and experienced music teachers. However, my focus here is on music education within the Arts and Culture learning area in historically black schools in township and rural areas, where there is generally little capacity in music education, and teachers' tertiary training in the arts is limited or insubstantial.

The disjuncture between playgrounds and classrooms as "sites of practice" (Pahl and Rowsell 2005) in township schools is emblematic of a wider set of problems and contradictions in South African music education. Outcomes Based Education (OBE) was introduced after South Africa's first democratic elections in 1994 and aimed to redress the inequities of the past and transform South Africa's education system (Harrop-Allin 2007: 3).

Although the Arts and Culture curriculum includes experiencing diverse musical cultures, in the case of music, government's interpretation of the curriculum to mean learning staff notation is immobilizing teachers who often have little subject knowledge or training. It is producing a dislocation between school music education and the rich and varied musics that form the fabric of South African's social, spiritual, and cultural lives. A failure to connect "music in everyday life" (DeNora 2000) to conceptions of musical knowledge, or to recognize music-making as embodied practice, presents a debilitating crisis for Arts and Culture educators trying to implement OBE. The result is enormous contradictions between policy and practice, between curriculum ideals and their interpretation, between schools and government, teachers and learners, music-making and music education.[1]

My work in Soweto primary schools as a teacher-educator attempts to address some of these contradictions. In this chapter I will suggest that "accessing learners' repertoires as a starting point in Arts and Culture education" (Andrew 2006: 10) can potentially bridge the disjuncture between children's musical play, the musical identities their play embodies, and current classroom learning. More specifically, I investigate the potential for using children's musical games as resources for teaching and learning. In promoting a closer relationship between pedagogy and children's musical practices, I demonstrate that the musicality exhibited in township children's games can be harnessed to deepen and alter music pedagogy. My approach is grounded on the assumption that educators can recruit elements of children's musical play for transformative learning.

GLOBAL RECOGNITION OF
CHILDREN'S MUSICKING

The global recognition that children's own music-making has important implications for music education is largely absent in South Africa. I therefore draw on an international body of research that stresses the necessity to relate children's musical identities and practices to formal learning (Harwood 1998; Campbell 1998, 2002; Davis 2005; Temmerman 2005;

Marsh and Hallett 2000; Jaffurs 2006; Barrett 2005; Green 2008; and Marsh 2008). For example, Green (2008) considers how to incorporate informal popular music-learning practices into formal music education in a secondary school context. In her recent and extensive study of the transmission of children's musical games and chants in different countries, Kathryn Marsh (2008) gives valuable recommendations for developing pedagogies that develop children's "musical communities of practice." Barrett's emphasis on the potential of children's games to inform school learning is particularly pertinent for the South African context. She highlights that understanding children's musical play holds "the potential for a further development of our understanding of the meaning and value of music in the lives of children and the ways in which this may be promoted in both school and community settings" (2005: 262). In South Africa itself, Minette Mans proposes "an increased use of play . . . not only as content, but as the form of all musical learning activities" (2003: 195). Mans contends that by focusing on play in music education, we may engage with our own and other cultural forms as "doing rather than knowing, process rather than product" (2002: 59). Her emphasis on play as musical action is instructive for developing a way for pedagogy to relate to children's games.

However, in practice South African music education does not, in my view, reflect such research. I propose that the gap is methodological: teachers need tools for "engaging with musical play" in the classroom. The first step is to recognize that what children are doing in their play is a form of music. The next is to identify that the musicality displayed in their games is recruitable for pedagogic practice.

WHY FOCUS ON TOWNSHIP CHILDREN'S GAMES?

Children's musical games exhibit several features that relate to musicianship and musical identity. First, they reveal who children are musically and socially: games embody the musical interests, experiences, and interactions that constitute learners' musical identities. Second, township learners' games are particularly compelling practices: drawing on local and global resources, township children play with music, movement, and language in order to relate to each other. Third, children's "practice-specific musicianship" (Elliott 2005: 54) inherent in their games displays elements of what might be termed musical knowledges-in-action that pedagogy aims to teach.

In this chapter I describe and analyze one of the many games children played at one Soweto primary school that I documented in 2006. The games I video-recorded on the playground were viewed by older students who played similar games as children and who, as cultural insiders, became co-interpreters in my research. Based on the description and analysis of one game, I first illustrate how township children are musical in multiple ways. I then explore the potential for recruiting children's musical games as resources for music education in ways that enhance teaching and learning. Documenting and analyzing township children's games reveals a layered set of musical functions and meanings that provokes a rethinking of pedagogy.

The description is located in the context of Soweto—South Africa's largest urban township, home to over 1.6 million people.[2] Soweto's complex history of social and political upheaval, violence, and poverty is still palpable, but its cultural, communal vibrancy is equally marked. In the micro-communities of school playgrounds, children's games epitomize young urban township culture.

BANA, ETLONG RETLOBAPALA (CHILDREN, COME LET US PLAY): A GIRLS' CLAPPING GAME ON A SOWETO PLAYGROUND

When I arrive at *Mohloding* Primary School, the bell rings and the fourth-grade class of nine- to ten-year-olds rush out of their classrooms. As adult interest in township children's play is unusual, the children are keen to demonstrate their music and dance repertoires. The learners soon notice the camera and gather in pairs or circle groups to show the *umlungu* (white) teacher their games. Some are highly organized, structured, and choreographed; others are more spontaneous. Most are noisy and vigorous, virtually always accompanied by dance moves and gestures.

Here, I focus on one game that girls at Mohloding Primary School play as part of an extended medley. Gathering under a tree, ten girls organize themselves into two lines facing each other. In shrill voices they begin singing the almost comic chorus of the pop song "Barbie Girl."[3]

Table 10.1. Text and Translation of "Barbie Girl"

Words	Translation	Actions and Musical content
I'm a Barbie girl, in a Barbie world		On "girl" and "world," learners do a circular motion with their hands around their faces, indicating a girl. Words are sung to the tune of the pop song.
I have a boyfriend; my boyfriend is a *tsotsi*		On "boyfriend", the learners gesture to their chins to indicate a man's beard.
Ma s'hamb' se y' tjontja amaswitsi	Let's go and steal some sweets	Pair cross-clapping pattern on word syllables
Ang-i-fu-ni	I don't want to	Sung melody to part of the "Barbie Girl" song, accompanied by a gesture, wagging forefingers to communicate "I don't want to"
Asamb' se y' tjontja amaswitsi	Let's go and steal some sweets	
Ang' fu-ni, ang' funi		Syncopated rhythm; word are pitched *doh, te, doh; doh, te, doh* (a melodic fragment from the song)

"Barbie Girl" is an adaptation of a Zulu clapping game to suit its urban, contemporary context. It uses the tune and text of a pop song, combined with gestures and movements associated with township culture. Retaining the pop song's melody, girls change the original lyrics to "I have a boyfriend, my boyfriend is a *tsotsi*." This is a colloquial South African word for street thugs or gangsters, which refers to a thief, petty criminal, or "clever, street-wise hustler" in the township (Coplan 2008: 444). On the word *tsotsi* the gesture pointing to a man's beard indicates a boyfriend in township gestural language and also suggests the riskiness implied in having a *tsotsi* boyfriend. The girls extend the word *angifuni* (I don't want to), singing it to the descending melody of the original song words "uh oh uh oh." Wagging their forefingers and rocking their hips from side to side on each individual syllable of *angifuni* emphasizes the word's connotations. The drawn-out stress on the word, combined with the "no" gesture, accentuates a sense of defiance and control over the *tsotsi* boyfriend, who tries to lure the "Barbie Girl" into stealing sweets (in the game's lyrics).

Table 10.2.

Words	Translation	Actions and Musical content
Sampilipili sam poro poro		Back and forth pair clapping pattern on the pulse
Salahl'ikhand' e he!	We throw our heads back	On "*e he*" they nod their heads back
Sampilipili sam poro poro		Clapping pattern
Salahla sandl' e he!	"We rest our elbow" or "put our elbows out" (On the side of the taxi)	Girls lean out with their arms. The action connotes a relaxed, laid-back stance
Sampilipili sam poro poro		Clapping pattern
Sahlala phans' e he	We sit down	Some girls push their skirts under as though they are about to sit down but there is confusion as other girls twirl around
Sampilipili sam poro poro		Clapping pattern
Salahl' unyawo e he!	We stretch out our legs	Girls kick one leg up to the side
Sampilipili sam poro poro		Clapping Pattern
Sazenza zonke e he!	We do it all!	The girls do each of the above actions in sequence at the end
Bang' thum' edolobheni *Bang' thum' edolobhen' -*	They sent me to the "dorp" (meaning "town" in Afrikaans)	Clapping pattern resumes in a faster tempo. Words are chanted words, no longer sung to the Barbie tune
I say: viva, viva, viva ANC! I say: viva, viva, viva ANC!		Shouted suddenly, swinging their arms overhead like a victory signal.

Accentuating each fast pulse of the song, instead of the song's four-beat meter, results in rapid alternative clapping back and forth across the two lines of girls. Their gestures replace claps on words like girl, *tsotsi*, and *ang'funi* (elided to make it fit the tune), so that individual actions are integrated into the rhythmic texture. The game increases in tempo, pitch, and loudness on the shouted chant, "I say, viva, viva, viva ANC" as the girls swing their arms overhead together in victory. This reference to political sloganing, copied from the "struggle" film *Sarafina*, underlines the girls' expression of power, although it seems they simply enjoy shouting it.[4] "Viva ANC" signals a transition to the next part of the game, which they begin with renewed vitality. (See table 10.2.)

This section of the game loosely describes the sounds and movements associated with traveling in a township minibus taxi—the main form of public transport for the majority of South Africans. The onomatopoeic sounds, fast tempo, and rhythmic excitement in the clapping communicate the speed and busyness of township travel. The girls chant "*sampilipili sam poro poro*" in a rapid dotted rhythm that emulates the sounds of a car hooter (car horn), accompanied by a fast back-and-forth pair clapping pattern. *Sampilipili sam poro poro* is the equivalent of "toot toot" in English. The sounds and movements imply that the game's actions take place inside a taxi, while the speed and rhythmic excitement of the word-actions convey forward movement. The word instructions indicate a series of laid-back, relaxed actions or poses of a taxi passenger. On each action-word a quick action replaces a pulse that is normally clapped. Rather than accompanying the words, the actions in the game are foregrounded in the rhythmic texture so as to be equally important as the words.

The children's musical motivation is clear in the way they subordinate the "correct" Zulu words to rhythm and movements in this game. Children change words like *angifuni,* to *ang'funi* and elide words like *si ya hamba* (we are going) to correspond with the Barbie tune. This in turn enables a regular clapping pattern. Altering words to fit into the beat is the organizing principle of the game, because it enables cooperative clapping and actions. The girls seem to be motivated by, and derive satisfaction from, being able to remember and synchronize fast actions in the correct sequence in unison. On the words *sazenza zonke* (we do it all) at the end of the game, girls perform each action in rapid sequence, exclaiming "*e-he*" on each one. They whoop, laugh, and fall to the ground as the game finishes. The coordinating of actions with words, the gesturing in between pair clapping patterns at the right time, and the laughter accompanying "do all the actions at once" bring the girls together in a cohesive group based on cooperative interaction.

MANIFESTING MUSICAL SOCIALITY
AND MULTIMODALITY

Games like "Barbie" convey who children are socially, who they are musically (their musical identities), and how they are musical (what they are doing musically). Although there are many kinds of "work" here related to children's identities, gender, relationships, communication, and meaning-making, I focus on this game as a manifestation of musicality. I suggest that this game displays children's musicality in two senses: socially and multimodally. Multimodality "is concerned with how human beings use different modes of communication, like speech, writing, image, gesture and sound, to represent or make meanings in the world" (Stein 2007:1; Kress 2000). I use this concept because the learners' musicking is innately multimodal—their games combine melody, rhythm, dance, gestures, and language—but also because of the way their games display children's awareness of "what modes can do, their affordances and how they work together in multimodal ensembles" (Stein 2008: 25). Clapping games such as Barbie link children's sociality with their music-making because successful musical participation enables successful social participation. For girls in particular, learning how to play the game provides entry into peer groups and connects their music-dance capacity with social identity. What is integral to children's musicality on a social level is *musical* sociality: musical cooperation, interaction, and communication.

Girls' games tend to be collaborative and inclusive (Opie and Opie 1985). Clapping games in particular involve close relationships between musical and social interactions (Grugeon 1993). For girls, synchronizing complex clapping patterns with a partner and other pairs is often more important than a game's textual meaning. And individual skills are less important than collaborative ability. What is meaningful is being able to play the game *together*. Through shared aesthetic performance, clapping games function as a "medium of friendship" for young girls (Factor 2001: 29). By becoming "apprentices to older girls," who pass down children's folklore, little girls are "drawn into a cooperative girls' culture" (Grugeon 1993: 29). Entering into a social group requires proficiency while successful participation in clapping games reinforces peer group solidarity. In games like "Barbie Girl," developing musical identities and relationships is intimately connected to developing social identities.

It is not only playing the game together, but playing *with* the game that is significant. This relates to the second way in which the game manifests musicality. In its combination of sound, movement, and words, the Barbie game is an embodiment of multimodality fundamental to music-making. In general, township children's games are multimodal in both content and creative process. They highlight *how* learners are musical in the way they play with the game: appropriating and incorporating elements from popular culture, the media, and traditional music and dance practices. Children add the "Barbie Girl" tune to an inherited game, modify its actions, and incorporate township sounds and signs. It thus embodies children's creative processes of adapting musical games to suit their identities and interests. It epitomizes the way in which township children draw on a range of resources appropriate for their expressive, communicative, and game-playing purposes.

As such, "Barbie Girl" highlights key features of hybridity in township children's games, produced by modifying, mixing, and matching styles. These processes are simultaneously a creative method and a reflection of children's urban township environment. Soweto culture is characterized by cross-over styles, hybrid music and dance forms, and localized communicative and expressive practices. Children are particularly invested and interested in township culture, and this is evident in the way they include township sounds, musics, characters, and signs in their game.

"Barbie Girl" uses the sounds and movements of its locality. Children incorporate the elements of urban township *kwaito* music—South Africa's version of electronic house music combined with rap and hip-hop. *Sampilipili sampolopolo* emulates the familiar township sound of a taxi hooter and its dotted rhythm follows the fast, repeated drum patterns of *kwaito* and South African house music. Children integrate the communicative practices associated with taxi travel into their clapping and circle games, like hand signs indicating direction and hooter signals representing place. In townships, the *tsotsi* reference carries representational meaning as a gangster—a risky man, both a criminal and someone revered for his style. Linked to township fashion and taste are its nonverbal communicative forms, particularly gestural language. In "Barbie Girl," gestures indicating boy (pointing to a beard), girl (pointing to breasts), and defiance (wagging the forefinger in front of your face) carry symbolic meaning for insiders. The game thus exemplifies how children integrate local "communicative and representational literacies" into their games to create their own meanings through music (Stein 2008).

The reworking of these discrete elements is a noteworthy practice in children's games because they utilize the mix-and-match practices associated with township youth culture. Children's combined deployment of multimodal resources in their musical play represents a sophisticated, layered set of meanings and communicative expression. Because children's choices relate closely to their interests and who they are, the multimodal materials they choose and how they integrate these in their games articulate their musical identities. Analyzing "Barbie Girl" thus reveals who township children are musically and how they are musical. Uncovering their prior musical knowledges and recognizing the innate musicality of their games emphasizes "how musical [children] already are without expert guidance" and prompts the question "how musical they may become through teaching" (Campbell 1998: 96).

How does teaching "engage musical play"? Although many music educators advocate relating children's existing musical practices and identities to pedagogy, I suggest that a method for doing so is often absent. *How* do we connect the domains of musical play and classroom teaching and learning? How can teachers incorporate children's musical play into the classroom in productive, generative ways?

I propose that a methodology of recruiting children's musical games as resources for teaching can address the dislocation between in- and outside-school knowledges and practices by bridging sites of practice *methodologically*. The Multiliteracies Pedagogy serves as a source for this concept (New London Group 1996; Cope and Kalantzis 2000). The Multiliteracies approach provides a way for teachers to build on learners' "Situated Practices," which are the resources learners bring to the teaching and learning context (ibid.). The elements of the Multiliteracies Pedagogical Framework—Situated Practice, Overt Instruction, Critical Framing and Transformed Practice—represent different teaching and learning orientations (New London Group 1996; Cope and Kalantzis 2000). Recruitment, in the Multiliteracies' sense, implies developing rather than reiterating children's games in the classroom, for potential transformation.

In practice, recruitment happens through a process of incorporating, developing, and changing the games in the classroom. Recruiting township learners' games as "Situated Practices" implies drawing on the aspects of multimodality and sociality their games display. With reference to games like Barbie, I propose that recruitment operates on a number of levels:

First, teachers can recruit children's specific musical and dance capacities displayed in the game. These include children's ability to coordinate complex clapping patterns, layer rhythmic textures, and connect sounds with movements. Then, teaching can capitalize on children's ability to collaborate musically. Pedagogy can use the way musical participation and cooperation operate in a game; it can use the fact that playing games gives children meaningful reasons to work together musically and socially. The actual dance steps and melodic or rhythmic elements from the games can be sourced to form the basis for creating new poems, songs, or dances. Teaching can also build on children's abilities to source and combine multimodal materials to create new musical designs. Here, we are recruiting learners' ability to work with the "affordances" of the aural and kinetic modes (Gibson 1979; Kress 2000). Teaching can employ the way in which music and movement functions for children: each mode presents opportunities to create narrative, to relate to each other, to explore and organize new sound-movement relationships. Last, music pedagogy can build on learners' "designing" (New London Group 1996; Cope and Kalantzis 2000), which is the ability to choose and shape available musical and movement resources effectively for expressive, performative, or representational purposes. When the *Mohloding* girls choose elements of the "Barbie Girl" tune, add their own words, integrate township sounds and signals, and use all of this to create a clapping game, they are already designing because they are drawing on and shaping available sound resources into new sound designs. A music pedagogy can utilize learners' ability to design in this way, and extend it in a process of design and redesign.

The purpose of recruiting and developing the capacities children's games exemplify in multiple ways is potential transformation. A pedagogy based on recruitment for transformation extends children's ability to design by helping them to redesign. It provides a means of incorporating children's games in pedagogy in ways that produce new musical knowledge and promote new kinds of learning. The desired result is to deepen the musicianship children already have and develop new kinds of musicianship in new musical contexts.

In attempting to bridge the dislocation between playground and classroom practices described earlier, I worked with three Soweto Arts and Culture educators, introducing a pedagogic innovation based on the theories and methods underpinning the Multiliteracies approach. In my trial of this approach with teachers and their learners, learners' games underwent a series of musical transformations to produce new musical designs (Harrop-Allin 2007). Drawing on the existing music and movement resources of their games, learners applied the new skills and ideas learned in their teachers' "Overt Instruction" (Cope and Kalantzis 2000) to create new games and rhythmic poems. Their new musical designs showed increased sensitivity to sounds, to each other, focusing listening, reflection, and a conscious awareness of how "we can make our own music."

The pedagogical intervention demonstrated that recognizing, recruiting, and developing children's musical identities, and the capacities their games embody, can result in transformation. It showed how to extend the agency and control children exhibit in their musical play into classroom learning. Recruiting children's designs (their games) and their ability to design entails recognizing the agency inherent in design. Applying these aspects of the Multiliteracies Pedagogy to music education in Soweto schools indicated the potential for music education to become a more creative, generative process build on learners' (and teachers') agency.

In aiming to bridge the disparities between learners' and teachers' practices described at the beginning of this chapter, recruiting children's games for pedagogy enabled teaching to work with the specifics of children's musical potential. It enabled teaching to "play"; to begin using the affordances of multimodal music-making and connect more fully to children's musical identities. In seeking to address the contradictions and challenges of teaching music in South Africa, recruiting children's games as resources for pedagogy proposes a new way of teaching music that responds particularly to South African teaching and learning environments, but which I suggest has broader application.

Notes

1. More broadly in South Africa, research confirms that many of the National Curriculum Statement's teaching and learning goals are not being achieved. (See, for example, Chisholm 2000 and Morrow et al. 2005.)

2. The township of Soweto was formally a separate black area, physically divided into ethnic areas under apartheid legislation. It is now amalgamated with Johannesburg, but the population remains overwhelmingly black.

3. "Barbie Girl" was released by the Danish-Norwegian "bubble-gum" pop group Aqua in 1997. The song topped the international pop charts at the time (http://en.wikipedia .org/wiki/Barbie_Girl, accessed 18 March 2009). The song is from the album *Aquarium* (MCA label, ASIN B000002P72).

4. Mbongeni Ngema's *Sarafina* tells the story of a young activist during the struggle against apartheid. It was a hit stage musical in South Africa and internationally during the late 1980s, and was later made into a film.

References

Andrew, D. 2006. Learners and Artist-Teachers As Multimodal Agents in Schools. Unpublished paper presented at the Namibia Institute for Educational Development Conference, Okahandha.

Barrett, E. 2005. Musical Communication and Children's Communities of Practice. In *Musical Communication*, ed. D. Miell, Raymond, A. R. MacDonald, D. J. Hargreaves, 261–281. Oxford: Oxford University Press.

Bishop, J. C., and M. Curtis, eds. 2001. *Play Today in the Primary School Playground*. Buckingham and Philadelphia: Open University Press.

Bogatsu, M. 2002. "Loxion Kulcha": Fashioning Black Youth Culture in Post-Apartheid South Africa. *English Studies in Africa* 45 (2): 1–13.

Campbell, P. S. 1998. *Songs in their Head: Music and Its Meaning in Children's Lives*. New York: Oxford University Press.

———. 2002. The Musical Cultures of Children. In *The Arts in Children's Lives: Context, Culture and Curriculum*, ed. L. Bresler and C. M. Thompson, 57–69. Dordrecht, the Netherlands: Kluwer Academic Publications.

Chisholm, L., ed. 2000. *A South African Curriculum for the Twenty-First Century: Report of the Review Committee on Curriculum 2005*. Department of Education: Pretoria.

Cope, B., and M. Kalantzis, eds. 2000. *Multiliteracies: Literacy Learning and the Design of Social Futures*. South Yarra: Macmillan.

Coplan, D. 2008. *In Township Tonight! Three Centuries of South African Black City Music and Theatre*, 2nd ed. Johannesburg: Jacana Press.

Davis, R. 2005. Music Education and Cultural Identity. *Educational Philosophy and Theory* 37 (1): 47–63.

DeNora, T. 2000. *Music in Everyday Life*. Cambridge: Cambridge University Press.

Elliott, D. 1995. *Music Matters: a New Philosophy of Music Education*. Oxford: Oxford University Press.

Factor, J. 2001. Three Myths about Children's Folklore. In *Play Today in the Primary School Playground*, ed. J. C. Bishop and M. Curtis, 24–36. Philadelphia: Open University Press.

Gibson, J. J. 1979. *The Ecological Approach to Visual Perception*. Boston: Houghton-Mifflin.

Green, L. 2008. *Music, Informal Learning and the School: A New Classroom Pedagogy*. Aldershot, UK: Ashgate.

Grugeon, E. 1993. Gender Implications of Children's Playground Culture. In *Gender and Ethnicity in Schools*, ed. P. Woods and M. Hammersley, 11–34. London and New York: Routledge.

Harrop-Allin, S. 2005. Ethnomusicology and Music Education: Developing the Dialogue. *SAMUS: South African Journal of Musicology* 25: 109–125.

———. 2007. Recruiting Learners' Musical Games as Resources for South African Primary School Arts and Culture Education Using a Multiliteracies Approach. Master's thesis, University of the Witwatersrand, Johannesburg.

Harwood, E. 1998. Music Learning in Context: A Playground Tale. *Research Studies in Education* 11: 52–60.

Jaffurs, S. 2006. The Intersection of Informal and Formal Music Learning Practices. *International Journal of Community Music.* Available at http://www.intljcm.com/articles/volume%24/Jaffurs (accessed 4 December 2006).

Kress, G. 2000. Multimodality. In *Multiliteracies: Literacy Learning and the Design of Social Futures,* ed. D. Cope and M. Kalantzis, 182–203. London and New York: Routledge.

Mans, M. 2002. To '*Pamwe*' or To Play: The Role of Play in Arts Education in Africa. *International Journal of Music Education* 39: 50–64.

———. 2003. Play in Musical Arts Pedagogy. In *Musical Arts in Africa: Theory, Practice and Education,* ed. A. Herbst, K. Agawu, and M. Nzewi, 195–212. Pretoria: University of South Africa Press.

Marsh, J., and E. Hallett. 2000. *Literacy and Popular Culture: Using Children's Culture in the Classroom.* London: Paul Chapman.

Marsh, K. 2008. *The Musical Playground: Global Tradition and Change in Children's Songs and Games.* New York: Oxford University Press.

Morrow, W., M. Jiya, and M. Samuel. 2005. *Report of the Ministerial Committee on Teacher Education: A National Framework for Teacher Education in South Africa.* Pretoria: Department of Education.

New London Group. 1996. Pedagogy of Multiliteracies: Designing Social Futures. *Harvard Educational Review* 66 (1): 60–92.

Opie, I., and P. Opie. 1985. *The Singing Game.* Oxford: Oxford University Press.

Pahl, K., and J. Rowsell. 2005. *Literacy and Education: Understanding the New Literacy Studies in the Classroom.* London: Paul Chapman Publishing.

Small, C. 1998. *Musicking: the Meanings of Performing and Listening.* Hanover, N.H.: Wesleyan University Press.

South African Department of Education. 1996. *Curriculum Framework for General and Further Education and Training.* Pretoria: National Department of Education.

Stein, P. 2007. Multimodal Instructional Practices. In *Handbook of Research on New Literacies,* ed. D. Leu, J. Coiro, M. Knobel, and C. Lankshear. Mahway, N.J.: Lawrence, Erlbaum.

———. 2008. *Multimodal Pedagogies in Diverse Classrooms: Representation, Rights and Resources.* London: Routledge.

Temmerman, N. 2005. Children's Participation in Music: Connecting the Cultural Contexts—An Australian Perspective. *British Journal of Music Education* 22 (2): 113–122.

ELEVEN

Personal, Local, and National Identities in Ghanaian Performance Ensembles

TREVOR WIGGINS

Anyone who has visited Ghana in West Africa will probably have encountered music and dance in performance. The events generally appear happy and celebratory, with little sense of the occasion as a nexus for a range of decisions around cultural identity that may be embodied in the style of the event, choice of material, and response to the context. This is of course a naïve view, as all musical identities are complex, drawing together a web of influences, references, and diverse styles. Each element has a derivation, a meaning, and symbolism that attach to it. There are many performance ensembles in Ghana, often referred to as "cultural groups," which present music/dance activities, perhaps intertwined with story-telling. This chapter will focus on three groups in the south of Ghana: the Brotherhood cultural group based in Alajo (a suburb of the capital, Accra), the Bɛwaa group at Mary Queen of Peace Catholic Primary School in Cape Coast (a regional center eighty-five miles west of Accra), and the Kukyekukyeku (pronounced Coo-chi-coo-chi-coo) Bamboo Orchestra, based in Mosmagor (a village in the Kakum forest reserve twenty miles north of Cape Coast). I have been associated with the Brotherhood group continuously since 1989, recording their performances and talking to the leader and group members, and I have similarly engaged with the Mosomagor group since I first encountered them in 1995. My relationship with the school group was more limited, conducted through recordings and interviews of the teachers and members in 1999. These represent three contrasting examples of the educational role of such groups, particularly in relation to the tensions in Ghana between national education and diverse regional cultural identities. In order to understand the decisions the leaders of these groups have made about their musical identity and the relationship to learning and teaching, it is necessary to understand something of the evolution of Ghanaian national culture.

Ghana comprises a large number of ethnic and linguistic groups, brought together in one state through the force of colonial power. One of the issues that confronted Kwame Nkrumah, Ghana's first president following independence in 1957, was to persuade the people to commit to the new state rather than pursue their own factional interests. With the cessation of colonial rule, there was a strong sense of new nationhood, but also many long-standing enmities and rivalries between ethnic, cultural, and linguistic groups, and none of them were prepared to subsume their identity or to agree to the ascendancy of another group over their own. Nkrumah was well aware of the role that education, sports, and the arts play in creating a national identity, often seen through iconic institutions such as a national university and an arts council, both of which he set out to establish.

There was a considerable debate in Parliament about how an arts council should be set up, its remit and role. As the minister of education asserted: "We all have an interest in seeing that our nation makes its proper contribution to the artistic and cultural life of the world" (Arts Council of Ghana bill [ACG], column 300). Although this point was agreed, the nature of the relationship between the Arts Council and the government was more contentious—"The Bill . . . is going to give power to the Government to control arts in the country. We must remember that art is culture and anything cultural should not be placed under the control of the government" (ACG, column 303). There was a commitment to representation of the different ethnic groups in Ghana on the Arts Council, but the practical issue of what constituted the national culture, particularly in a post-colonial setting, continued to exercise the minds of the members of Parliament. The minister was advised that: "The first place he [the minister] should look for development of this [the arts] is the villages. Encourage young people in the villages because the villages are the true repositories of our cultural heritage" (ACG, column 306). There was also a commitment to and an expectation of a broader national knowledge of arts rather than the transmission and preservation of an individual heritage within its cultural location. "On special occasions . . . residents from neighboring and distant areas of Ghana should be invited because it is not enough to know the heritage of your own individual tribal grouping; it is not enough. We must expand and be true exponents of Ghanaian culture *in toto*" (ACG, columns 306–307). At this time, traditional Ghanaian music scarcely featured in the curriculum of schools, with English national songs or hymns in a European style being more likely. The minister of education evidently understood these concerns when he came to sum up the debate: "We are going to do all we can to encourage the different kinds of art and culture and usages of all the people—and I repeat all the people—of Ghana" (ACG, columns 319–320). The Arts Council was subsequently enacted and included regional offices, but the power struggle between local and national identities was recognized rather than resolved.

There was some parallel in Nkrumah's relationship with the newly constituted University of Ghana. The academics believed they should offer a cogent public critique of government policy; Nkrumah felt they too often strayed outside their academic purview into politics, while expecting to retain their academic freedom of speech. Nevertheless, it was to two members of the university, the musician and musicologist J. H. Kwabena Nketia and the choreographer Mawɛre Opoku, that Nkrumah turned for help in setting up a national dance company in the early 1960s. As Nketia related it in a personal interview in December 2006:

> Guinea Ballet and others had already shown that a national dance company would be a good thing. . . . Everywhere [else] you took your accomplished performers, dancers, and musicians, and brought them together to form the company. . . . We said we would do it differently. Nkrumah agreed; we would train our dancers and musicians and form a dance company and the idea [was] that we would bring the culture together in this way.

The strategy that Nketia and Opoku agreed on was to make a selection of dancers and musicians locally, then bring in specialists from other ethnic groups around the country for residencies with the dance company to teach traditional dances from elsewhere. Regional dances were then adapted into a more "national" idiom by choreographing the dance more specifically and similarly standardizing the music. Dances from different parts of the country could be structured into a performance sequence, often linked by a simple moral narrative. The way in which this evolution answered the concerns expressed in the parliamentary debate, through taking regional identities and transforming them into a polyglot national style, is clear. This style of musical dance drama evolved by Nketia and Opoku quickly became the model for instructors sent out by the Arts Council, which, combined with the status of the National Dance Company, meant that Nketia and Opoku's innovation of combining a variety of dances from different parts of the country became a national ideal for performance groups. Expertise in local musical forms was expected, but additional kudos attached to a high level performance of dances from a variety of locations.

As was suggested in the parliamentary debates about the Arts Council, music and dance scarcely appeared in the school curriculum. However, expertise in music and dance had a significant community status, particularly as chiefs at the local, regional, and even national level wanted their own retinue of performers. Such groups fulfilled a dual function, entering national competitions that became common from the 1960s and offering status and praise in support of a chief at major social and community events such as a *Durbar*. (This word is from India, or possibly Iran, where it described the court of the princely ruler. The British adopted this in India for ceremonial occasions, such as the Proclamation Durbar in 1877 to celebrate Queen Victoria's elevation to Empress of India, and it was later introduced to other colonies as a celebration of culture at the behest of the rulers. It has subsequently lost most of its colonial association and is generally used in Ghana; "a durbar of chiefs" describes the opening ceremony of a major cultural event.) It thus became common to find performance groups, often termed "cultural groups," associated with schools, youth organizations, specific villages/towns, or powerful and high status figures in the community. Groups were supported by their sponsors with resources such as instruments, costumes, transport, or the cost of entry to competitions. The development of these performance groups could be perceived as communities responding to an evolving sense of nationality or, as Coe (2005: 83) suggests, "Drumming and dancing became the way the nation appropriated cultural traditions and engaged many of its citizens, particularly schoolchildren."

Since the 1960s the national situation has evolved. Although at one level enmity between different groups has decreased (probably particularly in the case of younger people whose cultural models may now be more oriented toward the United States or Europe), there is still limited trust at levels of political power. Senior figures in the chieftaincy or government are expected to promote their area economically, and "cultural" activity is often used to demonstrate excellence—with an implication of superiority. As the occasions for music and dance as part of rites of passage or for informal recreation decline, there has been an increase in the number of cultural festivals organized by individual towns. These typically involve a celebration of local culture before invited national representatives, together with a competition for performance groups. The largest model is NAFAC (National Festival of Arts and Culture), which is organized biennially in regional rotation. Although this is a celebration of culture, there are evident political maneuvers in which the artists are implicated. (The national agenda was also evident in the slogan adopted by NAFAC in Wa, Upper West Region, in November 2006: "Culture: a vehicle for wealth creation.") The music and dance for these occasions has to be particularly loud and energetic, a hyper-real version of the tradition so it can be heard across a large outdoor arena and make an impact in only a few minutes.

At the same time, the tradition can be innovative and include novel elements, such as drawing on music from elsewhere and incorporating them into the traditional style. This might be done using non-Ghanaian material to show an international perspective or appeal to young people, or it might use music from elsewhere in Ghana, in homage but also to demonstrate that the group can master other musical styles as well as their own, with an implication that the other musical style is not so difficult. It is within the context provided by regional and national festivals, cultural competitions, the model developed by the National Dance Ensemble and the intention of the Arts Council (and its successor) to create a national culture that performance groups operate. Since many of the groups are primarily aimed at young people, there is also the context of the National School Curriculum, where music and dance are located as part of the Religious and Moral Education [RME] syllabus. The RME curriculum is mostly knowledge-based, with an emphasis on "good" practices and behavior with some invitations to explore local and national cultural practices. Opportunities for practical work are included but are pragmatically constrained, as I will discuss later.

THE BROTHERHOOD CULTURAL GROUP

The Brotherhood Cultural Group is based in Alajo, a relatively poor area of Accra, and is directed by its founder, Johnson K. D. Kemeh. Johnson started the group in 1976 and since 1977 has been employed as a drumming instructor at the University of Ghana. Johnson learned to drum in his home town of Dzodze in the Ewe area of southeast Ghana. His learning was traditional in that he did not have instruction other than encouragement and support from an older master drummer. By the time he auditioned at the university aged twenty-six, he could play more than twenty-five different pieces/styles, mostly Ewe but with some from neighboring regions, learned aurally. As part of his audition, he was tested on the quickness and accuracy of his ability to learn music from elsewhere in Ghana (author interview, December 2006). At the university he was one of a group of instructors who represented some of the larger ethnic groups in the country. The instructors, as well as teaching primarily their own culture, would also play for dance classes and the resident dance ensemble of the university, so Johnson quickly learned a "national" repertoire. Although not primarily a dancer, he also learned the dance steps for these pieces, as the drummers have to know the dance in order to give the cues to the dancers to change the step at appropriate moments. There was, of course, a difference in the nature of his knowledge of Ewe material from that he learned at the university. Within the Ewe style he had in-depth knowledge of the traditions of Dzodze and the differences between these and other towns in the area. With material learned at the university, he learned the version played by another instructor (perhaps extended and mixed with observations of another visitor from the region) but had less knowledge of the scope of that music/dance or its regional variations.

The Brotherhood group does not have a fixed number of members but is typically fifteen to twenty-five strong, ranging in age from five to twenty-five. Children join usually as dancers and are expected to prove their commitment by learning the current program within six to eight weeks. Once accepted, they effectively become members of an extended family with rights and responsibilities. The group knows a number of traditional dances, predominantly Ewe but with a considerable mix from elsewhere in Ghana, and has appropriate costumes for these. The dances chosen are mostly recreational in character, and the children receive a basic knowledge of their origins or meaning. Johnson choreographs dances based on his learning over many years, using traditional steps that he adapts and updates for the group and his potential audiences. Johnson described the basis of his knowledge to me:

> [Before I started the group] I had already heard some of the dances from the north, some of the dances from Ashanti and other regions, then I've been hearing more here. So nobody came to teach my group, I taught my group myself. By so doing, I adopted some strategies of teaching the students other pieces from the north, Ashanti, Fanti, and other regions. All the ten regions, I was able to teach the music from there, even though I didn't visit some of the regions before, but I can teach and give them the history [of the music].

Following the Opoku/Nketia model, dances are used with short narratives to construct a dance-drama. The storyline typically follows a standard West African formula (also seen in many Nigerian films), with an evil character leading the hero astray until rescue is provided by a return to Christian values and forgiveness. In the group, the drummers are usually older boys, with both boys and girls singing, dancing, or perhaps playing a rattle. Johnson will generally not play except to demonstrate a particularly difficult section. Learning is by observation and imitation for both dancing and drumming, with younger children perhaps being shown something by the more experienced group members. Although this is an entirely voluntary club rehearsing evenings and/or weekends, there is a friendly but strict sense of discipline, reinforced with a quick tap on the head with a drumstick when needed. The group is highly successful and performs regularly by invitation in Accra, in the Ewe area of Ghana and on occasions in Europe.

MARY QUEEN OF PEACE SCHOOL

A different sort of performance group for children is found at Mary Queen of Peace Catholic Primary School in Cape Coast. This region is primarily

Fanti-speaking, but a significant number of Dagara people live in Cape Coast, and the school is unique in having its own Bɛwaa group (Bɛwaa or Bawa is a recreational dance from the Dagara area of Ghana, six hundred miles north) organized by two Dagara teachers. The adult Dagara community in Cape Coast also has a performance group, performing mostly Bɛwaa. In the north, the tradition (established for over forty years) is that each village has a Bɛwaa group of young people, who dance and sing mainly during the harvest period, when work is complete and there are often moonlit evenings. The Cape Coast adult group has two main reasons for its existence: it provides a social focus for the Dagara people to meet, but it is also sustained by the fact that it is perceived as exotic and unusual by local people who pay the group to perform for special occasions. The leader of the school group, Frank Dongbetigr, used to be the leader of the adult group and plays the xylophone that provides the music for this dance. The other teacher, Agnes Bewaale, takes the role of lead singer. The children's roles are to dance and sing the responses to Agnes's lead.

The children are from several ethnic/cultural groups: most are Fante, with some Dagara and some Ewe. The school's US headmistress, Sister Mary Ann, is committed to supporting the group as a public example of the school policy of intercultural education, and the group is asked to represent the school on "cultural" occasions. The children, of course, come more for enjoyment—they said they especially liked the "bumping" (part of the dance where hips are bumped together). This group rehearses after school and has quite a limited repertoire of four to six songs/dances. These are not linked thematically nor is there a narrative, as this is not the tradition with Bɛwaa. The children know the dances as a series of movements and recognize the songs enough to make responses they have learned phonetically, but they understand in only a rudimentary way what they are singing (with the exception of the Dagara children, of course). The group learns everything by rote and is heavily reliant on the two teachers in performance. This is perhaps not surprising in a junior school where most pupils will be less than twelve years old. (Some equivalent schools in the north have groups where all the roles are taken by children, but they are still reliant on having a xylophone player who has learned at home, as there is no opportunity for this level of specific instruction in school.) The children in the group learn little about the Dagara music and dance beyond a brief and limited experience of its simpler expressions, but they have enjoyed the experience, and it has probably moved them away from stereotypical conceptions of the "other," which are still very common.

MOSOMAGOR VILLAGE

North from Cape Coast is Kakum, a reservation of moist semi-deciduous trees and plants, which also provides refuge for rare animals. Historically in this area (still Fanti-speaking), the forest dwellers would clear an area for cultivation, then move on after a few years when the soil became exhausted to repeat the process, hunting to supplement their farming. With the advent of the reserve this mode of subsistence has been severely restricted, and the village of Mosomagor has been in the same place for at least twenty years, trying to develop more sustainable agriculture and limiting hunting. At the same time, the Ghanaian government has been promoting ecotourism in places like Kakum (see, e.g., www.touring-ghana.com/ecotourism/kakum.asp [accessed 29 July 2009]), so members of the village decided to try to utilize this for their economic benefit. The Kukyekukyeku Bamboo Orchestra was started in January 1995 by its present leader, Bismark K. N. Amoah in collaboration with a Danish-funded development project based in Cape Coast. The project provided a mentor/advisor to assist with the process of developing the local traditional music and dance into a performance that could be offered to tourists visiting Kakum. The instruments used by the ensemble are various sizes of bamboo ranging in length from around one to four feet, played by being struck on a block of wood to give a tuned note. Each player may have one or two instruments so, combined with a bell as timekeeper, they can imitate the sound of most drum ensembles. These are traditional instruments in this area, and the groups play dances such as *Sikye* and *Adowa*. Following their initial performances at Kakum and because the group wanted to appeal to a variety of tourists, they then added other Ghanaian rhythms, such as the Ewe *Agbadza* and the Ga *Kpanlogo*. As the group leader, Bismarck, said:

> Sometimes, we hear some rhythms and music from different people in the different areas. In fact, it was very surprising the way people enjoyed the rhythms and the music at the Kakum park and not there only but also other places we perform.

Bismark also felt that it was good for the group to practice these different rhythms to extend their experience and knowledge. The group has continued to add more rhythms, partly inspired by the positive responses from visitors to Kakum, but also as a way of continuing to develop repertoire. Group membership is through a combination of invitation and interest. Sometimes they will invite someone with good existing skills to join and extend their experience, while with younger members who show an interest, they offer a more structured training and induction. The majority of this group are adults, with a small number of teenagers. The dancing is quite limited in both extent and numbers of participants, and the main interest is the sequence of songs in different rhythms. The group displays high levels of energy and accuracy, playing at great speed and placing more emphasis on part singing in the ensemble than the other groups. In spite of this being principally an adult group, there is still a strong hierarchical discipline. An English student was surprised to be hit smartly on the head with a drumstick when she forgot the words of a song and was told that the pain would help her remember next time.

SCHOOLS AND FORMAL LEARNING

Each of these three ensembles trains group members in the acquisition of performance skills and is passing on an aspect of Ghanaian culture in a way that is not found in most schools in Ghana. Music still scarcely features on the curriculum for most students, and there are few trained music teachers in schools. Teachers may move around regions in Ghana; it is not uncommon to find that some teachers know little of the local culture because they grew up in a different area. So within the school curriculum, under the RME heading, music and dance are mainly presented as general objects of study, and children are asked to find out about their local traditions on their own. Schools are also encouraged to bring in local culture bearers to talk about and demonstrate traditions, but this can cause problems of payment, of resources, and of conflict with religious beliefs in some areas (see Coe 2005: 109–134). Many schools encourage cultural activities outside the classroom, but this relies on the commitment and expertise of one or more teachers to run a group. Few teachers are able to live solely on their salary, so they may be reluctant to stay voluntarily after school when they could work on their own land or be paid for tutoring individual students. Necessary resources of instruments and dance costumes are also a drain on a school budget that may be struggling to buy textbooks, so while there is a strong commitment to "cultural activities," the reality is often very limited.

CULTURAL PERFORMANCE AND IDENTITY

The school Bɛwaa group is run by teachers but is not transmitting local culture. There is no parallel group for Fante culture, nor any perceived need or role for one. The children benefit from a limited engagement with another Ghanaian culture; the school has a unique performance group for the area, but there is little progression for the pupils, and the existence of the group is mostly due to the presence of teachers with the specific skill. The materials used are a few well-known and relatively simple songs from the north composed around forty years ago. Although the headmistress is concerned with issues of multicultural education, the group itself is more pragmatic, and issues of national or regional identity are not a significant explicit issue for the children.

The Mosamagor Bamboo orchestra is in a different position. The original materials are local music and dance, adapted and arranged for a more commercial context. The performances at places like Kakum are designed mainly for tourists from outside Ghana or the relatively small number of wealthy Ghanaians who visit. Bismark, the leader, will be judged on the effectiveness of his offering in getting further paid engagements or selling recordings of the group. This is part of a package offering ethical ecotourism to the visitor—but anything that does not get an enthusiastic reception will quickly be replaced, whether local, traditional, or not. Audience reaction tends to select the most energetic performances with good ensemble, so the aesthetic is driven by the visitors. At the same time, there is evidence that the group is influenced by the Nketia/Opoku model in the inclusion of rhythms from different parts of Ghana, although these are presented discretely and not put together into a narrative sequence. Members of this group are there for personal and group benefit, and the repertoire continues to evolve despite there being no progression for group members into other roles nor any perceived benefit other than economic.

The Brotherhood group is the closest in conception and material to the Nketia/Opoku model—not surprisingly, as its leader is based at the university. Although the group knows material from many different regions, this is used to create a cultural smorgasbord in which the origin of the elements is less important. The leader has to make a substantial financial contribution in order to buy costumes and maintain drums, so there is still a strongly commercial element in looking for paid performances. So this group again favors high-energy dancing and drumming, achieving standards that challenge many adult groups. There is a good progression for members into future employment, with a number of former members now employed at the university or other cultural locations such as the National Theatre.

Guss (2000: 8–12) discusses the attributes of "cultural performance." He notes, "What is important is that cultural performances be recognized as sites of social action where identities and relations are continually being reconfigured" (2000: 12). All of these groups are engaging in cultural performance, recreating in a performance environment materials that would formerly have comprised ritual or recreational occasions of life. In the traditional setting, the materials would have been learned almost exclusively by observation. This methodology is still significant in the learning, but with a more active role for the teacher in organizing learning, demonstrating, and specifically correcting mistakes. Sessions are closely directed by the teacher, with none of the apparent chaos seen in spontaneous peer-group learning typical of more autonomous occasions but potentially leading to a different understanding of the material (see Green 2008: 53–54 for a discussion of this).

The traditions that are passed on are all Ghanaian, but these are losing some of their specificity of location, and at least two of the groups are engaging strongly with the notion of culture for "wealth creation." Nketia offered me a summary of the current situation in terms of national identity:

At the higher level of culture, we are Ghanaians, so that means that on the second level you will recognize the identity of ethnic groups, but each ethnic group then becomes a unit in a higher complex. So anything that is good, from any ethnic group, can represent Ghana. We never really thought of Ghanaian national culture as an integrated one . . . even though it has emerged that we are using materials from here and there, but it was not to create one uniform culture but to have a common point of reference. So that, in a creative work, if you have a little bit of that and that, it is Ghanaian. If it is one good thing from one area, it is still Ghanaian.

Guss (2000: 9) observes, "The same form [of cultural performance] may be used to articulate a number of different ideas and over time can easily oscillate between religious devotion, ethnic solidarity, political resistance, national identity, and even commercial spectacle."

These Ghanaian groups engage with issues of ethnicity, national identity, and the commercial need for spectacle, as well as teaching, learning, and transmission, in a thoroughly postmodern arena that deserves to be further investigated from the perspectives of both teachers and children. Schooling and all forms of education are moving inexorably toward a more standardized pedagogy that is knowledge-based and seen as the best basis for future economic development, which, everyone agrees, is necessary. Cultural activities were always seen to be the location for the development of *individual* identity through learning, and any thought of copying another person made no sense and was frowned on. The current generation of group leaders has learned mostly in this traditional way but they are now engaged in more direct, task-orientated pedagogy in response to diverse motivations. Children are apparently relative innocents in this forum, trying to develop their identities somewhere between possible aspirations to various "pop" models, local and national traditions, and Ghanaian political opinion, typically expressed by the Ashanti regional minister at NAFAC: "We must defend ourselves against globalization that is destroying our culture."

References

Agawu, Kofi. 2003. *Representing African Music: Postcolonial Notes, Queries, Positions.* New York: Routledge.

Arts Council of Ghana bill. Second Reading 9/10 December 1958. Source: Parliamentary Debates, First Series, vol. 12, session 1958–1959. Accra: Government Printer.

Campbell, Patricia S. 1998. *Songs in Their Heads: Music and Its Meaning in Children's Lives.* Oxford: Oxford University Press.

Campbell, P. S., J. Drummond, P. Dunbar-Hall, K. Howard, H. Schippers, and T. Wiggins, eds. 2005. *Cultural Diversity in Music: Directions and Challenges for the 21st Century.* Brisbane: Australian Academic Press.

Coe, Cati. 2005. *Dilemmas of Culture in African Schools: Youth, Nationalism, and the Transformation of Knowledge.* London: University of Chicago Press.

Green, Lucy. 2008. *Music, Informal Learning and the School: A New Classroom Pedagogy.* Aldershot, UK: Ashgate.

Guss, David M. 2000. *The Festive State.* Berkeley: University of California Press.

Lentz, Carola, and Paul Nugent, eds. 2000. *Ethnicity in Ghana: The Limits of Invention.* New York: St. Martin's Press, and Basingstoke: Macmillan.

Nketia, J. H. Kwabena. 1961. Continuity of Traditional Instruction. In *The Preservation of Traditional Forms of the Learned and Popular Music of the Orient and the Occident,* ed. William K. Archer, 203–213. Urbana: Center for Comparative Psycholinguistics, Institute of Communications, University of Illinois.

Wiggins, Trevor. 2003. *Ghana, Cape Coast: Changing Traditions.* AIMP/VDE-Gallo (VDE CD-1135).

———. 2005. An Interview with J. H. Kwabena Nketia: Perspectives on Tradition and Modernity. *Ethnomusicology Forum* 14 (1): 55–79.

TWELVE

Music Festivals in the Lapland Region

Constructing Identities through Musical Events

SIDSEL KARLSEN

The huge crowd that I am a part of has just made a big transition. From sitting quietly on the large green courtyard lawn, having a cheerful and cozy picnic, we are now jumping, dancing, and roaring wildly—twenty-five hundred people ranging in age from ten to seventy-five, behaving like mad teenage fans. While the previous "picnic-music" certainly supported this kind of behavior, being a happy, summery mix of Latino-inspired music and reggae, the band's female singer had experienced a hard time getting anyone on their feet. Her eager encouragements of "Up, up—you can dance" left us sitting, chatting, and calmly eating—waiting for what would come next. The music playing now is nothing of that kind. On the stage a bunch of middle-aged men is playing moderately good and not particularly swingy folk rock—and yet we dance, clap, and shout passionately. Although I am a researcher at work in the middle of my festival observations, scribbling down field notes, it is impossible not to join in. Still, I cannot help reflecting on my behavior while acting like the rest of the crowd. Thoughts like "Why are we doing this?—this music isn't even catchy!" run through my mind, until I start listening to the lyrics and the band members' talk in between the songs. Then it suddenly strikes me: this is not about the music, at least not the music *per se*. This is about the stories, mediated *through* and *in between* the music, of what it means to be an inhabitant of the Lapland regions—this is about *who we are*, we, the strange fellows who choose to live our lives close to the Arctic Circle. And for the first time since I moved to this area a year and a half ago, I feel ready and willing to take on the identity of a *Pitebo*—an inhabitant of Piteå, a small town in North Bothnia, a county in Swedish Lapland—and learn, deeply, what it means to be one.

MUSIC FESTIVALS—WHAT ARE THEY ABOUT?

Each year, hundreds of music festivals are arranged all over Scandinavia, and probably thousands all over Europe and other parts of the world. People gather in large towns as well as small out-of-the-way places to see their favorite performers and hear their favorite music—for a few days they take on a role as members of the audience and become immersed in the festival atmosphere. Why are they there? What are they doing? And, as music educators, we cannot help asking: if they are immersed in music for several days—what are they learning?

From the field of festival research we know quite a bit of what music festivals can be about, economically speaking (see, e.g., Aronsen 2006; Maughan and Bianchini 2004). However, as several festival researchers have pointed out (e.g., Formica 1998; Quinn 2005), we know very little about festivals' social and cultural impact and meaning, whether for their host municipalities, the attendees, or even the performers.

As music educators, we have a large body of research to lean on when it comes to the teaching and learning of music that takes place inside the formal classroom. With the new millennium, an understanding of what is going on, in terms of the development of skills and knowledge in the informal arenas for musical learning, has also started to emerge (see, e.g., Green 2002; Karlsen and Brändström 2008; Söderman 2007; Wingstedt 2008). However, when it comes to such exceptionally "open" learning environments as those found in a music festival, only a few investigations have been made (e.g., Karlsen 2007; Pitts 2005; Snell 2005), and much is left to explore. Still, we know that in a festival context the processes of learning and identity formation are likely to be "integrated, mutually dependent and overlapping" (Karlsen 2007: 2) both in time and content.

Looking back on my festival experiences described above, and connecting them with the ideas of Small (1998), they illustrate well how the primary meanings of music "are not individual at all but social" (ibid.:

8), and how rituals, including musical performances, can be used as acts of affirming, exploring, and celebrating community—telling ourselves who we are, trying on identities "to see who we think we are" (ibid.: 95), and rejoicing "in the knowledge of an identity not only possessed but also shared with others" (ibid.). Small further claims that each musical performance articulates the values of a particular social group "at a specific point in its history" (ibid.: 133) no matter its size, economic status, or power. Transferring these thoughts to a music festival context, it implies that such an event may also be one of the means that social groups utilize for educating their own members (Karlsen 2009).

Taking these ideas as a point of departure, the aim of this chapter is to look into festival-related identity work on the communal level and investigate how three particular music festivals, situated in the Lapland region, become vehicles for the expression of collective identity through musical events. Believing in the interdependency of identity and learning processes, I will also undertake to discuss what kind of learning outcomes may be available for the audiences when they enter the informal arena that the festivals constitute. The three festivals that will serve as the chapter's cases are the *Festspel i Pite Älvdal* (Festival in the Pite River Valley), Sweden; the *Festspillene i Nord-Norge* (Festival in the North of Norway), Norway; and the *Jutajaiset Folklorefestivaali* (Jutajaiset Folklore Festival), Finland. What these events have in common is that they are situated quite far from their respective countries' capital areas and thereby from their countries' cultural and economic centers. They are also similar in the sense that they are some of the largest, most visible and vivid festivals in the area in which they operate. While the three festivals certainly can be characterized as *music* festivals, all with large bodies of different kinds of musical performances, two out of three also incorporate other art forms. Still, the basis for the festivals is a plethora of concerts and gigs, featuring a wide variety of musical styles and genres.

INVESTIGATING MUSIC FESTIVALS— THE PRACTICALITIES OF RESEARCH

When a project is designed as a case study on premises such as the present, the practicalities of research involve taking earlier investigations as a point of departure and benefitting from the prior development of theoretical propositions to guide data collection and analysis. Consequently, before choosing the research tools with which I planned to collect my data, I needed to engage in the work of mapping the field and deconstructing, for the purpose of employing them in practical fieldwork, the theoretical concepts relevant for my research. Searching through the earlier research and theory concerning music festivals and communal or collective identity, I reviewed a large body of literature from the interdisciplinary field of festival research, and found two main themes. First, festivals were seen as *outward manifestations* of community identity, functioning as image-maintainers or image-makers and putting places "on the map" (Delamere 2001; Hjemdahl, Hauge, and Lind 2007; Quinn 2005). Second, they were also seen to contribute to the reinforcement of cohesiveness *within* a community, strengthening the bonds between its members (De Bres and Davis 2001; Ekman 1999). A leitmotif of the research was hence that of the festivals' contribution to the development of local identity in their host municipalities, happening in an outward as well as an inward mode.

North and Hargreaves (2008) surveyed a range of studies utilizing social identity theory to explore the functions of music in constituting different aspects of collective identity. However, since earlier research concerning festivals suggested that the collective identity function seemed to be more on a communal or even a municipal level, a sociological framework was chosen for the present study. Hence Giddens's (1991) ideas about the formation of self-identity in the late modern age were transferred to the collective level. This implied, among other things, that a community's identity was seen to be located in and maintained through the narratives by which it represents itself to the "outside" world as well as its own inhabitants. Furthermore, communal identity was perceived as possibly incoherent; in other words as existing in several parallel and even contradictory (Hall 1992) narratives. Consequently, when thinking about identity work in the context of music festivals becoming vehicles for the expression of collective identity on the communal level, this will appear when the festival is able to mediate, through its concerts and other performances, stories about its host municipality. An important task for the researcher, then, is to figure out a way of capturing this festival-related story-telling.

In the present study, the main methods for collecting data were those of participant observation, semi-structured interviewing, and analysis of documentation. I attended in total fifty-eight festival performances as an observing researcher, interviewed four festival directors/artistic leaders as well as six official representatives from the festivals' host municipalities, and gathered festival programs plus information from the festivals' websites. (Regarding the *Festspel i Pite Älvdal,* I also conducted a survey among 350 festival attendees and interviews with sixteen of the survey participants. However, the findings from these play only a limited role in this chapter). In the processes of data collection and analysis, I aimed at capturing, unveiling, and interpreting the stories mediated through the festivals about their host communities or municipalities. In the following, I present one such story for each of the three festivals and examine it in order to show how, in different ways, music festivals may become vehicles for the expression of collective identity.

FESTSPEL I PITE ÄLVDAL: EMPHASIZING THE MUNICIPALITY AS A CENTER IN ITS OWN REALITY

The *Festspel i Pite Älvdal* takes place in four municipalities, and in three of those it appeared to function to some extent as an outward image-maker (see Karlsen 2007). However, this was not the most striking identity mode attached to this particular festival. More important was its ability to contribute to the reinforcement of "inner" community identity by drawing on shared stories and cultural practices and ideals (Ekman 1999). To illustrate one such story, I have chosen to draw on observations of one particular performance that took place in the town of Piteå.

The event that I want to bring to the foreground is the combined Latino music and folk rock concert described in the opening of the chapter. The concert gathered a lot of families—young and old—which in itself is seen as a festival feature that will promote cohesiveness (De Bres and Davis 2001). While the band described first, Latino-inspired and professional, was obviously not able to engage the audience, the second band, the local, semi-professional one, certainly did. What was their secret? First, I believe the answer is to be found in the fact that the latter band had been local and regional heroes a decade ago, and that this performance was their revival concert. Secondly, their songs, not to mention their talk in between the songs, concerned what it meant to be an inhabitant of

North Bothnia in general and a *Pitebo* in particular. For example, the refrain of their signature song, "We can do it ourselves," nicely captured the "Piteå spirit," characterized by a strong, joint agency and resistance against anything that may have been forced upon this municipality, especially from the capital area. I quote from my field notes:

> The band takes the little man's perspective ... engages the audience (much more than [the Latino band]) ... offers stories in between the songs, not about musicians, but about places and people [in North Bothnia].

Thus the songs concerned, for example, the battle of North Bothnia against the rest of Sweden; informal economy as a proper way of surviving in smaller communities; and the resistance against whatever the Swedish government would come up with concerning this northern region. As can be seen from the introduction, the message reached its target group, and even I, originally an "outsider," was captured by what a local journalist called the "revivalist meeting atmosphere ... [and] the strengthening power of togetherness" (Pettersson 2005). In short, this concert exemplified what Frith (1996: 111) describes as social groups getting "to know themselves *as groups ... through* cultural activity."

Even though the *Festspel i Pite Älvdal* featured quite a number of national and even international artists, the main impression gained through the fieldwork was that its most important function was to produce and reproduce local knowledge (Ekman 1999), through its different performances, by deepening, retelling and prolonging already existing community narratives. In the case of Piteå, this entailed emphasizing the story of the local municipality as a center in its own reality, instead of as peripherally positioned against the capital.

FESTSPILLENE I NORD-NORGE: STRENGTHENING THE URBAN DIMENSIONS AND DISPLAYING STRONG, INTERNATIONAL BONDS

As opposed to the *Festspel i Pite Älvdal*, the *Festspillene i Nord-Norge* is seen to be of vital importance when it comes to the outward marketing of its host municipality, the town of Harstad. The ability of the festival to make the town visible in the national media was especially emphasized by the interviewees, and it was seen as the town's strongest trademark by far. As one interviewee put it, for example:

> If you removed the *Festspillene i Nord-Norge,* Harstad would appear as quite naked . . . I would say more stripped than just by the disappearance of a festival . . . if the one thing that makes your town known outside the town itself disappears, you've got a problem . . .

As Delamere (2001) points out, such image-enhancement is one of the most common perceived social benefits of festivals, at least when seen through the eyes of the inhabitants in the festival's host municipality. As such, the *Festspillene i Nord-Norge* represents an excellent example of how a music festival may function as a vehicle for the outward expression of the local collective (Quinn 2005).

I indicated above that communal identity, as mediated through festivals, might exist in parallel or even contradictory narratives. This was the case with the *Festspillene i Nord-Norge.* During the fieldwork I found three main storylines in the festival. However, for reasons that have to do with the limited format of this chapter, I choose to focus on the most evident one, namely the story of a Northern and seemingly peripheral, but still urban and internationally well-connected municipality.

While the *Festspel i Pite Älvdal*-related municipality narratives were disseminated through particular performances, the story-telling of the *Festspillene i Nord-Norge* happened on a more overarching level. The festival program contained a myriad of artistic and musical expressions from a variety of nations and cultures, and the host municipality's status as "international" was highlighted already in the mayor's speech at the opening ceremony. According to the festival director, the festival's international character was also emphasized in the feedback he received from the audience: "People will come up to me and say: 'Finally, you've got the world to come to Harstad'." During the festival, this was evident in the presence of featured artists from all over the world—from New York to Siberia and from Mexico to Armenia. Some acts were rather traditional, such as a performance of Mahler's Fourth Symphony or a string quartet playing Grieg; others featured pop, rock, and jazz, or folk and world music. The diversity also included avant-garde theater, New Circus performances, children's concerts, and a festival café dedicated to public discussions among the performers. Altogether, this vivid mixture signaled a late modern urbanity with strong international features. Waterman (1998) recognizes that a festival linking global and local facets is quite common. Furthermore, Wenger emphasizes how this local-global interplay, in other words "negotiating local ways of belonging to broader constellations . . . and broader styles and discourses" (1998: 149) is integral to the formation of identity, also on the collective level. Interestingly, the collective self-image of "international urbanity" as captured through observations of the *Festspillene i Nord-Norge* events contrasted with the "everyday identity" of the host municipality as expressed by the interviewees. In their opinion, Harstad was a rather dull commuter town with petit-bourgeois features, and not especially lively:

> The people living here are not so good at making their own town a lively place . . . we need someone from outside to do that, because we are too busy sitting on our expensive sofas.

A possible interpretation of the discrepancy between the festival-envisaged and the interviewee-disseminated communal identity may be that the former represents an attempt at negotiating potential and prospectively achievable collective self-images. Hence, the *Festspillene i Nord-Norge* example illustrates how music festivals may become vehicles not only for expressing existing versions of collective identity but also for suggesting possible routes for future identity development.

JUTAJAISET FOLKLOREFESTIVAALI: EMPHASIZING CONNECTIONS TOWARD OTHER PERIPHERAL AND RURAL COMMUNITIES

The *Jutajaiset Folklorefestivaali*, like the *Festspillene i Nord-Norge*, is one of the factors which makes its host municipality, Rovaniemi, visible in the national media, and it is also utilized strategically to market the town. As one of the interviewees expresses it, this is a two-way operation that benefits the town as well as the festival: "Rovaniemi will market the festival, and so the festival itself will market Rovaniemi." However, as with the *Festspel i Pite Älvdal*, this may not be its most important function when it comes to the matter of collective identity. Reading about its history on the festival web pages, it appears that the festival is designed to bring together resources from all over Lapland, to "forward traditions and to create new culture" (*Jutajaiset Folklorefestivaali*). As such, it mirrors the views of Frisby and Getz (1989), claiming that most festivals are held in order to promote and preserve local culture. According to one of the interviewees, this is also what actually happens during the festival, through its different performances:

> [The festival] has raised up from the folklore, folk music and dance, local people and their identity . . . Lappish nature, Lappish people, Sami people . . . many stories about local identity . . . exist in the songs and the dances in the performances . . . when you go deeply into those concerts, you move beyond history.

The events observed during the fieldwork largely corresponded with the view of the festival as expressed through documentation and interviews. Many of the performances mediated stories about the Finnish, and above all the Lappish uniqueness, musically as well as through other artistic expressions. A major Jubilee Concert featured Lappish amateur choirs; entire concerts were dedicated to the accordion and the *kantele*—both instruments considered to be "typically Finnish"—and local myths were shared through musical stand-up acts. Also, through folk dances performed by locally based dance groups, local stories about cultural conflicts were shared that emphasized the tension between the "Finnish" population and the inhabitants of Sami origin. I quote from my field notes:

> At first there are Sami singers, *joik* and dance, then they are chased away by a "Finnish" couple with an accordion. A slow dance—the dancers use some kind of handkerchiefs. More couples join in. Is this a way of displaying local, cultural conflicts?

As such, the *Jutajaiset Folklorefestivaali*, like the *Festspel i Pite Älvdal*, functioned as an arena for drawing on shared stories, cultural practices, and ideals (Ekman 1999) in order to establish community cohesiveness. However, to an even larger degree, it also showed, especially through the dance performance, how collective identities might be shaped through in-group and out-group categorizations (North and Hargreaves 2008).

As indicated in the heading of this section, the *Jutajaiset Folklorefesti-vaali* did not only mediate stories connected to its host municipality. An international dimension was added, which extended the locally bound identity toward a broader community—that of peripheral, rural, and east-bound municipalities. Folklore ensembles from Mongolia, Mordovia (a Russian republic), and Hungary participated in joint performances with the Finnish musicians and dancers. The common denominator between the two latter groups and the Finnish contributors, namely the fact that they all spoke a Finno-Ugric language, was emphasized both by the per-formers themselves and the presenters, thereby making visible their kin-ship. Hence, these festival performances also became a way of displaying a joint experiential dimension and celebrating a shared, rural heritage (De Bres and Davis 2001).

FESTIVAL-ENHANCED COLLECTIVE IDENTITY AND LEARNING—WHAT IS AT STAKE?

A premise of the festival study was, as pointed out previously, the belief that processes of identity formation and learning are interdependent and intertwined. Theoretical support for this claim was found in the theories of Wenger (1998: 215), explaining how learning occurs through peripheral participation in communities of practice, and stating that learning is an experience of identity because it "transforms who we are and what we can do." Conversely, identity work also entails learning. Taking this as an epistemological point of departure, what kind of learning is offered through the work of expressing, shaping, and celebrating collective iden-tities as part of attending music festivals? Reiterating Small (1998), who states that each musical performance articulates the values of a specific social group, and adding the thoughts of Frith (1996: 111), who argues that music is not a way of expressing ideas, "it is a way of living them," it may be claimed that the outcomes of the festival-related collective iden-tity processes described in this chapter must be connected to learning about the social and cultural heritage of the festivals' host communities (De Bres and Davis 2001) and the broader ethical codes and social ide-ologies that underlie the particular aesthetic practices that the festival performances constituted (Frith 1996). The data from the broader survey and interview study among the *Festspel i Pite Älvdal* attendees support this claim, suggesting for instance that what the folk rock concert, referenced above, afforded in terms of learning was not the music in itself, but "mainly what it meant to be an inhabitant of North Bothnia" (Karlsen 2007: 204).

The format of this chapter makes it impossible to go into all the different aspects of learning found among the festival attendees, both in terms of learning strategies and outcomes (for a broader account of this, see Karlsen 2007). Moreover, since the attendees' actual experiences in this respect were only investigated at the *Festspel i Pite Älvdal,* the potential learning outcome when it comes to the *Festspillene i Nord-Norge* and the *Jutajaiset Folklorefestivaali* can only be understood in relation to my own experiences as an observing researcher and as theoretical constructs. A weakness of this is of course the possible bias that this may have caused, which might have been reduced by undertaking more extensive empirical investigations.

As mentioned in the beginning of this chapter, the plethora of music festivals constitutes an important feature of contemporary cultural life; still, we know little about the social and cultural meaning and impact of these festivals on the collective as well as on the individual level. Considering the recent development in the field of music education research toward attempting to understand learning strategies and outcomes in informal arenas, one of our discipline's future tasks should be to investigate further the processes of music festival–related learning. That would imply looking into musical as well as nonmusical outcomes, and even, as shown throughout this chapter, touching upon what, according to Merriam (1964: 225) is one of the basic functions of music, namely to contribute "to the continuity and stability of culture." Hopefully, the findings derived from such research would also shed more light on what kinds of experiences, skills, and knowledge our students take with them when they enter into formal music educational settings.

References

Aronsen, Mats. 2006. *Quart o6—Mer enn musikk. Verdiskaping og ringvirkninger* [Quart o6—More Than Music. Appreciation and Cumulative Effects]. Kristiansand: Agder Research.

De Bres, Karen, and James Davis. 2001. Celebrating Group and Place Identity: A Case Study of a New Regional Festival. *Tourism Geographies* 3 (3): 326–337.

Delamere, Tom A. 2001. Development of a Scale to Measure Resident Attitudes toward the Social Impacts of Community Festivals, Part II: Verification of the Scale. *Event Management* 7: 25–38.

Ekman, Ann-Kristin. 1999. The Revival of Cultural Celebrations in Regional Sweden: Aspects of Tradition and Transition. *Sociologica Ruralis* 39 (3): 280–293.

Formica, Sandro. 1998. The Development of Festivals and Special Events Studies. *Festival Management & Event Tourism* 5: 131–137.

Frith, Simon. 1996. Music and Identity. In *Questions of Cultural Identity,* ed. Stuart Hall and Paul du Gay, 108–127. London: Sage Publications.

Frisby, W., and D. Getz. 1989. Festival Management: A Case Study Perspective. *Journal of Travel Research* 28: 7–11.

Giddens, Anthony. 1991. *Modernity and Self-Identity: Self and Society in the Late Modern Age.* Stanford, Calif.: Stanford University Press.

Green, Lucy. 2001/02. *How Popular Musicians Learn: A Way Ahead for Music Education.* Aldershot: Ashgate.

Hall, Stuart. 1992. The Question of Cultural Identity. In *Modernity and its Futures,* ed. Stuart Hall, David Held, and Anthony McGrew, 274–316. Oxford: Polity in association with the Open University.

Hjemdahl, Kirsti M., Elisabet S. Hauge, and Emma Lind. 2007. *Festivaler på Sørlandet. Kultur i kraftformat* [Festivals at Sørlandet. Powerful Culture]. Kristiansand: Agder Research.

Jutajaiset Folklorefestivaali. At http://www.jutajaiset.fi (accessed 12 June 2009).

Karlsen, Sidsel. 2007. The Music Festival as an Arena for Learning. Festspel i Pite Älvdal and Matters of Identity. PhD diss., Luleå University of Technology.

Karlsen, Sidsel, and Sture Brändström. 2008. Exploring the Music Festival as a Music Educational Project. *International Journal of Music Education* 26 (4): 363–373.

Karlsen, Sidsel. 2009. Learning through Music Festivals. *International Journal of Community Music* 2 (2/3): 129–141.

Maughan, Christopher, and Franco Bianchini. 2004. *The Economic and Social Impacts of Cultural Festivals in the East Midlands of England. Final Report.* Leicester: De Montfort University.

Merriam, Alan P. 1964. *The Anthropology of Music.* Evanston, Ill.: Northwestern University Press.

North, Adrian, and David Hargreaves. 2008. *The Social and Applied Psychology of Music.* Oxford: Oxford University Press.

Pettersson, Birgitta. 2005. Ett fall för filosofiska rummet [A Case for the Room of Philosophy]. *Piteå-Tidningen,* 12 November, editorial.

Pitts, Stephanie. 2005. *Valuing Musical Participation.* Aldershot, UK: Ashgate.

Quinn, Bernadette. 2005. Arts Festivals and the City. *Urban Studies* 42 (5/6): 927–943.

Small, Christopher. 1998. *The Meanings of Performing and Listening.* Middletown, Conn.: Wesleyan University Press.

Snell, Karen. 2005. Music Education through Popular Music Festivals: A Study of the OM Music Festival in Ontario, Canada. *Action, Criticism and Theory for Music Education* 4 (2). At http://act.maydaygroup.org/php/archives_v4.php#4_2 (accessed 25 May 2009).

Söderman, Johan. 2007. Rap(p) i käften. Hiphopmusikers konstnärliga och pedagogiska strategier [Verbally Fa(s)t. Hip-hop Musicians' Artistic and Educational Strategies]. PhD diss., Lund University.

Waterman, Stanley. 1998. Carnivals for Elites? The Cultural Politics of Arts Festivals. *Progress in Human Geography* 22 (1): 54–75.

Wenger, Etienne. 1998. *Communities of Practice: Learning, Meaning and Identity.* Cambridge: Cambridge University Press.

Wingstedt, Johnny. 2008. Making Music Mean: On Functions of, and Knowledge about, Narrative Music in Multimedia. PhD diss., Luleå University of Technology.

THIRTEEN

Shaping a Music Teacher Identity in Sweden

EVA GEORGII-HEMMING

All students in Swedish high schools are obliged, irrespective of which theoretical or vocational courses they undertake, to study an aesthetic subject. Students can typically choose between music, art, and drama. The course is approximately thirty hours, and the national curriculum only describes a few general objectives that students should achieve upon completion. The aim of the course is to

> develop and stimulate the students' creativity and desire to use aesthetic means of expression to express thoughts, emotions, and actions. The subject also aims to evoke interest in and understanding of culture and creative activities in a wider perspective. (ES 2000: 5)

The content and delivery of music education should be designed so that these objectives are met, but it should also consider the interests and needs of students, as well as local conditions. However, the curriculum does not provide any concrete directives for the content, methods, or repertoire of the courses. Nor is there any national reading material for music education in high school that could guide teachers in their lesson planning.

The need to examine what constitutes, or should constitute, a formal music education from a Swedish perspective is evident; but there are also issues of more general relevance. Teachers always need to consider how educational content should be designed and in what kind of (musical) knowledge schools should engage. However, the problem is accentuated as the world becomes increasingly pluralistic and globalized. As in many other countries, in our current education system, students and teachers with different origins, backgrounds, and plans for the future meet, all of them with shifting personal, social, and cultural identities. Out of this freedom and complexity, a number of essential issues around music educational choice and starting points become apparent. One important issue, which is addressed in this chapter, is to examine music teachers' views on the functions and goals of music education in relation to a concept of "music teacher identity." This concept can be understood as involving a dialogue between different experiences of music in various social, educational, and musical contexts found in Sweden.

The chapter presents empirical data I collected between 1999 and 2003 for the purposes of a PhD thesis, with the aim of exploring the relationships between music teachers' personal experiences and their choices as professional teachers (Georgii-Hemming 2005). I have reanalyzed the data in order to illuminate the multifaceted factors that together form a professional identity as a music teacher. The study consists of *life stories* written by five high school music teachers, fictitiously named Clara, Hanni, Brigitte, John, and Michael, who have six to twenty years of work experience. It also involves repeated in-depth interviews, dialogues via e-mail, and observations of teaching. The period of data collection spanned more than two and a half years. The next phase after data collection events and first stage analysis was the writing of five *life histories* portraying the teachers. The teachers received these and had the opportunity to comment and further develop the material. Further stages of the analysis and interpretation were carried out by the researcher alone.

The life stories written by the teachers prior to the first meetings were developed in a relatively flexible fashion. The teachers were asked to describe "musical experiences as a private person as well as a teacher." All of the interviews throughout the years took place in locations chosen by the teachers, usually in their workplace. However, some meetings also took place in two of the teachers' private homes. The life stories as well as previous conversations were discussed and problematized during the deep interviews. Events described by the teachers were contextual-

ized in various ways (e.g., how teachers interpreted a specific experience that influenced their teaching) in order to increase the researcher's
understanding.

Structural studies and explanations are not incompatible with this
research perspective. Life history research that only presents a few stories
based on "local anecdotes" has, on the contrary, become the Achilles' heel
of the methodology (Goodson and Sikes 2001; Roberts 2002). Teachers
live their lives in both a historical and a social context. The data needs
analyzing and contextualizing in order for their individual stories to create a foundation for further critical discussion and for them to become
integrated into the ongoing discourse. This study makes use of music
education theory (e.g., Nielsen 1998) as well as music philosophical theory
(e.g., Elliott 1995; Jorgensen 1997 and 2003; Reimer 1989; Small 1998).

MUSICAL IDENTITY IN PRIVATE LIFE

Brigitte, Clara, and Michael are all specialist music teachers with an educational degree from a Swedish School of Music (higher education institution). Hanni is also a specialist music teacher but educated in another
European country, whereas John began his career as a general teacher
(teaching children age six to twelve). When the study started, Brigitte
(born 1971) had the least work experience, six years of music teaching
experience. Michael (born 1957) and Hanni (born 1967) had taught music
in high school for eleven years, whereas Clara (born 1961) had the most
work experience—fifteen years in total. However, John had the longest
work experience in total; he had worked as a teacher for more than twenty
years, including nine years as a music teacher in high school.

Musical backgrounds and directions have clear gender-related relationships (Green 1997; Jorgensen 2003; O'Neill 1997). All these teachers
started piano lessons at the age of six and also studied other instruments,
focusing on Western classical music. In addition, the male teachers also
engaged in more varied genres, forms, and contexts, compared to the
females. The females' musical experiences were mainly formal—connected to education and rehearsals—and their repertoires consist mainly
of Western classical music (Folkestad 2006; Green 2008). Clara is aware
of this issue, and her self-description as "a typical music girl who plays
classical piano and Western concert flute, and organizes choirs" also fits

well for Hanni and partly for Brigitte, whose experiences and interests are slightly broader. Apart from playing the flute and piano and leading a choir, she is also interested in West African music. Brigitte is also the only female music teacher who had been involved in musical ensemble, over and above the obligatory group playing during their teaching education. Her experiences from being a flautist in an amateur group playing medieval music are vivid and reoccurring in her life story. Also, John and Michael have learned to play through private lessons and music education at school, but their most important experiences have derived from informal and voluntary contexts. In these contexts they have been involved in rock, jazz, sound technologies, and new digital media—both with friends and alone. Both play a large number of instruments—piano, guitar, drums, bass, and so on. However, Michael is extreme; he also plays trombone, saxophone, cornet, trumpet, cello, and violin. Out of the five teachers, only Michael and Brigitte arrange and compose their own music; Michael writes pop and jazz, and Brigitte theatrical and medieval music.

All five teachers grew up in families that stimulated their musical and cultural interests. However, a major difference among them is related to their motivations for continued engagement in music.

Brigitte seems to be a lively, energetic, and sociable person, whose musical identity is strongly connected to social contexts. When she describes musical experiences she particularly recalls good friends, joy, and a sense of belonging that has come from her engagement with music. In her early teenage years, Brigitte often felt "different" as a result of her interest in both music and history. Boys were "only" interested in motors, and girls were mainly interested in boys. The turning point came in high school when she became a "fanatical member of a medieval music ensemble that consisted of 'weird' people." She has always enjoyed trying out new instruments and believes that this fact relates to her disinterest in focused rehearsals.

Michael's musical identity is influenced by play and experimentation. His life story is completely centered on all the bands, in which he played various instruments. His impressions of courses in free, experimental improvisation during the 1970s are also reoccurring themes. Michael started to build his own instruments early on, and during his teenage years his most important instrument was a tape recorder. During this period he used to record his own songs and "strange" sound experiments. His artistic ideals are broadness and skills acquisition. He has been involved in folk music from the whole world, theater, dance, and art. Despite being educated at a School of Music, he considers himself self-taught:

> My tape recorder that I used to experiment with recordings in different speeds, my homemade "drum kit" made of cookie jars filled with marbles and lampshades of glass, all jam sessions and courses in expressive dance and improvisation. And all these rock bands in particular. That is my education. That is the first thing I think about when you ask about my education.

In John's family, playing music was considered a part of a good upbringing. They always played together at family gatherings during the holidays. In the same way, it was considered natural to be involved in the choir in the independent Christian church to which the family belonged. John describes himself as having been an obedient child. Despite the lack of passion for music (and as a result, slow musical development), he continued to take lessons throughout his whole childhood and teenage years. His musical interest was first evoked when at the age of eighteen he discovered chords and playing by ear. This resulted in a growing confidence in his musical ability and a strong curiosity for learning more instruments and techniques. He learned to DJ and also started rapping at the age of forty. Even though John's musical life is deeply involved with social contexts, including family and church, he prefers to play alone, sitting in front of his computer, although he does accompany group singing on the piano.

Clara wants to make other people happy through music, and she has a strong sense of social engagement. While growing up, she performed for people in nursing homes and prisons. However, music is mainly connected to her individual and private experiences. Clara spends a relatively small amount of her leisure time playing and listening to music, but she sometimes uses music for the purposes of private needs. Music for Clara is a way to communicate and vent emotions:

> Life is difficult. People are not made to absorb unlimited amounts of emotions or information. It needs venting; it needs to be let out in some shape or form. My own well-being depends on whether I can

practice playing piano or not. Yet, at the same time, I have always played guitar and sung in front of people, even as a kid. But I don't do it in front of my students.

DeNora (2000) connects individual uses of music in everyday life to self-regulation and identity enhancing strategies. Music can help the individual to shift from one mood to another, to increase physical energy or relaxation, or to "just let off steam." This is what Clara does when she plays the piano.

Hanni has been involved in music since she was a child, and has played piano, harpsichord and Western concert flute. She has never strived to become a musician, but did set high goals for herself and practiced a lot. Her ambitions had negative consequences. They manifested mainly as feelings of insecurity, anxiety, and nervousness, as well as frustration with other peoples' lack of competence, and dominated her life story. Hanni has preferred to accompany others, as it allowed her to be important without being the center of attention. Since she started teaching she has more or less stopped playing in private. She talks about her personal experiences of music, but without focusing upon the actual music. Without a doubt her musical activities have taken up a lot of time, but Hanni is unwilling or unable to verbalize her motivations for playing music. Most descriptions are also viewed from a music educational perspective, as competences or learning processes.

Despite differences in time spent practicing, all teachers agreed that music is not about perfect playing. Music is a function, a means of communication and also connected to a situation (Small 1998).

MUSICAL IDENTITY IN AN EDUCATIONAL CONTEXT

The kind of music education that Brigitte, Hanni, John, and Michael practice is fairly similar in terms of content and methods. Music performance is prioritized over factual knowledge. None of them teach history, and music listening rarely occurs. John is the only one who teaches basic music theory—to those who wants to learn. John argues that his teaching gives students the possibility to discover their abilities, but that it is also the individual's responsibility to "cultivate their gifts":

JOHN: But it's based on self-determination. Every pupil's got to be able to make their own decision, and that's the moral education part of it. A person alone can do almost anything. But you can't know what gifts you've got till they've been tried out. That's what I try to drum into them—they mustn't bury the gifts they may have.

John's students are allowed to influence teaching in all groups; they help to decide the content and methods of the course, and can choose relatively freely what songs to play. The musical material that completely dominates lessons is selected from the rock and pop repertoire. Classes are divided into "bands" that are left to practice relatively independently in well-equipped rehearsal rooms. There they rehearse songs in a similar manner to garage bands (Green 2008). Those who want could also play music individually. John tries to broaden musical content through using DJ-equipment and karaoke programs, and he explains:

> They all get the "tools": they play some chord instrument, learn a few notes on the bass and some drum beats. They do covers of songs they've chosen themselves or they sing to prerecorded backgrounds. The ones who want to can do their own recordings or music videos, or they can use the computer programs or the DJ equipment. Diversification and providing the tools, that's what it's all about.

John, Hanni, and Michael *offer* students the chance to compose their own music, but it is less of a central component in their classes and few students take advantage of their offer. Brigitte also lets her students sing in a choir and is the only teacher who includes composition as an obligatory element, whereas Clara does not even mention composition. Michael wishes that more students would want to create their own music. He is not demanding this in the shape of an obligatory course component, as he does not want to "offend" students through forcing them to do something against their will. He feels that music lessons should be pleasurable and also function as a "break" from the academic everyday life of students. Therefore, it is seen as "more important that they work practically rather than artistically."

A central element to Hanni's teaching is that all her students are expected to play or sing in front of each other, individually or in small groups. The performance event—which she calls "the concert"—ends the course, and lessons prepare students for this event musically and mentally. The aim is to improve students' self-esteem and for them to be seen and heard. During the concert, Hanni is completely focused on the student performers on stage.

Brigitte and Michael problematize the narrow genre selections in their lessons. Even though both are familiar with several genres, they are not using, for example, folk music, jazz, or medieval music in their lessons. Michael believes that Western classical music is probably disappearing, sadly, and that he contributes to this development. Both teachers believe that "it cannot be helped," as students interests must be prioritized, and because lessons should be pleasurable.

Clara differs from the rest of the teachers. A reoccurring argument is that students' *needs* must direct the activities. For Clara, "students' needs" is only marginally conceptualized as equal to their individual musical level, and is not at all synonymous with cultivating their musical interests. Activities are directed from booklets that Clara has designed. They consist of play and theory exercises based on uncomplicated tunes. Every student must learn to play a simple tune on an instrument, through reading the notation in the booklet. Using the tunes as a starting point, theory is transformed into practice and students are mainly practicing to solve intellectual problems motorically. Teaching is almost completely individualized and students practice alone, regardless of how large the groups are.

Clara's respect for the individual student is related to integrity rather than cultivating individual students' leisure interests or music preferences. Students should not be forced to make their emotions public— emotions that music can transform as well as give rise to. As Clara cannot know when a student needs to work through their emotions, she chooses to refrain from musical activities in groups:

> My lessons can be a bit dry; it does not have to be fun and games all the time. Music education is about allowing students to work with whatever they need to release. You can become very exposed when you're playing music, but I don't want to force students to expose themselves. Not like the way you expose yourself when you play or sing together.

The objective with music education for all five of the teachers is to give students opportunities to sing, play different instruments, and, the teachers hope, continue to engage in music throughout their lives. The overarching goal is that the education should develop "whole," open human beings with plenty of self-esteem. Brigitte explains that she has gradually realized the importance of this goal:

> The more I think about it, the more important I think it is to develop people holistically, and to develop social skills and cooperation. You are helping to "create" *human beings*. Yes, I think people are obsessed about science! Do we really want a society where everyone is a scientist?!

Through studying this topic, students can understand that skills and forms of knowledge beyond intellectual ones—practical, emotional, and/or artistic—have a value. The music lesson is a space—both a physical and a mental one—where the student can experience acceptance of being different and thinking differently (Ruud 1996; Nielsen 1998). If students become familiar with music, and are therefore not afraid of participating in social contexts in adult life, and if they have access to tools to vent their emotions, society will become richer. John expresses most strongly the view of culture as "building bridges"—between past and present, and between life inside and out of school. All teachers believe that music should be accessible for everyone, and that culture should not be excluding. The most important thing is not to further a given musical heritage, but instead to *create* individual cultural identities through local everyday experiences (Frith 2002; Swanwick 1999).

SHAPING A MUSIC TEACHER IDENTITY
—A THEME WITH VARIATIONS

The relationship between an individual's musical identity and a music teacher's identity is complex. Content and design of the course are relatively similar, apart from Clara's, and are influenced by teachers' perceptions of how contemporary music education "should" be shaped. When teachers argue and justify their choices, they all refer to the idea of "student centeredness." However, the definition of this concept varies, as do expectations of the results. The uniform discourse is influenced by contemporary pedagogical debates, whereas teachers' personal motivations for music engagement influence their view of (and arguments surrounding) the value of music and educational objectives. Their personal motivations also influence interpretations of the value of music and educational objectives, and how these issues are defined.

Teachers' personal, "real," musical experiences are thus not primary influences for their educational strategies, but there are some relationships between the private lives of the teachers and how teaching is being conducted. Michael, for example, whose background is strongly influenced by jazz and rock bands, lets students work in groups. Clara, on the other hand, lets them work individually.

Previous research and national evaluations suggest that Clara's teaching methods are rare in Sweden (Karlsson and Karlsson 2009; Skolverket 2004). The majority of Swedish music education is conducted similarly to the way the other teachers work—with pop and rock music, in groups. Teaching is probably designed as much according to expectations of music education in contemporary life as according to teachers' own experiences.

There are even weaker relationships between their teaching and *what* musical activities teachers themselves have engaged in. Even if a teacher would like to include more genres or more varied musical activities—for example, improvisation or composition—it is rarely prioritized in lessons. The (pedagogical) discourse of "student centeredness" stands out whenever there is a conflict between teachers' own interests and education as it occurs in daily life.

It can be said that teachers in this study strive for valuable meetings; between people in the group, between individuals and music. Therefore, they have situated the student in the center. Music is an important tool for individuals who need to vent creativity, passion, and/or emotions, but music can also be a form of knowledge among others—including measurable components or possibilities for practitioners to be seen and heard. Teachers argue that music activities are pleasurable, and this is essentially because music has socializing functions and can be a way to meet other people with similar values. In musical contexts, some values are belonging, relationships to other people, and existential significance. The varied and integrated relationships, views, and attitudes to music activities (e.g., whether engaging in music means listening/playing alone or with others) are portrayed and prioritized in the music educational practice. Whether music for one individual teacher consists of playing together and values of joy and a sense of belonging, or whether it means individual playing that can channel emotions, this is what will be prioritized in that teacher's lessons. Types of music, forms of musical activities, and learning strategies used in the past are subordinate to the actual experiences and what these experiences are thought to give others.

In order to explain and justify these visions, shaped by teachers' personal motivations, the teachers speak of "individual needs." This refers to how teaching needs to be adapted according to students' personal and musical preconditions, as well as to how students should develop and grow as human beings.

Ambitions for wanting to see, and center around, each student—to merge students' personal experiences with the kind of knowledge development that schools offer—permeate openly formulated documents on several levels. A gradual move toward individualized ideals and personal freedom has, since the 1990s, become increasingly more pronounced, not only in educational politics, but also in society in general (Baumann 2002).

In this study, the identity of a music teacher is thus shaped through an interaction between personal experiences, professional everyday lives, and contemporary discourse. These results are consistent with previous research and therefore not surprising (Krüger 2000). However, the strength of these music teachers' underlying perceptions, as well as the level of their influence, is striking.

Studies of life histories demand time and engagement from participants, which affects participant selection. The methodology described in this chapter requires teachers who are willing to engage in an open dialogue about sometimes sensitive matters. This has in turn possibly resulted in five relatively positive stories from music teachers who have stayed in their profession for an unusually long time (see Bladh 2002 for further discussion of correlations between teacher identity and the probability of remaining in the music teacher profession). In addition, because life-history research involves detailed work, it is only feasible to research small samples of participants—the study in this chapter builds on stories from only five participants. However, there is nothing to say that these stories could not adequately reflect other teachers' experiences. The teachers presented in this chapter prioritize musical breadth and enjoyment, as well as the social dimensions of musical engagement, rather than technical perfection. In other words, they identify themselves more as teachers than as musicians. It would be interesting to further study how these musical and educational ideals influence job satisfaction. How do teachers with high levels of job satisfaction view music, people, pedagogy, and the role of education? How do values systems shape the pedagogical identity of a teacher?

One way to describe the shaping of identity (whether we are talking about the identities of music teachers or of other human beings) is to express identity formation as a meeting between the individual and "the other," as formulated by G. H. Mead (1972). The study described in this chapter enhances the portrait of how deeply personal a musical identity can be. While it focuses on the identities of music teachers, the findings have implications also for the identities of students: they suggest that students' identities and musical experiences are important resources that need to be both respected and utilized. In order for students to be able to meet, understand, and collaborate with people from a variety of cultures—whether these are ethnically, socially, or culturally defined—music education must enable them to occupy a perspective from the point of view of "the other." Possibilities for increasing understanding lie in meeting with what has previously been unknown (Gadamer 1997; Georgii-Hemming and Westvall 2010; Swanwick 1999).

References

Baumann, Zygmunt. 2001. *The Individualized Society.* Cambridge: Polity Press.
Bladh, Stephan. 2002. *Musiklärare—i utbildning och yrke: En longitudinell studie av musiklärare i Sverige.* Diss. Göteborg: Institutionen för musikvetenskap.
DeNora, Tia. 2000. *Music in Everyday Life.* New York: Cambridge University Press.
Elliott, David J. 1995. *Music Matters: A New Philosophy of Music Education.* New York: Oxford University Press.
ES 2000:05. Estetiska programmet. [National Curriculum]. Stockholm: Fritzes.
Folkestad, Göran. 2006. Formal and Informal Learning Situations or Practices vs. Formal and Informal Ways of Learning. *British Journal of Music Education* 23 (2): 135–145. Cambridge: Cambridge University Press.
Frith, Simon. 2002. Music and Identity. In *Questions of Cultural Identity,* ed. Stuart Hall and Paul du Gay, 108–127. London: Sage.
Gadamer, Hans Georg. 1997 [1960]. *Sanning och metod.* [Truth and method] I urval. Göteborg: Daidalos.

Georgii-Hemming, Eva. 2005. *Berättelsen under deras fötter: Fem musiklärares livshistorier.* [The Story Beneath Their Feet. Five music teachers' life histories] Örebro: Örebro University.

———, and Maria Westvall. 2010. *Music Education—A Personal Matter? Examining the Current Discourses of Music Education in Sweden.*

Goodson, Ivor F., and Patricia J. Sikes. 2001. *Life History Research in Educational Settings: Learning from Lives.* Buckingham: Open University Press.

Green, Lucy. 1997. *Music, Gender, Education.* Cambridge: Cambridge University Press.

———. 2008. *Music, Informal Learning and the School: A New Classroom Pedagogy.* Aldershot: Ashgate.

Jorgensen, Estelle R. 1997. *In Search of Music Education.* Urbana: University of Illinois Press.

———. 2003. *Transforming Music Education.* Bloomington: Indiana University Press.

Karlsson, Carl, and Stefan Karlsson. 2009. *Lagom svåra och hyfsat moderna.* ['Not too difficult and quite modern'. A study of repertoire in compulsory music education amongst 13 to 15-year-old pupils.] Bachelor's thesis in Music Education, Örebro University: Örebro.

Krüger, Thorolf. 2000. Musikundervisningens epistemologi [Music Education and its epistemology]. In *Nordisk musikkpedagogisk forskning* [Nordic Network for Music Educational Research, Yearbook 3], ed. Frede V. Nielsen, Sture Brändström, Harald Jørgensen, and Bengt Olsson, 55–77. Årbok 3. Oslo: Norges musikkhøgskole.

Mead, George Herbert. 1972 [1934]. *Mind, Self, and Society: From the Standpoint of a Social Behaviorist.* Chicago: University of Chicago Press.

Nielsen, Frede V. 1998. *Almen Musikdidaktik* [Pedagogy for Music Education]. Köpenhamn: Akademisk förlag.

O'Neill, Susan A. 1997. Gender and Music. In *The Social Psychology of Music*, ed. David J. Hargreaves and Adrian C. North, 46–63. Oxford: Oxford University Press.

Reimer, Bennett. 1989. *A Philosophy of Music Education.* 2nd ed. Englewood Cliffs, N.J.: Prentice Hall.

Roberts, Brian. 2002. *Biographical Research.* Buckingham: Open University.

Ruud, Even. 1996. *Musikk og verdier* [Music and Values]. Oslo: Universitetsforlaget.

Skolverket. 2004. *Nationella utvärderingen av grundskolan 2003* [Swedish National Agency for Education. 2004. National evaluation of the compulsory school in 2003. A summary main report]. Rapport 253. Stockholm: Skolverket.

Small, Christopher. 1998. *Musicking: The Meanings of Performing and Listening.* Hanover, N.H.: University Press of New England.

Swanwick, Keith. 1999. *Teaching Music Musically.* London: Routledge.

FOURTEEN

Icelandic Men and Their Identity in Songs and in Singing

ROBERT FAULKNER

There is a tendency to portray contemporary masculine identity as being in conflict with singing and song, especially in formal educational settings (Adler 2005; Harrison 2008). Even research on the benefits of singing in relation to health and well-being reports gender differences (Clift and Hancock 2001). For the Icelandic men who are the central focus of this chapter, singing plays a very significant role in everyday life and identity, and rather than threatening their masculinity, it is more likely to enhance it and be intricately entwined with it. This chapter provides a comparative ethnography of two contrasting all-male singing groups in Iceland. It discusses the configuration and representation of self-identity in relation to singing within Iceland, and examines how these particular men articulate key identity concepts through and about their music-making and learning: versatility versus specialism; the individual versus the collective; cross-generational and cross-genre issues; the representation of mothers, love, and relationships in Icelandic culture and lore; and the role of Icelandic landscape and locality.

The first group is a large male voice choir with over fifty choristers based in the remote northeast of Iceland. Male voice choirs dominated early twentieth-century public music performance space in Iceland, playing a crucial role in emerging national identity and independence that was finally attained in 1944 (Björnsdóttir 2001). Over the past twenty years this particular choir, known as *Hreimur* or Accent, has enjoyed widespread popularity as one of the more active of many male voice choirs in Iceland. It has toured in the UK, Finland, Germany, Switzerland, Austria, and Italy, has recorded several full-length CDs, and is regularly played on Icelandic radio. On average, members of the choir are around fifty years old. While younger choristers may even include the occasional teenager, restricted high school, tertiary education, and employment opportunities see a steady stream of young people drawn toward larger urban centers in Akureryi and Reykjavik. Regardless of age, though, singing in the choir appears rather to accentuate than threaten the choir-members' masculinity. As one of them said, in describing the singing of a slow, sustained, unaccompanied four-part song:

> **BALDUR (ACCENT):** Singing [this is] gentle, beautiful and clean, pure and beautiful. You're not less of a man for that, you're more.

The other group featured in this chapter has an average age of thirty-five, with its youngest member at age twenty-five. On their blog, *Ljótu Hálfvítarnir*, or the Ugly Halfwits, describe themselves as an "Icelandic punkish folk band." Made up of nine men, all from the same county of Thingeyjarsýslu as the male voice choir, the group prefers the less literal translation of "the Stupid Bastards said with weary affection." With a strong emphasis on folk and a large number of songs in triple time, they defy conventional pop music expectations. Nevertheless, the Stupid Bastards have enjoyed considerable national success since their formation in 2006. They have had several top ten hits in national charts and perform regularly all over the country.

There is a long tradition of overseas musicians living and working in Iceland in the extensive community music school programs, in church music, and as performing musicians. So it was that, after moving here from London in 1996, I lived and worked among men from both Accent and the Stupid Bastards for two decades. Apart from my work in Iceland as a music educator in settings that ranged from kindergarten to tertiary education, I was musical director of Accent for a great deal of that time and carried out ethnographical research with them over several years. In addition to very substantial open interviews and my field notes from observations and experiences, the men in Accent also kept vocal diaries, making regular entries about singing in their everyday lives. This investigation formed the data for my PhD dissertation, completed in 2006. My research with the Stupid Bastards is more recent and less extensive, although I have known or been acquainted with most of the men who make up the choir for many years. The data relating to the Stupid Bastards within this chapter comes from observations at an open-air performance in Húsavík—just south of the arctic circle—in 2009. Subsequent conversations and e-mail correspondence with a group member, Oddur, along with music and lyrics from recordings and YouTube videos, also form data for analysis and discussion. What follows is an examination of the extent to which findings from the long-term ethnographic study of the male voice choir Accent, about self-identity and its central themes and constructs, find resonance in the very different kind of male music-making of the Stupid Bastards.

EVERY ICELANDER A SPECIAL CASE—THE INDIVIDUAL AND THE COLLECTIVE

One of the most striking impressions from watching the Stupid Bastards' performance in the summer of 2009 is that no single individual stands out. A solo singer in one song is playing a bassoon or bass guitar in the next, drums the next, backing vocals and a cabasa in the next. It is hard to pin people down, and this, Oddur insists, is:

> **ODDUR (STUPID BASTARDS):** one of the hallmarks of our band. We play everything possible and impossible, and it is rare for the same person to play the same instrument for two songs in a row.

In a contemporary anthropology of Iceland, Durrenberger (1996) developed the notion of every Icelander as a special case, and in my work on the male voice choir Accent, I observed how important that concept is to dynamics within it (Faulkner 2006). In such settings, "specialness" is achieved by an equal presence. Even though the choir regularly sings with soloists—including several from its own ranks—and with a conductor for formal rehearsals and concerts, superior airs are not tolerated for long. A range of strategies are used to maintain equity, not least the spontaneous invention and recitation of short satirical poems or *vísur* with strict rhyme and rhythmical and alliterative structures. Men in the male voice choir humorously challenge, rebuke, subdue, or even ridicule individuals into less prominent positions. In any case, observation of these men at informal gatherings, parties, and dances indicated that they have no particular need of a "qualified" leader to engage in singing— even in four-part harmony singing. Individual voices who "stand out" are frowned upon, and producing a homogeneous, well blended sound is considered the highest level of achievement. This is particularly evident in soft, sustained singing in harmony, which is seen as the main source of "peak aesthetic experience" in far greater preference to rousing opera choruses and calls to arms!

Members of Accent even articulate a learning process, especially in informal settings, that is not dependent on a formal teacher, but on the joining in and matching of fellow singers through close physical proximity. Men see this process as one of being "sensitized" to others:

> JÓN (ACCENT): I'm not very quick to learn exactly . . . but with the help of the good guys in second tenor . . . it went OK and you could feel it was beginning to sound, beginning to harmonize and resonate . . . and then it became really fun.

In informal settings like birthday parties or in the band-break at a ball, harmony is improvised in a kind of vocal jamming session. Physical intimacy, which in informal settings will even extend to sustained body contact, appears as an embodiment of "singing in harmony" (Faulkner and Davidson 2004: 239). Rarely, if ever, content with unison singing, many men articulate why harmony matters so much to them:

> ÚLFUR (ACCENT): You feel much better in harmony with others. Then you get that kick, that's how it is supposed to be.

> GUÐMUNDUR (ACCENT): We're talking about experiencing something in harmony and we experience something specific toward each other.

No surprise then, that men are resentful about the Lutheran church's recent efforts to introduce unison singing. When men sing, harmony must be made: if it is not known, it will be invented, and aural and vocal ability like this is not seen as exceptional.

As Faulkner and Davidson (2006) have illustrated, men in the choir use a wide range of competitive and collaborative strategies in the learning and performance of music. There are many extremely able singers in the group and they are able to support less able singers in the conjunctive task that choral singing is (Faulkner and Davidson 2004: 243).

> SIGURÐUR (ACCENT): I always thought I was pretty poor . . . my voice is thin . . . and it doesn't work by itself.

> ÞÓRARINN (ACCENT): I've always thought it good to sing with somebody that's got a good voice.

Noticeably, the Icelandic Male Voice tradition is devoid of the formal competitive elements of, say, Eisteddfods in Wales or Australia, the Barbershop tradition in North America (Stebbins 1996), or the Isicathamiya in South Africa (Erlman 1996). Nevertheless, there will still be lighthearted banter and inter-voice rivalry in the choir:

> GUÐMUNDUR (ACCENT): We have our sound and it works with yours and you'll jolly well give it to us right . . . it's done for fun . . . people often say, "bloody tenors, they can never learn anything."

Collaboration and egalitarianism are central to the Stupid Bastards, too.

> ODDUR (STUPID BASTARDS): Democracy is honored. We discuss the problem and try to find a collective solution. . . . practices can be time-consuming, irritating, and fun!

Like members of the male voice choir, the Stupid Bastards also have different strengths:

> ODDUR (STUPID BASTARDS): Eddi is great at finding good riffs. Bibbi and me are good on structure. Baldur is really good at complicating harmonies. Sævar is a really good critic of the lyrics. We are allowed to criticize, change, and improve. Sometimes we find in performance that it isn't working. Maybe it is enough to move just one instrument. It comes alive and works.

The tasks that the Stupid Bastards undertake are, of course, more complex than in Accent, but a fundamental and intuitive belief in collaborative and polyphonic—in Bakhtin's philosophical sense (Bakhtin 1994)—processes, identified in systems theories of creativity and learning, is central to both settings. The Stupid Bastards talk about the arranging of songs in similar ways to those identified in group composing processes in the classroom in this very same location (Faulkner 2003). People bring ideas at various stages of development to another group member and then to the whole group, where heuristic jamming processes, refine, develop, hone and polish songs, lyrics, and their performance.

> **ODDUR (STUPID BASTARDS):** Usually people compose at home, to begin with. Though we tend to play more together of late. We start a song . . . get somebody to help you. Recently, me and Sævar did a text together, me and Baldur did a song, so it varies a lot. Arrangements are always done as a group process. Somebody wants to pick up the bass and he does.

VERSATILITY VS. SPECIALIZATION

The notion that individuals are not to stand out as being "more special" than others is clearly reflected in the wide variety of instrumental skills that the Stupid Bastards have acquired and developed across the whole band. The performance I saw included bass guitar, acoustic guitar, balalaika, flute, mandolin, ukulele, oboe, trombone, banjo, bassoon, cor anglais, double bass, drum kit, cajon, piano accordion, melodica, chime bars, glockenspiel, recorder, mouth organ, jaw harp, and dozens of conventional and more exotic untuned percussion instruments.

The community music school system in Iceland provides an extremely high level of access to instrumental music for children in schools, and nowhere in Iceland, I suggest, has that access been greater over the past thirty years than in the particular area of the country where both Accent and the Stupid Bastards are based. It provided nearly all of the members of the Stupid Bastards with basic instrumental learning in instruments such as the recorder or guitar, and in several cases it provided considerably more than basic music skills. More importantly, though, the tradition of picking something up and having a go, and a strong emphasis on aural traditions, make the kind of creative experimentation evident in the Stupid Bastards an exemplar of an Icelandic outlook on learning and competency in general, and in music in particular.

ODDUR (STUPID BASTARDS): None of us are "well-educated" musically speaking. It's self-learned. It isn't stuff we learned at school. Just talent (laughs)! There are so many of us, you have to have something to do. Pick it up and learn it as you go.

There is a strong belief in the power of self-learning in Iceland. The country boasted 100 percent literacy and a remarkably high ratio of published books per capita long before the development of a modern Western schooling system (Canoy, van Ours, and van der Ploeg 2006). The late nineteenth-century music revolution is another case in point: the arrival of the harmonium ushered in Western four-part harmony and mercilessly threw out two-part vocal traditions rooted in pre-Reformation music of the medieval Icelandic commonwealth (see Ingólfsson 2003). Within a decade of its arrival in the area, and in spite of very limited formal instruction, almost every other local farmstead owned a harmonium, and a remarkable number of four-part choirs soon emerged (Jakobsson and Jónsson 1990).

Some Icelanders still have doubts about institutionalized learning, and the term *"sérfræðingur"* or "expert" is often greeted suspiciously. Versatility and breadth are considered virtues. Traditionally, Icelanders often had several jobs, and career changes have been considered healthy. It is still not uncommon for farmers to be part-time policemen, occasional carpenters, members of a "functions band" (playing at local dances, birthday parties, and the like) and so on. With a total population of less than half a million, extreme specialization is not likely, though the diversity and level of skills in contemporary Icelandic society is formidable. Nevertheless, popular speculation sees a lack of expertise in the financial sector as a key factor in the catastrophic collapse of the Icelandic national economy in 2008.

ODDUR (STUPID BASTARDS): We're all versatile-men (*fjölmenn*) and most of us have a go at writing lyrics and music.

Men in the male voice choir Accent have instrumental skills, too. More than ten perform, or have performed, in functions bands for the regularly held local dances and social events. Some play in Accent's own instrumental group that accompanies the popular repertoire it regularly sings as part of its widely varied program. Others take part in amateur dramatics, or write their own poetry and music. The choir has often performed songs written by its members and by other local amateur composers.

In the Stupid Bastards, Oddur illustrates that this kind of versatility is not a thing of the past: like many of his group he has a strong theater background, something they see as central to their performance identity. Oddur has played minor roles on national TV and at the National Theater in Reyjavík. He studied at the Bristol Old Vic Theater School in the UK and has directed numerous plays and musicals for amateur companies in Iceland. Significant grants are available for amateur societies to hire professional/semi-professional directors. In addition, Oddur has been a leading figure in the promotion of the Icelandic Yuletide Lads at the local Lake Myvatn, as an international tourist attraction. He has worked as a traditional stone wall builder, and presently he is completing a degree in theology with a view to becoming a priest in the Icelandic Lutheran church.

> **ODDUR (STUPID BASTARDS):** I hope playing in the band will fit in well with being a priest. Even if I become a priest I have no intention of stopping being Oddur. Being Oddur is singing, acting, feeling, and meeting people.

In this thought, he echoes the same sentiment that very many men in Accent had expressed:

> **BALDUR (ACCENT):** Life without singing would be no life at all.

CROSSING GENERATIONS AND GENRES

Just as there is a tendency toward versatility rather than specialization in terms of all kinds of skills, including musical ones, the small and scattered population mitigates against subculturalization too. That musical style is far less important in terms of age-specific identity than it is in many Western settings is illustrated by the fact that the same ball or dance may be attended by teenagers and their parents, and even their grandparents. The functions bands that often perform—and members of both the male voice choir Accent and the Stupid Bastards have regularly performed in such bands—might include cover versions of recent international and Icelandic hits, and a wide range of pop standards. These songs might be programmed alongside polkas, jives, English waltzes, and marches. None of this is to suggest that male voice choir concerts are regularly attended by teenagers, though some of their special events do attract a audience with a wide age range. The Stupid Bastards, on the other hand, are extremely popular across the entire lifespan, from very young children to senior citizens.

> **ODDUR (STUPID BASTARDS):** It is strange really. I think it is because we are honest on stage, we're likeable, and we absolutely love what we are doing and we show it. It is infectious. Our songs are happy and full of humor that people appreciate—unless they take themselves too seriously as artists! We are not for the art snobs. We are a band for ordinary people, for common people.

Admittedly, the summer evening open-air concert I attended, along with two thousand guests, was part of a family-oriented town festival, and even though it continued long into the night and alcohol was consumed fairly liberally, the atmosphere was relaxed and inclusive. This uni-age music is not a characteristic of all popular Icelandic music by any means. The last two decades have seen a proliferation of more genre-specific bands. Interestingly, the two most internationally renowned Icelandic music acts—Björk and Sigur Rós—are celebrated because of their remarkable international success and because they are Icelandic, but their music has limited popular appeal here. Notwithstanding the success of Sigur Rós's free outdoor concert in the local national park at Ásbyrgi in 2007, there is a sense in which their version of Icelandic nature and identity is seen by Icelanders as constructed for international consumption, as on their DVD about that tour (Sigur Rós 2007). For Björk and Sigur Rós, it is the power of Icelandic landscape and nature that identifies them as specially Icelandic, despite Björk's singing in English and Sigur Rós's invention of a nonsense language for one of their CDs. For the Stupid Bastards:

> **ODDUR (STUPID BASTARDS):** What makes us really Icelandic is the importance of the language. The lyrics are so important for us.

Stupid Bastards' texts are very important in terms of identity, and they are widely acclaimed for their wit and craft. Apart from regularly alluding to some of the alliterative conventions of Icelandic *vísur,* discussed earlier, the texts often include carefully disguised references to well-known Icelandic songs, even to songs sung by the male voice choir.

> **ODDUR (STUPID BASTARDS):** The references and links are fun. For the audience. When they get the joke, it's like they're in on it.

One of the Stupid Bastards' biggest hits reminds Icelandic listeners of the inter-generational tradition of country balls and dances that is still a fairly regular component of local recreation and socializing. *Mamma mín* or *My Mother* is a lively waltz, and it is not only its inclusive musical style and humorous lyric that locate it firmly in an Icelandic arena, but its subject matter of motherlove.

MOTHERS, LOVE, AND RELATIONSHIPS

In contrast to heterosexual love that dominates popular music, motherlove strikes a resonant chord with male voice choir repertoire too. It is a key theme of Icelandic nationalist identity, a product of a particular historical masculinity and its dominance of public performance space. The importance of the reinvention of tradition in nineteenth-century nationalism is well documented (Hobsbawm and Ranger 1983). Iceland was no exception, and given the pivotal and powerful roles many female figures played in the medieval Icelandic sagas, it is unsurprising that one of the key inventions of the nationalist movement in Iceland itself was the Mountain Woman. Links between her as the mother of the Icelandic nation and nature are explicit, and poems about her are central to independence literature and identity (see Björnsdóttir 1996). Finding expression in vocal and choral settings in the early twentieth century and especially in the male voice choral tradition, this archetypal Icelandic madonna—a goddess with a "kind smile" and "golden tears"—features in songs, and in one in particular that is regularly sung informally by the male voice choir, to thank women for their support or to celebrate their birthdays. Another song, *Mamma ætla að sofna* (Lullaby for a Tired Mother), is one of the most popular songs in its repertoire and, significantly, it is one of the soft, sustained songs that men claim to enjoy singing most, described by one of Accent's members thus:

MAGNÚS (ACCENT): When you sing like that, you get this "ah yes!" feeling—this happiness, there's no other measurement for singing except that feeling.

The nostalgic image of motherhood is one of hard-working, unselfish, and courageous dedication to family and community. That this view is recognized in traditional Icelandic values is reflected in an international survey of characteristics and attributes associated with men and women, where Icelanders uniquely refuse to conform to a simple binary view of gender and qualities like compassion and courage (Gallup 1996). The Stupid Bastards sing a more contemporary, everyday version of "Mountain Woman," with a chorus:

> Mamma, you got in my way quite a bit
> Whatever I did, you had an opinion on it
> Yes, and mamma, you drove me really quite far
> But, mamma, I love you just as you are.
> [Author's translation]

With its detailed account of childbirth, the complications of growing up, and learning life's ways, the Stupid Bastards' most popular hit portrays mother, like the Mountain Woman, as responsible for turning Icelanders into humans. Like another of their songs about a boy going to school for the first time, it celebrates an Icelandic kind of motherlove, just as songs by Accent do.

While there are elements of heterosexual romantic love in some of the male voice repertoire, they are not numerous, and almost exclusively they are arrangements of pop ballads. At the open-air concert, the Stupid Bastards performed a song, "Another Love," that sounded for all the world like a stereotypical heterosexual love song, until the last sentence revealed that the love in question is for one of the band members, Arngrímur, who moved to Australia:

> Why did you leave me for another love?
> . . . Call from the windows, call out in the dark
> Arngrímur, stop this stupid lark
> Dump her now and come back home
> Australia's such a pathetic place to roam!
> [Author's translation]

The same kind of *filio* homo-social bonds are a key theme in many of the male voice choir members' accounts, too.

One of the Stupid Bastards' few references to heterosexual relationships is a fairly explicit parody of the historically very high incidence of children born outside of established relationships, let alone marriage, in Iceland. By the end of the song *Meðlag*, or Maintenance, the singer has told of sexual encounters with eleven women, who all become pregnant as a result. This sentiment would never be expressed in the idealized version of Icelandic womanhood found in male voice choir repertoire, as their discussion about their female accompanist, Juliet, illustrates. She has played a key role in the more formalized learning of repertoire, over the past twenty years. Unlike in the Stupid Bastards, a female figure is seen as important to the process of learning challenging songs and to public performance if it needs accompaniment. *She* makes them *presentable,* and men's repeatedly expressed view of *her* as supportive, nurturing, seated, and attractive is easily theorized as a further dimension of Green's notion of women as musical facilitators in other people's (men's) music-making or learning (Green 1997). In fact, local music history reveals a series of women conforming, I suggest, to the Icelandic notion of the Mountain Woman and motherhood, who have enabled men to sing together and thus made them "human" (Faulkner 2006). The phenomenon of women keyboard players accompanying and teaching songs to choral groups and societies (conducted by men) is surely widespread in Western societies, even if this explicit symbolism may be unique. The Mountain Woman brings us to the place of landscape in the identities of these two male groups.

LANDSCAPE AND LOCALITY

Many surprises await visitors to Iceland who venture beyond its capital, Reykjavík. Among them are enormous expanses of black volcanic sand around the island's rugged five-thousand-kilometer-long coastline and in huge areas of its uninhabitable interior, where they form a stark monochromic contrast with Europe's largest glaciers. These dramatic landscapes, and the dynamic forces of ice, wind, water, and fire that form them, visibly account for the central role nature plays in the construction of Icelandic identity—its significance in Icelandic saga and society and, as internationally renowned musicians like Björk and Sigur Rós explicitly illustrate, in Icelandic soundscapes. Icelandic nature, with its mountains and glaciers, waterfalls and lakes, birch forest, green valleys, and pastures, is a key theme in traditional Icelandic male voice choir repertoire too. Whether nature retains this position at the level of contemporary national identity is debatable—though recent protests about the building of a large dam in the highlands suggests it may. Nature and landscape feature strongly in songs that men sing in the choir Accent and in their extensive everyday vocal practices. As farmers search in the mountains for sheep, give hay to livestock, or lay nets in the lake, as men work at the lathe, in the abattoir, or driving trucks, natural landmarks call songs subliminally to mind and locate self-identity. Alternatively, songs call landscapes to mind to distract from a monotonous task or help entrainment with it (Faulkner 2006). Often these are songs by local amateur composers, even by members of the choir themselves. The metaphorical, if not literal, locating of self-identity through song in local and national landscapes is essential to accounts of song and singing given by men in Accent.

In contrast, few of the Stupid Bastards' songs are concerned with Icelandic landscape. While the sea figures in several of their songs, it is as a more socially dynamic site, where a theatrical parody of Icelandic masculine identity can be acted out in song. If the farmer and Icelandic small-holding were traditional sites of Icelandic masculinity—of which the male voice choir tradition was a component part in the first half of the twentieth century—there is a sense in which the modernization of the Icelandic fishing fleet, and the remarkable prosperity that fish exports brought to Iceland, moved that focus from the land to the sea (Durrenberger and Pálsson 1989). In a parody of the masculine values associated with the formidable challenge of fishing in these arctic waters, the song "Son of the Sea" talks about one band member who is unable to follow in the family tradition of going to sea. The song's video is shot in absolutely calm seas in Húsavík Bay with all nine musicians and instruments crammed into a desperately overcrowded traditional day-fishing boat. Seasickness becomes a laugh at the stereotypical image of the Icelandic fisherman. When grandmother offers to give her grandson a fishing boat, the grandson, with an eye on rock stardom, asks if he can have an electric guitar instead! Given that the Stupid Bastards are not a rock band, the irony about being a rock star is clear. Other songs also focus on Icelandic men at sea: low morale, being wet and cold, having to watch the same porn video once again, wives complaining every night on the radio, and a captain with Alzheimer's disease who is unable to navigate back to land.

So, while landscape plays different roles in the identity of these groups, local identity—being from the county of Thingeyjarsýslu—is central to who both groups think they are. Oddur explains:

> **ODDUR (STUPID BASTARDS):** It is clearly important to us that we are Thingeyinga. When we needed a replacement drummer [Aggi was the one who went off chasing a girl to Australia] we nearly insisted on finding another Thingeyinga, but in the end we settled for an experienced player from Reykjavík . . . until Aggi returned!

In his book *Brekkukot,* Icelandic Nobel Prize winner for literature Halldór Laxness (1966) wrote:

> Life has taught me to make no distinction between a hero and a little man, between great events and trifles. From my point of view, men and events are all more or less the same size. (Laxness 1966: x)

Changing social and historical contexts have subtly changed men's identities and vocal behaviors in this setting. Nevertheless, core constructs that emerged from the study of men in the male voice choir are fundamentally at play among the Stupid Bastards too. In contemporary Western settings clear distinctions are often made between different performers, audiences, musical objects, and musical behaviors themselves. That kind of differentiation is seen as essential to the identity constructed around a style or genre, individual artist, subculture, or behavior. Yet the Icelandic view of singing and music-making in this setting reveals an inclusive, everyday version that enables a male voice choir and a male pop group to share essential constructs of musical and masculine identity. Whatever distinctions are made between them upon first impressions turn out to be relatively superficial.

Rural and agricultural settings were traditionally seen as dominant sites of Icelandic identity and the cultural and political cradle of nineteenth-century nationalism. But with the development of the Icelandic fishing industry after independence and World War II, economic and political influence moved from the land to the sea to fishing towns, and to the Reykjavík conurbation. This change in the balance of economic and political power has been accompanied by a gradual change in musical styles and in subject content, though certainly not the dramatic shift that might have been expected. The Stupid Bastards suggest that there has not been any radical transformation of the fundamental qualities of Icelandic individualism and collectivism, versatility and specialization. Musical inclusion is still paramount. Parodying the Icelandic fisherman hero and stereotypical masculinities resonates with the Stupid Bastards' refusal to build up their own "rock stars" and with Accents' intolerance of "prima-donna-ish" behavior and their vocal autonomy. Versatility, inclusion and equity, and an emotionally wide-ranging expressive content are key constructs of the self-identity produced and represented by men in both these singing groups. So, while nature dominates how outsiders see Icelandic identity and even how Icelanders represent it in music for international consumption in particular, nature remains only one element in a complex, ever-changing kaleidoscope.

Having an effect on other people—by singing with them or for them—and regulating self-identity through singing are key motivating factors for both groups of men in this study. The timing of my research with the Stupid Bastards coincided with the most significant national crisis here since independence. The global financial crisis of 2008 and onward has transformed a nation from the top of the 2007 United Nations Human Development Index to one of the most indebted economies in the Western world. I had just returned to Iceland after more than a year's absence; I expected to see severe strains and concerns, and I did. But people were still intent on "singing ourselves away from anxiety and worry." So in the early hours of the morning after the Stupid Bastards concert, I sang in harmony for an hour with an impromtu assembly of twenty old friends in a local home. None were willing to discuss the present crisis, though I knew many of them had been severely impacted by it. Similarly, the following evening I attended a family barbeque organized by the male voice choir and I was invited to conduct and sing with them. In little more than twenty-four hours I had been reminded how men singing together, in the kinds of ways outlined above, are still central to this regional Icelandic version of self-identity, to Stupid Bastards and to local Accent.

References

Adler, Adam. 2005. Let the Boys Sing and Speak: Masculinities and Boys' Stories of Singing in School. In *Sharing the Voices: The Phenomenon of Singing IV—Proceedings of the International Symposium, St. John's, Newfoundland, Canada, June 26–29, 2003*, ed. Ki Adams, Andrea Rose, and Leon Chisholm, 1–15. St. John's: Memorial University of Newfoundland.

Adler, Alfred. 1992. *Understanding Human Nature*. Trans. Colin Brett. Oxford: Oneworld.

Bakhtin, Mikhail Mikhailovich. 1984. *Problems of Dostoevsky's Poetics*. Ed. and trans. Caryl Emerson. Minneapolis: University of Minnesota Press.

Björnsdóttir, Inga Dóra. 1996. The Mountain Woman and the President. In *Images of Contemporary Iceland: Everyday Lives and Global Contexts*, ed. Gísli Pálsson and E. Paul Durrenberger, 106–125. Iowa City: University of Iowa Press.

———. 2001. Hin karlmannlega raust og hinn hljóðláti máttur kvenna: Upphaf kórsöngs á Íslandi [Masculine Voices and Silent Women: The Origins of Choral Traditions in Iceland]. *Saga* 39: 7–50.

Canoy, Marcel F. M., Jan C van Ours, and Frederick van der Ploeg. 2006. The Economics of Books. In *Handbook of the Economics of Art and Culture*, ed. Victor A. Ginsburgh and David Throsby, 721–761. Amsterdam: Elsevier.

Clift, Stephen M., and Granville Hancox. 2001. The Perceived Benefits of Singing: Findings from Preliminary Surveys of a University College Choral Society. *Journal of the Royal Society for the Promotion of Health* 121 (4): 248–256.

Durrenberger, E. Paul. 1996. Every Icelander a Special Case. In *Images of Contemporary Iceland: Everyday Lives and Global Contexts*, ed. Gísli Pálsson and E. Paul Durrenberger, 171–190. Iowa City: University of Iowa Press.

Durrenberger, E. Paul, and Gísli Pálsson. 1989. Forms of Production and Fishing Expertise. In *The Anthropology of Iceland*, ed. Paul E. Durrenberger and Gisli Pálsson, 3–18. Iowa City: University of Iowa Press.

Erlmann, Veit. 1996. *Nightsong: Performance, Power and Practice in South Africa*. Chicago: University of Chicago Press.

Faulkner, Robert. 2003. Group Composing: Pupil Perceptions from a Social Psychological Study. *Music Education Research* 5 (2): 101–124.

———. 2005. Men's Ways of Singing. In *Sharing the Voices: The Phenomenon of Singing IV: Proceedings of the International Symposium, St. John's, Newfoundland, Canada, June 26–29, 2003*, ed. Ki Adams, Andrea Rose, and Leon Chisholm, 67–75. St. John's: Memorial University of Newfoundland.

———. 2006. The Vocal Construction of Self: Icelandic Men and Singing in Everyday Life. PhD diss., University of Sheffield.

Faulkner, Robert, and Jane W. Davidson. 2004. Men's Vocal Behaviour and the Construction of Self. *Musicae Scientiae: The Journal of the European Society for the Cognitive Sciences of Music* 8 (2): 231–255.

———. 2006. Men in Chorus: Collaboration and Competition in Homo-Social Vocal Behaviour. *Psychology of Music* 34 (2): 219–237.

Folkestad, Göran. 2006. Formal and Informal Learning Situations or Practices vs. Formal and Informal Ways of Learning. *British Journal of Music Education* 23 (2): 135–145.

Gallup Organization. 1996. *Gender and Society: Status and Stereotypes—An International Gallup Poll Report*. Princeton, N.J.: Gallup Organization.

Glaser, Barney G., and Anselm L. Strauss. 1967. *The Discovery of Grounded Theory: Strategies for Qualitative Research*. Chicago: Aldine Publishing Company.

Green, Lucy. 1997. *Music, Gender, Education*. Cambridge: Cambridge University Press.
———. 2001/02. *How Popular Musicians Learn: A Way Ahead For Music Education*. London: Ashgate Press.
Harrison, Scott D. 2008. *Masculinities and Music: Engaging Men and Boys in Making Music*. Newcastle, UK: Cambridge Scholars Press.
Hobsbawm, Eric J., and Terence O. Ranger, eds. 1983. *The Invention of Tradition*. Cambridge: Cambridge University Press.
Ingólfsson, Árni Heimir. 2003. "These Are the Things You Never Forget": The Written and Aural Traditions of Icelandic Tvísöngur. PhD diss., Harvard University.
Jakobsson, Garðar, and Páll Heimir Jónsson. 1990. *Fiðlur og tónmannlíf í Suður-þingeyjarsýslu* [The Violin and Musical Life in South Thingeyjarsyslu (Iceland)]. Reykjavík: Jakobsson and Jónsson.
Laxness, Halldór. 1966. *The Fish Can Sing* [*Brekkukotsannáll*]. Trans. Magnus Magnusson. London: Methuen.
Smith, Jonathan A., and Mike Osborn. 2003. Interpretative Phenomenological Analysis. In *Qualitative Psychology*, ed. Jonathan A. Smith, 51–80. London: Sage Publications.
Stebbins, Robert A. 1996. *The Barbershop Singer: Inside the Social World of a Musical Hobby*. Toronto and Buffalo: University of Toronto Press.

Film Recording

Sigur Rós. 2007. *Heima: A Film by Sigur Rós* [Home]. Director: Dean DeBlois. Klikk Production, EMI 5099951041991.

FIFTEEN

Discovering and Affirming Musical Identity through Extracurricular Music-Making in English Secondary Schools

STEPHANIE PITTS

For well over fifty years, a defining characteristic of English secondary school music education has been its extracurricular activities—those collective musical endeavors undertaken voluntarily, outside the school day, by students and staff with a particular enthusiasm for music. Historically, these have included orchestras, choirs, and musical productions, with opportunities later broadening in response to changing musical and school cultures, to encompass samba groups, "battle of the bands" contests, and music technology clubs. Often these extracurricular experiences become the most vividly recalled memories of music in school, and they can lay the foundations for continued participation in adulthood. They are therefore a valuable focus for research, offering insight on the opportunities beyond the curriculum that shape young people's understanding of what music is, and whether it is for them.

In a study of musically active British adults' recollections of their formative musical experiences, the challenges and successes of extracurricular music emerged as the most prominent factor in lifelong musical interest and activity (Pitts 2008). Written responses from over seventy adults illustrated the ways in which friendships, teacher influence, and the acquisition of musical skills and identity were closely intertwined:

> Middle school ensembles [ages nine–thirteen] always went to music festivals, usually doing well, and school concerts were always

very well prepared and good fun. There was an inter-form competition each year where each form [grade level] had to put together a program including a few solos and a whole form piece. All of this was run by one very energetic music teacher who sadly died last year. I had seen her the previous year and both her and her husband (my piano teacher) had always been keen to hear about my progress as well as that of almost all the other pupils she would have known. Over three hundred attended the funeral and she will be greatly missed. [Life history study, respondent 51, age twenty-nine]

This description is representative of many similar accounts of tireless and much-loved music teachers providing opportunities for instrumentalists and singers in their schools, and shows how the teacher's musical identity, as much as their students', is manifest in collective musical activity beyond the classroom. Gordon Cox (1999) has shown through interviews with teachers that the satisfaction of using and developing their own musical skills, as well as providing opportunities for their students, helps teachers to retain their identities as musicians as well as educators. By doing so, they present valuable role models for their students, communicating inclusive values for music by revealing and modeling the processes of musical learning.

If that all sounds too idealistic, it must indeed be acknowledged that not all children are fortunate in having such nurturing experiences of extracurricular music. Even among the musically active adults involved in my life histories study, some had retained memories of disappointments and missed opportunities:

The first music teacher I encountered [at grammar school] was a rather forbidding character, and at eleven years old I felt rather nervous of him. The whole class was auditioned for the school choir, taking pupils two at a time. I was not accepted, much to my great disappointment. This must have had quite a negative impact on me because I did not try again through all the years I was at the school. [Life history study, respondent 13, age fifty-eight]

Perhaps the greatest drawback of extracurricular music-making is that it typically involves a small proportion of a school population, often selected through audition. This selection process means that those who had wanted to join in but have been denied access can suffer a serious blow to their musical confidence. Similarly problematic are the cases where students are eager for musical opportunities, but those provided within the school are insufficient for their needs, thus creating a disjunction between the musical identity that is nurtured by parents and instrumental teachers, but that appears invisible within the school context:

> In the senior school the standard of music was very high but I was disappointed that the head of music seemed only interested in children who learned instruments in school and I was never allowed to play in assembly like them and I felt, rightly or wrongly, that my music was inferior. […] It was only in the last three years at school when I learned the double bass there that I felt part of school music as the teacher was very encouraging. [Life history study, respondent 17, age sixty-five]

The experiences reported here of failing the choir audition and not being allowed to play in assembly share the common characteristic of seeking (and not finding) a teacher's recognition of an already emerging musical expertise and interest. While both of these adults have subsequently pursued their musical activities elsewhere, it is clear that the school music teacher was an important potential source of affirmation, and that the denial of his or her approval caused them to doubt either themselves or the value of school music provision. Music teachers might be felt to have enough pressures to face without feeling responsible for the confidence and future involvement of their students—but perhaps this is in fact their most fundamental responsibility, and should be at the heart of curriculum and extracurricular decisions. In order to explore this further, I turn now to some contemporary accounts of extracurricular musical involvement, focusing in particular on the musical values and attitudes that are communicated through the teacher's role in different extracurricular settings.

ROLES AND ATTITUDES IN
EXTRACURRICULAR MUSIC-MAKING

The large-scale musical production, once a staple feature of English secondary school extracurricular music, has increasingly had to compete for students' and teachers' energies with the pressures of external examinations and assessed coursework. The time and effort involved in staging a public performance is a significant commitment for all involved, and it requires managerial support if those efforts are to be recognized and justified. In some schools such an undertaking may not be appropriate or possible, given the limited access to instrumental tuition for the economically disadvantaged, as well as the problems with school engagement and motivation among pupils with low attainment or aspirations. That said, extracurricular activity has been shown to improve school engagement in a range of contexts (Mahoney et al. 2003), allowing previously marginalized pupils to find new routes to success and popularity (Kinney 1993: 30) and increasing teachers' expectations and thus, indirectly, their levels of support for such pupils (Van Matre et al. 2000). Students' identities as learners are therefore strengthened by such involvement, but rather less has been written about the potential effects on their identities as musicians.

As the retrospective accounts discussed above illustrate (see also Pitts 2008; 2009), extracurricular involvement at school can offer a life-changing opportunity to experiment with an identity as musician, and to have this affirmed by teachers, peers, and audience members. In some schools this still occurs through the staging of large-scale musical works, while in others student-led improvisation groups or technology-based workshops have become more central to musical life beyond the classroom. The discussion that follows here examines these diverse contexts more closely, considering the teacher's changing role in supporting students' emerging musical identities.

HIGH SCHOOL MUSICAL: *ANYTHING GOES* IN A SELECTIVE GIRLS' SCHOOL

In 2005 I carried out a study of a production of Cole Porter's *Anything Goes* in a private girls' school in the northern English town of Sheffield. I explored the experiences of teachers and pupils involved in the show to compare these with adult amateur musicians (Pitts 2005) and thus consider the effects of the school context on musical participation. In addition to a questionnaire survey of participants and non-participants, designed to investigate the impact of the show on the wider school community, I asked participants to keep audio diaries that captured the day-to-day frustrations and pleasures of rehearsals (see Pitts 2007 for full description of methods). Through the audio diaries, the participants spoke to one another about their experiences of being in the show, gathering rich qualitative data through peer-to-peer questioning that was far more direct than anything that could ethically have been undertaken by a visiting researcher (including speculation about the "stressful look" on a teacher's face and tales of backstage antics during performances). The honesty of these diary accounts is a useful reminder of the researcher's obligations and constraints in this area of research: as with music therapy or community music projects, there is an unstated moral pressure to find evidence of the benefits of an activity that has taken such huge commitment from its organizers, for whom external validation would be a welcome consequence of the research. In this case, the enthusiastic descriptions of the participants and their obvious sense of withdrawal when the show ended provide exactly that; but there are nonetheless uncomfortable questions to be faced about the impact of the production on those who were not involved, and more fundamental premises to be examined over the provision of extracurricular opportunities in less privileged school settings.

In the questionnaire and diary responses, there was clear evidence of participants' changing musical skills and attitudes between Year 7 (ages 11–12) and Year 10 (ages 14–15). While even the Year 7 respondents all had past performing experience on which to draw, they noted that they had acquired new musical skills, such as "being able to learn a song quickly" or to "understand how well melodies and harmonies fit together." The older participants (Year 10, ages 14–15) described their musical learning more in terms of refining existing skills, such as "singing in different accents," and emphasized the non-musical benefits of participation more strongly—acquiring new and deeper friendships and having "fun within a non-formal school environment." It seems that between the ages of eleven and fifteen, musical identities have become more fixed: those Year 10s involved in the production are confident of their skills and musical status, while non-participants of the same age are similarly adamant in their views that "I don't sing" or "I don't like those kinds of shows." Among Year 7 students, the most common reason given for not participating was related to missing or failing auditions, and many of those non-participants stated that they would be interested in taking up similar opportunities in future. For Year 10s, however, there was a resigned sense that "the same people always get the parts" and although they were largely supportive of the school putting on musical productions, most stated that they would not be going to watch the performance.

The changes in attitude demonstrated by these two year groups suggest that receptiveness to musical opportunities decreases through secondary school for many reasons. One may simply be an increase in self-evaluation and reduced risk-taking tendencies: one of the Year 7 participants had realized "I'm not as good as I think I am," but many of those who had failed the audition were bitterly disappointed, and therefore unlikely by the age of fifteen to run the risk of further failure. Academic and time pressures undoubtedly increase over the school career too, and those Year 10s who felt unable to commit themselves to hours of rehearsals were making what many of their teachers would consider to be a wise decision. In a high-achieving school such as this one, pupils are encouraged to pursue their strengths; and while many of the non-participants remained musically active into Year 10, they had also discovered other, higher priorities within or beyond school. To some extent this is to be expected: just as adults have varying levels of musical interest and involvement, so the acquisition of strong musical identities by some young people is matched by similar enthusiasm for sport or study in others—and, sadly, by the absence of any such discovery for a significant number too. The case study of *Anything Goes* shows that the provision of opportunity, and of diverse routes back into musical engagement where interest or activity has lapsed, must be a priority for ensuring that all pupils have the chance to discover and develop a musical identity.

NEW FORMS OF EXTRACURRICULAR ENGAGEMENT

In the *Anything Goes* production discussed above, the extracurricular activity was teacher-directed: decisions about the choice and timing of the musical were made by staff, the auditions placed the teacher in an authority role, and rehearsals—though involving some input from older students—were scheduled and directed by the music and drama teachers. This state of affairs was totally accepted by the students, and indeed they reflected on the pleasures of working with their teachers outside the classroom, forming "more friendly" relationships with them as they worked toward the shared goal of a public performance. For the teachers too, working with students without the constraints of formal assessment brought real benefits: as the head of the music program stated: "The girls are under so much pressure and sometimes I think it's good to do something for the pure excuse of having a good laugh." Extracurricular music-making in this traditional model therefore offers valuable opportunities to blur the boundaries of classroom hierarchies by giving greater attention to individual students' abilities and achievements, and by working toward mutually agreed musical goals.

The school production model is heavily dependent on the musical expertise and authority of the teacher, and on the students' willingness to engage for many voluntary hours in a teacher-led activity. In the privileged environment of a selective girls' school, the activity is congruent with the school ethos: the majority of non-participants agreed that "having shows in school is a good thing," and participants were fully aware of the enrichment to school life that their participation afforded. Not all schools, though, have such a tradition or ethos to draw upon in providing extracurricular opportunities. Where there are challenges of student engagement, parental support, or economic deprivation, a willingness or ability to spend additional school hours in rehearsals cannot be relied upon. The cultural values of a high art musical might seem remote from the music encountered in class lessons or in the wider community, and so the messages of inclusion and identity affirmation offered by staging a pre-composed show in the girls' school context will be absent or contradictory in a more diverse school community. Alternative ways must be sought to achieve similar musical outcomes, involving the reappraisal of the teacher's role as well as the broadening of musical styles, genres, and activities designed to connect more readily with students' musical lives out of school.

In exploring new kinds of extracurricular music-making, some schools in England have formed partnerships with community musicians, bringing in expert DJs, rappers, or songwriters to supplement teachers' typically more classically oriented musical backgrounds. The Musical Futures project has documented some instances of these activities (Kaiserman et al. 2007), including a student-run songwriting club, training in professional sound studios, and fusion workshops with punk, ska, and reggae musicians. Kaiserman et al. emphasize the importance of consulting students in order to provide personalized extracurricular opportunities that meet their current needs and relate to the musical activities and interests that they already pursue outside school. Arguably, the *Anything Goes* musical in the private high school context does that too, since students in that population were widely experienced in stage performance and formal singing training, in ways that students in the Musical Futures report were not. The principles are therefore similar, with teachers in all settings aiming to provide opportunities that begin with their students' current musical identities and enrich these through expert role models and the pursuit of a musically authentic outcome.

The Musical Futures community music projects, and other comparable activities around the country, make more explicit the teacher's role as a broker of arts opportunities, by stating that "young people require an exposure to a whole range of professional music expertise, and they need this in a variety of different contexts" (Kaiserman et al. 2007: 9). One risk in this approach is that the teacher's own musical expertise is overlooked by students, and the presence of an approachable role model in school is overshadowed by the novelty value of working with community practitioners on short-term projects. Kaiserman et al. offer reassurance that the place of music in schools is still critical to young people's musical development:

> With the possible exception of a small minority, only in the school is there a guaranteed, universal entitlement to music learning, whatever form that might currently take. Certainly, young people are exposed to, and create for themselves, a huge variety of musical experiences outside the school (and additionally, many of course are driving their own learning) but the school is in a unique position to create a solid foundation for a lifelong engagement in music—for those for whom it will remain part of their general cultural life, as well as for those who choose to develop their interest further. (Ibid.)

Evidence of the impact of new forms of extracurricular music-making is provided by James Cross, a teacher in Sheffield working a few miles away from the *Anything Goes* school, in a state comprehensive school with a mixed urban intake and a reasonably active music department. In a case study written for Musical Futures concerning the use of the informal learning model (Green 2008) as an extracurricular activity, Cross (2009: 183) describes having identified the need to broaden the extracurricular activities of his department to reach students who "clearly had an interest in music, but didn't play an instrument." Drawing on his own expertise in music technology, Cross established My Sound, an informal lunchtime and after-school club in which students could book studio time and consult their teacher about creative musical projects of their own devising. He describes the effects on the participating students:

> Students would come to me armed with ideas for backings, lyrics scribbled on the back of worksheets from other subjects, and enthusiastic pleas for as much studio time as they could get their hands on. Students who had long lists of behavior incidents and exclusions were choosing to stay after school to make music. Students who struggled in English lessons were spending hours of their own time writing lyrics. Students of all ages who never would have dreamed of taking part in extracurricular music were thriving. One even begged, "Sir, please phone my mum and tell her I've got a detention," as he was worried that his mother would never believe he had stayed in school by choice, and would assume he was up to something that he shouldn't be! (Cross 2009: 184)

It is worth noting in passing the validity of a case study such as this in contributing to research on extracurricular music. Undoubtedly, accounts provided by practitioners will be biased toward positive reports, since teachers (like any other professionals) are unlikely to make public any instances of difficult or unsuccessful activities. Nonetheless, the aspects of a case study that teachers choose to report are interesting data in themselves: Cross emphasizes the motivation of his students in relation to their wider school attitudes, and in fact says rather less about their musical progress, showing that he recognizes personal development to be an important, perhaps even central, part of the project. We therefore learn something of the teacher's values—his care for his students as individuals, not simply as competent musicians—as well as witnessing examples of the students' changing behavior that support this outlook. Cross's account can be cross-referenced with published studies, where his findings are consistent with established views on the contribution of extracurricular activity to school engagement (Mahoney et al. 2003). While there is certainly a need for more rigorous and extensive research into the activities documented by Cross and the Musical Futures team, practitioners' accounts offer a useful way in to understanding contemporary experiences of music education, and can help to generate the research questions for more extensive studies using longitudinal data collection to explore students' experiences in greater detail (cf. McGillen 2004).

From the brief accounts given here, it can be seen that students, teachers, researchers, and the wider musical community have much to learn from extracurricular music-making. While David Bray cautions against the tendency to see extracurricular activity as "the barometer of the musicality of a school environment" (Bray 2009: 10), those activities in which teachers and students choose to invest their time and energies voluntarily highlight the musical attitudes and values that are given priority by participants, and so offer a way in to understanding the construction of musical identity within that community.

For students, the opportunity to participate in extracurricular music can be an important step in acquiring or affirming a sense that music is "for them"—they are welcome to participate; they have something to contribute. The *Anything Goes* study showed students' recognition that this inclination would not be equally distributed through the school community, but nonetheless acknowledged that having such opportunities was a valuable part of school life, even for non-participants. Those most at risk of musical disaffection were the young people who had failed an audition; and the life histories study illustrated that the memories and effects of this could be long-lasting. Teachers therefore need to balance the aims of different extracurricular activities, ensuring that a focus on achieving a high musical standard on specific occasions is matched by the chance for all comers to participate in other events. There also need to be clear pathways back in to music-making for those who do not engage musically at the start of their school careers, since the *Anything Goes* study also revealed an entrenchment of attitudes between the ages of eleven and fifteen, which could make it harder to encourage the exploration of new musical activities in later adolescence.

Teachers make a strong investment in extracurricular activities, and a shift toward using more community practitioners to provide these opportunities could represent a threat toward the professional satisfaction found in nurturing and modeling musical skill and enthusiasm. However, testimonies from teachers who have been involved in learning new musical skills alongside their students show that this can bring its own source of musical and professional growth: as Christopher McGillen, a teacher-researcher member of the student-led band Jungle Express, puts it, "It is the relationships that are formed within a learning environment that will lead to the kinds of profound engagement, task identification and mutuality to which we all aspire" (McGillen 2004: 291). The life history responses cited in this chapter show the close interaction between working informally with a teacher and coming to share their musical enthusiasms. Even in a new mixed economy of extracurricular provision, teachers should not underestimate their own status as role models, communicating messages about the inclusivity and relevance of musical activity to their students. Consideration of those values is essential if they are not to be unwittingly exclusive: life history respondents had often learned as much from their teachers' attitudes to music as from their skills, and in many cases had carried into adult life a similar desire to share and encourage music-making with young people.

Finally, as a field for investigative research, extracurricular music offers a real chance to witness musical teaching, learning, and identity formation working together at their best, highlighting those practices that secure the enthusiasm of the next generation of adult musical participants. Despite the constantly changing nature of educational and musical life, the traditions of extracurricular music-making in English schools have at their heart a passion for music and a willingness to go beyond the confines of the formal school curriculum in providing authentic, appealing opportunities for young people to flourish as emerging musicians. Such activities deserve to be more thoroughly supported and celebrated—and the first step in doing this is to understand more clearly the characteristics and benefits of effective extracurricular practice. Practitioners and researchers therefore need to work together in documenting and critiquing the multiplicity of musical opportunities that currently exist in English schools, in order that their immediate and long-term impact can be recognized and properly valued in music education policy and practice.

References

Bray, David. 2009. *Creating a Musical School.* Oxford: Oxford University Press.

Cox, Gordon. 1999. Secondary School Music Teachers Talking. *Music Education Research* 1 (1): 37–45.

Cross, James. 2009. Case Study: High Storrs School, Sheffield. In *Musical Futures: An Approach to Teaching and Learning* (Resource Pack: 2nd ed.), ed. Abigail D'Amore, 183–184. At http://www.musicalfutures.org.uk (accessed 11 May 2009).

Green, Lucy. 2008. *Music, Informal Learning and the School: A New Classroom Pedagogy.* Aldershot, UK: Ashgate Press.

Kaiserman, Paul, and David Price, with J. Richardson, F. Pacey, and F. Hannan. 2007. *A Guide to Personalising Extra-Curricular Music.* London: Musical Futures/Paul Hamlyn Foundation. At http://www.musicalfutures.org.uk (accessed 3 January 2007).

Kinney, David A. 1993. From Nerds to Normals: The Recovery of Identity among Adolescents from Middle School to High School. *Sociology of Education* 66 (1): 21–40.

Mahoney, J. L., B. D. Cairns, and T. W. Farmer, 2003. Promoting Interpersonal Competence and Educational Success through Extracurricular Activity Participation. *Journal of Educational Psychology* 95 (2): 409–418.

McGillen, Christopher W. 2004. In Conversation with Sarah and Matt: Perspectives on Creating and Performing Original Music. *British Journal of Music Education* 21 (3): 279–293.

Pitts, Stephanie E. 2005. *Valuing Musical Participation.* Aldershot, UK: Ashgate.

———. 2007. *Anything Goes:* A Case Study of Extra-Curricular Musical Participation in an English Secondary School. *Music Education Research* 9 (1): 145–165.

———. 2008. Extra-Curricular Music in UK Schools: Investigating the Aims, Experiences and Impact of Adolescent Musical Participation. *International Journal of Education and the Arts* 9 (10). At http://www.ijea.org/v9n10/ (accessed 3 June 2009).

———. 2009. Roots and Routes in Adult Musical Participation: Investigating the Impact of Home and School on Lifelong Musical Interest and Involvement. *British Journal of Music Education* 26 (3): 241–256.

Van Matre, J. C., J. C. Valentine, and H. Cooper. 2000. Effect of Students' After-School Activities on Teachers' Academic Expectancies. *Contemporary Educational Psychology* 25: 167–183.

SIXTEEN

Scottish Traditional Music

Identity and the "Carrying Stream"

CHARLES BYRNE

Scotland, along with England, Northern Ireland, and Wales, is one of the four countries comprising the United Kingdom. Having a population of just over five million, it is unique among the four nations in that after a period of nearly three hundred years, it now has its own devolved Parliament once again. On 12 May 1999, the day of the Parliament's first meeting, emotions were running high when Winnie Ewing announced that "the Scottish Parliament, which adjourned on 25 March 1707, is hereby reconvened" (Scottish Parliament 2009). This event "brought with it a strong sense of cultural and artistic awareness and direction in our communities" (Sheridan 2000). A sense of national pride was evident at the time of the formal opening ceremony, and the sense of occasion was palpable.

The Scottish composer and academic Mark Sheridan, in an e-mail communication with the author in 2009, suggested that, as a nation, our growing interest in Scottish traditional music can be traced to the second half of the twentieth century with the establishment by Hamish Henderson and others of the School of Scottish Studies at Edinburgh University in 1951. Henderson's concept of the "carrying stream" is significant, reflecting the value and importance placed on the oral tradition of passing on the stories, songs, and tunes of the people for successive generations (Henderson 1992). There has been a huge increase in the numbers of young people engaging with their own musical traditions through the school curriculum, the work of *Fèisean nan Gàidheal*, and the Traditional Music and Song Association of Scotland, and numerous local associations, musical societies, and informal groups (Sheridan and Byrne 2008). It could be argued that to many people living, learning, and working in Scotland today, music plays a significant role in determining our sense of national identity. The spirited singing of our unofficial national anthem "Flower of Scotland" at international sporting events seems to bring about a sense of pride and passion that other songs cannot. It has been claimed that the use of the song was partly responsible for the grand-slam rugby victory over England in 1990 by sending them "homeward tae think again" (Purser 1992).

Music is now firmly established as a popular subject in Scottish schools, and the music curriculum in secondary schools is well equipped to cater to this increase in interest (Byrne 2005). The Scottish Government is committed to an ambitious program to "broaden the range of musical styles and learning contexts available as early access music-making experiences" (Scottish Arts Council 2006: 5) through the provision of tuition on a musical instrument for every child by Primary 6 stage (age ten–eleven). This agenda is being supported by government funding for both formal and informal education sectors. In many parts of the country, tuition is provided by organizations such as *Fèisean nan Gàidheal* on traditional instruments like the chanter, *clàrsach* (Celtic harp), fiddle and whistle, *bodhran* (Irish frame drum), and melodeon and for step-dance and Gaelic singing.

The aim of this chapter is to describe and analyze the experiences, thoughts, and views of a small group of traditional musicians who are key stakeholders in the continuing transmission of the Scottish music tradition. In addition, I will offer some comparisons between theory-based views (Sheridan and Byrne 2008) and the musical lives and work of the participants.

THE ONWARD TRANSMISSION OF CULTURE

In Scotland, cultural and educational policies set the context within which many of our young teachers and performers will work in the future, and there is some concern that the oral tradition of the transmission of culture and language will be maintained and preserved for future generations. It has been observed that "courses in higher education must not be solely concerned with students' success in their chosen music degree or other course, but also with their continuing development as musicians and their ability to sustain a meaningful and rewarding career" (Sheridan and Byrne 2008: 154). Many graduates with music degrees in Scotland will need to find a balance of different types of work, as performers, teachers, and recording artists, in order to sustain meaningful and rewarding careers while at the same time fulfilling their function of carrying onward the traditions and values of the music, poetry, and stories of Scottish culture. Are our undergraduates and graduates aware of this imputed role, or is this mere whim on the part of Scottish academics? If there is awareness of this cultural transmitter role, is there also an emerging sense of identity as a professional musician, and if so, how does this manifest itself? Is there a strong link between informal music making and a sense of musical identity, and to what extent is this evident in interviews with research participants? A sense of national identity is also linked with traditional music, and how this manifests itself will serve as a topic for discussion below.

The Scottish education system was subjected to major revisions in the late 1980s. This process introduced a new inclusive approach designed to broaden the range of styles and genres of music that young people were already interested in, giving rock, jazz, and traditional music a stamp of approval by adding them to the national examination syllabus. This shift in emphasis away from the classical music tradition also embraced Scottish traditional music, and "knowledge and understanding of the indigenous music of Scotland" (Scottish Examination Board 1988) was a requirement of the new course. Another significant development was the creation and support of five specialist music schools throughout the country. Plockton High School is the National Center for Excellence in Traditional Music, providing tuition for studies in bagpipes, fiddle, accordion, *clàrsach*, piano, guitar, whistle, flute, and Gaelic and Scots song.

THE PARTICIPANTS

Five participants took part in a semi-structured interview either via telephone or face-to-face. Their interaction with the formal and informal music education sectors in Scotland and their roles as performers and composers form the context for the study. Each is either a graduate or an undergraduate of the BA in Applied Music degree at the University of

Strathclyde in Glasgow, Scotland's largest city. Mark Sheridan established this degree in the early 1990s in response to the changes in the music curriculum in Scottish schools, catering to a wide range of musical styles and backgrounds; it was the first degree-level course in the country to encourage rock, traditional, and jazz musicians. Graduates from the course go on to teach privately and in the state school sector, and to perform and work in various branches of the music industry. The course is a crucible of talent, with many musical collaborations beginning there and lasting for many years into professional life. Bands have been formed while students are at university, and some musicians arrive as members of bands whose regular performances provide a means of financial stability while enduring the student life in a big city. This Strathclyde Applied Music network taps into the wider Celtic music network in Scotland and allows musicians to connect with a variety of fellow performers, promoters, and venues.

Typically, graduates go on to travel around the United Kingdom and the world. Some make successful recordings in jazz, traditional, and rock music, blending this with teaching, performing, and leading ensembles. Graduates from the BA in Applied Music program have performed in Spain, China, France, Germany, Belgium, and Poland. Several graduates have won the prestigious Glenfiddich Fiddle Championships, and many combine successful teaching careers with performances at concerts and festivals throughout the year. Many musicians as undergraduates have performed at the *Festival Interceltique* in Lorient, France, often returning once their university days are over.

The participants in this study each explored their musical background, influences, and interests during the course of the conversations. Ayrshire-born fiddler and teacher Alistair McCulloch's passion for Scottish traditional music was inspired by his father, who was a piper and fiddler. Alistair started playing the fiddle at the age of eleven and quickly became involved in the local Strathspey and Reel Society, being taught by its musical director, Wallace Galbraith. He graduated in 1998 and is in great demand as one of the country's finest fiddle players, having been national fiddle champion on three occasions. He balances teaching commitments at the University of Strathclyde and Royal Scottish Academy of Music and Dance (RSAMD) with performing and conducting all over the world. Alistair travels extensively, having visited all continents, and he is musical director of the Ayrshire Fiddle Orchestra and the young string group Innovation. He also manages to find time to tour with his *céilidh* band, Coila, and another band, the eponymous Alistair McCulloch Trio. He is an established composer in the traditional Scottish style and his albums include original tunes penned as tributes to friends and mentors. Rachel Hair is a *clàrsach* player who graduated in 2005 and now divides her time between a busy teaching schedule and performing with her own band. Rachel also records her own music and is very much a cultural entrepreneur, managing and marketing her own musical career. Siobhan Anderson plays the fiddle; Jennifer Austin is a piano player; and James Lindsay plays double bass. All three are embarking upon their third year of study in the Applied Music program at Strathclyde. Siobhan is from Perthshire. James, originally from Aberdeenshire, now lives in Glasgow, while Jennifer hails from the Orkney Islands, which lie off the northeast coast of mainland Scotland.

EMERGING THEMES

A number of themes have emerged from the literature, from previous research in the area of Scottish traditional music, and from the participants' own stories about their development. As a result, three important aspects of identity are revealed within the data: transmission of musical culture, musical identity in teaching and learning, and awareness of national identity within the lives of the musicians. Some of the participants' stories, along with analysis and commentary, will serve to illustrate each of these aspects.

HOW DO YOUNG MUSICIANS ACT AS TRANSMITTERS OF THEIR CULTURE?

Clearly, in order to play a full part in the onward transmission of Scottish traditional music culture, the tradition has to be passed on to the musicians in the first place, and this can often happen in subtle ways. Rachel describes her earliest experiences of music-making in the West Highland town of Ullapool.

> There was a lot of traditional music in the village. You know, you were just, I was never conscious of it when I was wee [small], it was just there ... the school in Ullapool has done very, very well for the amount of

traditional musicians that have come out of it. We've actually got a big concert in a few weeks' time, where a full week of events, there's four concerts in total, celebrating all the kind of success of it all.

As a busy working professional musician, Rachel will be involved in the local celebrations in her village; and while she may not have been fully aware of the level of musical activity around her while she was growing up, she is now making a conscious effort to play her part in celebrating the musical success of the village. Now, as a teacher, she is busy teaching *clàrsach* to many young people, and indeed to whole families.

A lot of the pupils that I teach I go out to their houses. You know how in the past, like, people would have a piano in the house and every child in the house would learn piano? Quite a few of the folk that I teach, they've got a *clàrsach,* and every child in the family learns the *clàrsach.*

In Ayrshire, there were different musical opportunities for Alistair, and while fiddle lessons took place in and during school, his first ensemble experience was in a community-based group.

ALISTAIR: I joined the Strathspey and Reel Society, but I'd only been playing for six months. I think I was eleven at the time . . . I've been playing solo since I was about twelve years old. The local Strathspey and Reel Society, I suppose that helped. I think at that age you don't really realize the sort of magnitude of what you're doing somehow.

Later, as a member of the Ayrshire Fiddle Orchestra, he has gradually taken on more responsible roles, first as soloist and then as conductor and musical director. Alistair has developed a strong identity as a musician who upholds both local and national musical traditions of fiddle orchestras, although he is aware that many young members of the orchestra are primarily violinists who take part in fiddle playing. The distinction is important.

ALISTAIR: That's a hugely successful organization, they're just about to go to China and this is the twelfth foreign tour they've done. All the kids have lessons at school, or have private tutors in the county, but there's actually very few who speak to them in the Scottish fiddle tradition.

Although from Ayrshire, Alistair has a keen awareness of different regional fiddle styles in the country.

> I was taught by Dougie Lawrence when I was at university. Probably the greatest living northeast fiddle player.

Perthshire also has a unique style of fiddle playing, although Siobhan is in the process of developing her own style of playing.

> SIOBHAN: I come from Killin in Perthshire, and I play the fiddle and I've been playing since I was about eleven years old, and I'm mostly interested in folk and traditional music. And playing gigs, but I'm also interested a little bit of classical and I play in an indie band as well. So a bit of everything really ... I got taught at school by a, it was more of a classical violinist. So I think I've kind of got a bit of a mixed-up style, 'cause she was a classical person teaching me fiddle music but, I don't know, I think I prefer the Highland style to the more traditional East Coast style of fiddle music, but I'd say I'm probably more of a player in that style. I think the kind of classical background can sometimes make me sound more East Coast so I'm a bit mixed up.

Fiddle styles may be linked with other forms of music-making, such as bagpipe music and vocalized dance music (*puirt-a-beul*). Scots Gaelic is spoken by a small proportion of the population, mainly confined to the northwest highlands and the western isles. Is there a link between the language, through which songs and stories are transmitted, and the tunes that are played on certain instruments?

> RACHEL: Yeah, quite a bit of it, because, which is the culture—you know, you'll find a tune and you go, "Oh wait, I know that as a song." I find that myself in my teaching as well. A lot of my pupils are fluent in Gaelic or they're Gaelic singers. One of the girls yesterday, I was teaching a tune which is a jig but it's also a Gaelic *puirt-a-beul* and I played it and she said, "Oh, I know that. I know how to sing that."

Composing music in the style of the tradition is mentioned by all participants not only as something that they value and enjoy but as an important part of carrying on the tradition. Musical compositions can take the form of simple tunes that are either hastily notated or committed to electronic data. In the best *céilidh* culture tradition, the tunes are designed for sharing, sometimes at band rehearsals or with other musicians in a more planned way. Alistair has published a book of his own compositions, and this is widely available in music shops. More extended compositions might form the basis of tracks for a planned album or might be the composer's first foray into the field. James's composition "Esson's Croft" has an interesting genesis:

> **JAMES:** I wrote a tune quite recently called "Esson's Croft" and it's about a colony that lived on Bennachie, which is a hill just around the corner from my home up in Aberdeenshire. I was quite inspired by their story so I just wrote it. Well, it's years and years ago, there was this plot of land on the hill that wasn't owned by anyone, that no one owned, so lots of folk just went and built their own houses and just lived off the land, and then they got kicked off pretty much when the Aberdeen folk came along and said, "This is our land." So most couldn't afford the rent and just left except for this one guy who was called George Esson. He just paid his rent and lived there for the rest of his life doing his thing, living off his own back.

All of the participants who compose do so very much in the traditional style, and their tunes are often influenced by places they have visited or people they have met. Tunes can also help preserve the culture for future generations, and all of the musicians felt it was important that good tunes help provide the learning experiences for the next generation of musicians.

MUSICAL IDENTITY IN TEACHING AND LEARNING

The professional identity of musicians can be formed in a number of ways: through performing, teaching, and composing. For many, performing in *céilidh* bands will provide a means of earning part or all of their income. Student life dictates that the very functional role of the *céilidh* band is quickly established in the lives of young musicians. Jennifer, for example, has formed a small band with some friends from the degree course. Sometimes the band is an ad hoc affair depending on the venue and requirements.

> **JENNIFER:** Somebody who is having a do, or a party, or a dance, approaches somebody and says, "I've got this *céilidh* I'm wanting to do, can you get me a *céilidh* band?"

Other, longer-term arrangements are also possible, and regular events such as tours and festivals form an important part of Alistair's year.

ALISTAIR: I've got a trio which is more sort of folk-based. So we do maybe one tour a year, odd gigs now and then, we record together under the name the Alistair McCulloch Trio. We've got a tour coming up round the Highlands and Islands.

Teaching, for the professional musicians, is an integral part of how they earn their livelihood. All participants recognized the need to develop this aspect of their professional role, and both Alistair and Rachel have established it in their work. A varied teaching portfolio suits Alistair:

I'm employed at the RSAMD as a fiddle tutor in the Scottish Music Degree. I do other sort of bits and bobs of work for the Academy as well, one being as a fiddle examiner. I also teach fiddle at Strathclyde, as you know. Apart from that I have about maybe eight or nine private pupils.

North and Hargreaves (2008: 313) remind us that in some societies "music is a natural part of everyday life: people sing, play, and dance from a very early age, and music accompanies many aspects of work and leisure." Céilidh culture in Scottish traditional music has already been discussed (Sheridan and Byrne 2008) with reference to the importance of music in rural communities. Musical gatherings of any type are important for the musical development of young people, and experienced teachers clearly recognize this. Jennifer describes traveling from the Orkney Islands to the mainland for an annual musical gathering with the group Gizzen Briggs at Tain Royal Academy.

JENNIFER: I went to it once, and it was because, my teacher Douglas Montgomery up in Orkney, I think the woman who runs Gizzen Briggs got in touch with Douglas and said, "If any of your people from Orkney want to come and play with us, that would be completely fine." So, he said do you want to go? and I said yes. So I did that one year and it was good fun. It was like a mass of folk, like loads of people, mostly fiddlers. They have a practice, I think it's like for like a day, and we put on a concert at night.

This event clearly had a major impact on Jennifer, and the importance of such experiences is recognized by her family, who has twice travelled to Cape Breton to allow her to take part in summer schools there. As previously mentioned, while opportunities for learning and practicing traditional music exist within the formal music curriculum, it is clear that the spark and excitement of the informal settings are what really motivate and engage each of the musicians in this study.

AWARENESS OF NATIONAL IDENTITY

The young musicians in this study often describe themselves as traditional or folk musicians, "folkies," or sometimes Celtic musicians. Reiss (2003) makes the point that "the existence of Celtic music as a global category cannot be denied" and that while this is often seen as a convenient marketing tool, the distinctions between this term "and the various traditional musics that constitute its core can and should be drawn" (Reiss 2003: 146). Participants are aware of how they learned their own instrument and of the various ways in which they learn to find their own unique voice. Yet there is a characteristic style of playing the instrument that is uniquely Scottish and therefore distinct from other traditional musics. For example, Rachel teaches some *clàrsach* pupils who are entered for music competitions in traditional Irish music, and she herself is happy to draw attention to her own family connections with Ireland. She sees this as a useful marketing tool, yet she is clearly able to make the distinction, suggested by Reiss, between Irish and Scottish traditional music.

Alistair, in his roles as fiddle teacher and Fiddle Orchestra director, acknowledges the importance of his teachers in providing him with a wide knowledge of the repertoire, which in turn informs his own playing and composing in the Scottish traditional style. He also makes use of available marketing tools to catch the attention of audiences and to make a connection with their awareness and expectations of a skittish performer.

> ALISTAIR: If I am touring in America we usually wear kilts. In Canada in particular, in New Zealand, Australia, there are so many ex-pats. A lot of the audience are made up of ex-pats.

National identity is preserved through the Gaelic language; Gaelic medium education is prominent in many parts of the Highlands and Islands, and this can coexist comfortably with the English language.

RACHEL: There was always kind of Gaelic songs about. We used to have a Gaelic choir in school that I went to in Primary 7 for a while. And then the choir in high school . . . there'd be, one minute we'd be doing *"Cànan nan Gàidheal"* ("The Language of the Gaels"), and the next we'd be doing "Don't Look Back in Anger" by Oasis at a concert.

So, use of the Gaelic language encourages a strong sense of Scottish identity. Within the formal music curriculum, young people can be taught traditional instruments at school and can go on to take national certificate examinations and university degrees, and this is indicative of the value that Scotland attaches to its own culture and traditions.

Tunes can also help preserve the culture for future generations, but there is a trend toward blending the old style with new musical ideas.

ALISTAIR: I think people who write the tunes in the traditional sense, although the tunes are written in the modern day they do stick to, very much, the conventions of the tried and tested music from the golden age of fiddling, I suppose the eighteenth and early nineteenth centuries. Whereas the modern-day tunes, they're considered as new, they are definitely of a different idiom.

The participants in this study are products of an ongoing musical genesis wherein the characteristics of traditional Scottish or Celtic music mingle with the sounds of jazz and hip-hop to create new musical fusions. The late Martyn Bennett, for example, was a pioneer of Celtic techno dance music, drawing upon many diverse musical influences, yet his music is unquestionably Scottish in both character and emotional content. The character of the music would not be identifiable as Scottish without a thorough understanding of the traditions, nuances, bowing, and ornamentations that mark the traditional style. Similarly, the emotional content of the music is driven by an understanding of the language, lore, stories, and songs. When experts meet with novices to share their knowledge of the tunes, they are indeed "carrying on a powerful aspect of common heritage" (Sheridan and Byrne 2008: 150). The musicians in this study have found that a rich and diverse Scottish musical heritage coexists alongside cultural influences from across the world.

Each of them is aware of the need to carry on the musical traditions, and they all assume their important roles as part of the "carrying stream" of Scottish musical culture. The two graduates sustain successful careers, and it is to be hoped that cultural and educational policies continue to benefit the professional and educational lives of the musicians in this study and musicians of this and subsequent generations throughout Scotland.

Further research is needed to gain a sense of how widespread this implicit or explicit sense of a "carrying stream" is among professional Scottish traditional musicians. While the tradition continues, a parallel development is that contemporary styles are emerging—but this is not perceived as a threat to Scottish music. The importance of community-based music is reinforced by the participants, but location is now less of an issue as communities are "no longer sonically isolated" (Reiss 2003). Musicians may use their mobile phones to record new tunes, and YouTube to learn others, but there is still an emphasis on the oral tradition of learning "by ear" from a variety of sources. Sharing or "having a tune" with other people and then passing it on to someone else will, it seems, remain one of the most important features of Scottish traditional music for some time to come, which in turn will feed into Henderson's "carrying stream."

References

Byrne, Charles. 2005. Pedagogical Communication in the Music Classroom. In *Musical Communication,* ed. D. Miell, R. A. R. MacDonald, and D. J. Hargreaves. Oxford: Oxford University Press.

Henderson, Hamish. 1992. *Alias MacAlias: Writings on Song, Folk and Literature.* Edinburgh: Polygon.

North, Adrian C., and David. J. Hargreaves. 2008. *The Social and Applied Psychology of Music.* Oxford: Oxford University Press.

Purser, John. 1992. *Scotland's Music: A History of the Traditional and Classical Music of Scotland from Early Times to the Present Day.* Edinburgh: Mainstream Publishing.

Reiss, Scott. 2003. Traditional and Imaginary: Irish Traditional Music and the Celtic Phenomenon. In *Celtic Modern: Music at the Global Fringe,* ed. M. Stokes and P. V. Bohlman. Lanham, Md.: Maryland Press.

Scottish Arts Council. 2006. National Youth Music Strategy 2006–2008. Edinburgh: Scottish Arts Council.

Scottish Examination Board. 1998. *Scottish Certificate of Education: Standard Grade Amended Arrangements in Music*. Dalkeith: Scottish Examination Board.

Scottish Parliament. 2009. At http://www.scottish.parliament.uk/vli/history/firstDays /1999firstMeeting.htm (accessed 19 May 2010).

Sheridan, Mark. 2000. *Cultural Development and Expansion: Beyond Preservation and Renewal*. Unpublished manuscript, Glasgow: University of Strathclyde.

Sheridan, Mark, and Charles Byrne. 2008. Cèilidh Culture and Higher Education. *International Journal of Music Education* 26 (2): 147–159.

SEVENTEEN

Performance, Transmission, and Identity among Ireland's New Generation of Traditional Musicians

JOHN O'FLYNN

While Irish traditional music has long been celebrated in terms of national culture, the past twenty-five years or so have also witnessed an embrace of this musical style within the mainstream of contemporary popular culture in Ireland and elsewhere. This chapter provides some snapshots of the practices and perspectives of a new generation of traditional musicians, with a view to providing insights into musical, social, pedagogical, and phenomenological aspects of their individual and collective experiences and identities. It further discusses these findings in the light of some of the issues facing music education in Ireland.

My research centers on the present moment of selected young musicians' lives, on their activities as performers and in some cases teachers, and on their perceptions of these activities in relation to wider sociocultural contexts and identities. It also inquires into their recollections of and reflections on past musical and pedagogical experiences. The data arises from four semi-structured interviews that I carried out with eight young musicians between the ages of seventeen and twenty-five in August and September 2009. Additional data emerges from observations made at subsequent events involving six out of the eight interviewees.

The fieldwork began by arranging interviews with four pairs of young musicians in the cities of Dublin, Galway, and Limerick, and in the east coast town of Drogheda. All of these pairs were made up of friends or siblings who regularly played together. Three of the interviews were followed by what could generally be described as a session, though not always in the exact sense as defined in *The Companion to Irish Traditional Music:*

> Session. A loose association of musicians who meet, generally, but not always, in a pub to play an unpredetermined selection, mainly of dance music, but sometimes with solo pieces such as slow airs or songs. There will be one or more "core" musicians, and others who are less regular. (Hamilton 1999: 345)

While the first three interviews took place in pubs immediately preceding sessions of one type or another, the fourth took place in the students' union office of a college of education. This last interview was followed shortly afterward by observations made at a series of fiddle lessons given by one of the participants. All eight interviewees gave consent for their names to be used in the account that follows.

JOHNNY AND DERMOT

The first interview was with Johnny (twenty-three) and Dermot (twenty-three) in the Skeff, a bar in a Galway city hotel where they would later perform with two other traditional musicians. This was in fact a paid gig attended mainly by hotel visitors and by other tourists. In spite of their holding university degrees, respectively, in civil engineering and in Irish language and history, Johnny and Dermot were working as professional musicians, largely though not exclusively with the touring ensemble Music at the Crossroads (which for marketing reasons changed its name to Celtic Connections when performing for American audiences). While both were multi-instrumentalists capable of performing in a number of styles, their initial "musical pathways" (Finnegan 1989) were quite different. Dermot's first musical encounters were steeped in the traditional music of his family and his home county of Mayo. His main instrument was the *bodhrán* (played on the night in question), although he also played drum kit and other percussion, and was proficient on the mandolin and guitar and on "any stringed instrument with a fret." Johnny came from a musically active family in East Galway, with his initial instrumental education based in classical style. He played guitar for traditional music but was also a classically trained flautist and pianist. Whereas Dermot identified himself as "a traditional musician," Johnny simply described himself as "a musician." When asked whether they sang or not, both reported that they sang "a bit." In fact, Johnny did more than this on the night in question when the group took time out from the traditional sets (groups of instrumental dance tunes) and he performed a ballad penned by West Virginian musician and songwriter Tim O'Brien. Dermot expressed little interest in music teaching while Johnny had several students, mainly for classical flute and piano.

BRÍD AND NIAMH

My second interview was with fiddle players and sisters Bríd (twenty-five) and Niamh (twenty-four), and took place in Dolan's, a renowned music venue in Limerick. They were joined throughout the session by another young female musician on keyboard and during some of the earlier sets by their father on fiddle and tin whistle. The session drew a good crowd for the middle of the week, with locals and tourists in roughly equal number. Although the bar owners had covered the musicians' basic expenses for the night, Bríd and Niamh considered the event more in the way of an informal session, as something that they did primarily for enjoyment and for practice. They informed me that their fiddle-playing heritage went back several generations on their father's side, and that they had been "steeped" in local musical traditions from an early age. Niamh was one of the first graduates of the University of Limerick's BA program in traditional music and dance, and had since been a member of the highly successful and acclaimed traditional group Beoga (Irish word for "lively"). Bríd had completed a master's degree in traditional performance at the same university but was presently pursuing a career in occupational therapy. The sisters' musical activities differed in two other respects. While Bríd would occasionally sing in vocal arrangements, she did not readily identity herself as a singer. Niamh, meanwhile, considered herself as much a singer as a fiddle player (and I heard her sing a fine rendition of the traditional ballad "Paddy's Green Shamrock Shore" that night in Dolan's). Bríd was not particularly interested in teaching music, possibly owing to her busy life in social and health care, whereas Niamh reported that she *loved* teaching whenever she could between recording and touring. Both sisters expressed gratitude for, and a strong sense of identity in, their traditional music heritage; at the same time, there were places in the interview where they were keen not to confine the conversation to traditional music alone.

CIARA AND DEIRDRE

Coincidentally, my search for research participants led to another interview involving two sisters, this time in Dublin with Ciara (twenty), a bachelor of education student, and Deirdre (seventeen), who had just begun her last year of secondary (high) school. Ciara played fiddle and Deirdre played concertina and harp, the latter in both traditional and classical styles. Neither was comfortable in describing herself as a singer, although they reported that they would contribute to vocal harmonies from time to time. The interview took place in Ciara's college, and while it was not followed by a session or gig, I later got to hear Ciara play at a very "traditional" session at Club *Conradh na Gaeilge,* the principal social venue of the national Gaelic Language Association. Although that particular session involved no monetary exchange, both sisters reported regular part-time income from standing in or "subbing" at professional sessions or from playing at other social events. Deirdre and Ciara presented examples of the largely hidden network of young traditional musicians in Dublin. Similar to all the musicians described so far, they had the benefit of a home full of music, as their father was an accomplished *uileann* (elbow) pipes player. They were also at various stages involved in the musical and social activities club *na Píobairí Uilinne* ('The Pipers' Club), *Comhaltas Ceoltoirí Éireann* (Association of Musicians of Ireland), and *Ceoltoirí Cluain Tarbh* (a local music club). Ciara's part-time work extended to teaching traditional fiddle, and I later had the opportunity to observe her teaching young children and teenagers during evening classes held in a local primary school. Deirdre and Ciara were unequivocal in identifying themselves as traditional musicians.

STEPHEN AND SÍLE

My last interview took place in Sarsfield's bar in Drogheda, and involved Síle (twenty) and Stephen (twenty-one), both BA students who knew each other through attending the same university college, and who played music together on an informal basis. The interview was followed by a session (in the loosest sense of that term) at the nearby Carberry's pub given by a large amateur blues band where Síle played fiddle (she also performed sets of Irish traditional tunes from time to time along with some of the other musicians). Although he came along to socialize and listen, Stephen did not play that night, since he was a keyboard player who almost exclusively performed for Irish dance *feiseanna* (competitions and/or festivals). Stephen stood out from all the other young musicians that I interviewed in several respects. First, he had grown a love for music not through family influence, but rather through his first passion, Irish dancing, for which he had already won many national and international awards. Second, with virtually no prior instrumental background he took up keyboard at the age of sixteen, was entirely self-taught, and was now sought after as a professional keyboard accompanist for the numerous dance *feiseanna* taking place in Ireland and in Britain. Thus, he described himself as "a modern *feis* musician" rather than as a traditional musician. Meanwhile, Síle came from a family where if you didn't play an instrument you would be "quietly ostracized." Her instruments were violin-fiddle, drums, guitar, piano, "and others that I sort of mess around with," and she practiced in traditional, classical, and other music styles. Not surprisingly, then, Síle described herself as an all-around musician. Síle and Stephen also did not identify themselves as singers, although in a similar way to Bríd, Dermot, Ciara, and Deirdre, on further questioning Síle reported that she participated in arranging and performing group vocal harmonies. She had a steady part-time income from playing at parties and other social events and also taught traditional fiddle on a regular basis. Stephen did not teach.

PERFORMANCE PRACTICES

NETWORKS

The interviews with the eight young musicians revealed a wide range of opportunities to play with family and/or friends, in informal and formal contexts, and in amateur and professional capacities. The musical connection with family remained particularly strong in the cases of Dermot, Johnny, Bríd, Niamh, Ciara, Deirdre, and Síle insofar as they had parents and siblings with whom they continued to play. This suggests that while

Irish traditional music has in recent decades evolved "as a genuinely youth-oriented 'popular' music" (Smyth 2004: 9), family networks and identities retain their importance, not only in enculturation (Green 2001: 22–25), but also in ongoing amateur (by which I also mean unpaid) musical encounters. At the same time, it is noteworthy from the descriptions above that all of the musicians were at some level professionally occupied. Johnny and Dermot had been auditioned four years previously when the touring group Music at the Crossroads was established. Their engagement with this company not only offered opportunities to play and tour with other young musicians; it also involved training in stage presentation and audience interaction. But along with Niamh (full-time member of the band Beoga), this involvement in professional gigs and interaction with transnational audiences did not displace their love of participating in more low-key informal sessions (see O'Flynn 2009: 79–82). At the other end of the spectrum, Deirdre and Ciara, while playing for the odd paid gig, were primarily interested in the more "traditional" settings of traditional music.

Most of the interviewees had been involved in radio broadcasts and in CD recordings at some stage of their young careers. Dermot, Ciara, and Deirdre had been part of traditional ensembles that featured in the RTÉ radio show "Céilidh House." As a member of Beoga, Niamh had contributed to several CD recordings in the past few years, as had Johnny and Dermot with Celtic Crossroads. Stephen was in the process of creating an interactive CD of Irish dance music for teachers, and all the interviewees had at some stage contributed to CD recordings produced by other parties. This level of media-related activity among the interview group illustrates the wide range of production and distribution facilities available to young traditional musicians in Ireland.

PERFORMANCE STYLES

Half of the musicians interviewed displayed multi-instrumental capabilities. This may simply have been a coincidence, but when considered against similar observations made recently by Waldron (2006) and Berrill (2008), it suggests that playing several instruments is not uncommon among young traditional musicians. Against this, just one of the musicians, Niamh, readily identified herself as a singer, in spite of the fact that most of the others also occasionally sang. This apparent downplaying of singing may have something to do with what has come to be regarded as the core repertoire of Irish traditional music, namely instrumental dance tunes, and this is perhaps one of the most significant differences between contemporary traditional music and contemporary popular music, insofar as it is the sung text that is central to the latter (Middleton 1990). But it also raises questions as to why Irish song traditions do not appear to have interacted with contemporary youth culture to the same extent that instrumental practices have over the past decades (Ó Laoire 2005).

While all of the eight musicians practiced traditional music, there were considerable differences when it came to the influence of other music styles. Ciara played only in what might be called "pure" traditional style although, as we shall see below, she was not averse to adapting classical teaching methods in her own lessons. Her sister Deirdre, primarily a traditional musician, had recently taken up formal lessons in "classical" Irish harp, but consciously kept it "separate from my traditional playing." Johnny distinguished traditional guitar from playing rock and folk, not only in terms of the DADGAD "Celtic" tuning (see Smith 2003), but also in terms of "a different mindset." Dermot was very interested in all forms of percussion playing, including "old style" (on the beat) and "new style" (syncopated) bodhrán playing, samba, and North African drumming. In earlier years he had learned to play drum kit for céilidh bands (groups of traditional musicians who play for communal dancing), which for me was a fascinating insight insofar as I had never before considered "traditional" adaptations of drum kit playing. Bríd and Niamh were also classically trained violinists, and both appreciated how one style could inform the other. As Niamh put it: "It's great to be able to apply them both to what you play, because music is music." At the same time, both sisters, particularly Bríd, left me with the impression that they felt most comfortable when playing in traditional style: "It's much more organic, it's much more embodied when you're playing Irish [traditional] music."

Síle didn't make as much of a distinction between the different styles she played, even though she identified her technique, including that used for traditional music, as classically trained. It seemed to me that Síle never quite conformed to the conventions of either classical music or traditional music. She rebelled against what she considered to be an overemphasis on technique while studying violin at the Royal Irish Academy of Music in

Dublin, whereas her style of fiddle playing perplexed adjudicators when she first began playing at traditional music *fleadhanna* (competitions/festivals): "my style was always a bit . . . odd." Indeed, Síle touched on something here that came through in all of the interviews, namely that individual background and experiences were considered to be more formative than any "received" style, regional or otherwise. Neither Ciara nor Deirdre considered her style to be of any one place, mainly because traditional playing in Dublin tends to absorb elements from all regions of Ireland. Interestingly, though, Deirdre reported that her concertina playing was thought by others to be in "piping style," referring to the chords she played, which sounded like those produced on the regulator of the *uileann* pipes; and this she put down to learning tunes from her father and from regular attendance at the Pipers' Club in Dublin. Johnny (guitar), Dermot (*bodhrán*), and Stephen (keyboard) all played "modern" traditional instruments that have been added relatively recently to traditional ensembles. For these musicians, the development of individual style was mostly based on interaction with other musicians from all over Ireland and beyond (as opposed to local influences). But to some extent, this was also the experience of Bríd and Niamh who originally emerged from a rich fiddle-playing background. Bríd's postgraduate studies at the University of Limerick brought her into contact with traditional styles of fiddle playing from other Celtic regions, while Niamh's undergraduate traditional music studies and subsequent full-time career with Beoga had led to myriad stylistic influences.

IMPROVISING, ARRANGING, AND COMPOSING

Some of the more conservative aspects of traditional music style (and I use the word "conservative" in reference to a relatively fixed repertoire of tunes) came through when I asked about improvising, arranging, and composing. There was much reticence when it came to the word "improvisation" among fiddle players Bríd, Ciara, and Deirdre. And certainly, their preferred term of "tune variation" was more in accord with conventional practices and with the discourse of traditional music. Beoga member Niamh considered improvisation rather differently, however:

> Yeah! I like to spiral out of control, I'd have no problem doing it . . . just to keep me interested. Yeah, I love it all!

Involvement in arranging depended very much on what kind of traditional music was played. Those who had a preference for "right on" traditional music, that is to say, for heterophonic or single melodic style, were not involved in arranging; those involved in more "modern" ensembles, which were generally larger and included accompaniment and percussion textures, invariably were, suggesting that the latter variant was more likely to lead to shared arranging in the way practiced by many young popular bands (see Green 2001/02: 43–44). Johnny and Dermot both affirmed that they practiced in improvisation and arrangement, although they pointed out that many of the arrangements for the Celtic Connections tour would have been prearranged. In a different vein, Stephen was particularly interested in the new possibilities opened up for *feis* (Irish dance) musicians, as the traditional combination of piano and accordion was gradually giving way to keyboard and accordion, allowing for melodic doubling and for variations in timbre and texture. He did not consider tune variation to be an option, though, insofar as it would likely put the dance competitors off their rehearsed moves!

Niamh was the only person interviewed who was regularly engaged in composing songs and tunes. Dermot had only recently begun to experiment with songwriting; Ciara and Síle had both dabbled in composing original fiddle tunes, though not in any consistent way. While it could be said, then, that there was a relatively low level of activity in original composition, none of the interviewees were averse to my question concerning the composition of "traditional" tunes and songs (see Dowling 1999).

TRANSMISSION AND EDUCATION

INFLUENCES

In most cases, family influence was the most critical factor in the early years of traditional music enculturation. Family influence also overlapped with community activities to a great extent, as the young musicians became involved in local traditional music clubs and in national music festivals. Dermot presented the following example:

> My dad ran the local branch of *Comhaltas,* so there was always sessions and stuff going on around the place . . . and North Connaught

is really good, especially during the summer, for smaller festivals. You could hop in the car and go off for the weekend and, you know, ten miles down the road there'd be a load of musicians come from all over the place. So it was kind of good like that, there was always something going on.

Similar stories were recorded by Deirdre, Ciara, Niamh, Síle, and Bríd. Johnny, who was initially immersed in classical music, came later into traditional music through a friendship group, much in the way that many teenagers become involved in popular music:

> JOHNNY: It was only when I was about fourteen or fifteen that a friend of mine just kind of coerced me into learning trad [traditional] guitar and accompany them, and that kind of got me into it.

Stephen, as already noted, began his keyboard playing at an even later stage and was entirely self-taught. His "community" for the most part involved observing other keyboard or piano accordion players who accompanied at dance *feiseanna,* with musicians like Damien McKee and Liam Bradley (now both members of Beoga) providing his initial inspiration.

Looked at together, these snapshots suggest a strong link between musical influences and musical identities. In most cases, the initial love for traditional music was picked up at home, though other routes were available, as reported by both Johnny and Stephen. As young adult musicians, all of the interviewees could be said to have identified with more than one affinity group (Slobin 1993), and these included family, friendship groups, and both real and virtual music networks.

For most of those interviewed, statutory music education had minimal influence on their development as traditional musicians. Indeed, there was a general criticism of secondary school music in two major respects. First, it was felt that music teachers generally came from a classical music background and therefore had little understanding of traditional performers, though some teachers could recognize and utilize students' stylistic knowledge, as Ciara recalled:

> When it came to learning about traditional music, the teacher was always asking, like, us to tell the class about whatever aspect of it . . .

On the other hand, both Ciara and Deirdre were very appreciative of the many traditional music friendship groups that they enjoyed in their school (this unusual concentration of traditional musicians in a Dublin school had much to do with its special *gaelscoil*, or Irish-language status). Second, the curriculum content of secondary school music was considered to be somewhat dry and out of touch with performance. As Síle described:

> Like, I could tell you loads about Mícheál Ó Súilleabháin (contemporary composer/performer and academic) but it's not really a traditional music education. It's more like learning stuff off for an essay. It's not natural in any way.

Furthermore, Ciara and Deirdre thought it quite amusing that they could opt to perform traditional music for their Leaving Certificate music examination in front of examiners who they believed had little or no knowledge of the performing standard or style (see O'Flynn 2009: 53).

A general lack of connection between university music programs and the performance practices of traditional musicians was expressed by all, the most cited exceptions being courses offered at colleges in Limerick, Dublin, and Dundalk. Bríd presented the following recollection of her first year studying for a general arts degree in college:

> **BRÍD:** I did first year [music]. I didn't go to full degree because I felt quite a negative attitude . . . toward traditional art forms. I felt there was fair bit of looking down their nose at us that played Irish music, and I just don't think that's good enough, to be perfectly honest.

It is indeed regrettable that a student practicing in any music style should encounter such a "hidden curriculum" (Bernstein 1997) and I can't help wondering if Bríd's music lecturers were aware that she would also have been a competent classical musician. I should point out that there were some positive statements made in relation to the development of traditional music in third-level institutions over the past decade, but overall, it appeared that university music programs were generally regarded as irrelevant to the needs, aspirations, and identities of young traditional musicians. Of course, this perceived "mismatch" could also relate to young classical and popular musicians, as Pitts (2004: 134–135) has observed.

METHODS OF TEACHING AND LEARNING

Everyone I interviewed had learned music by ear, whether through group or one-to-one teaching, or by listening to recordings. While the phenomenon of independent listening to and imitating recordings among young popular musicians is by now well documented (Green 2001; 2008), a pattern to emerge from this study was how imitating recordings can be utilized at home (by parents) and during instrumental lessons (by teachers) when exposing young musicians to new tunes. This supplemented rather than replaced live imitation, as the following interview extract illustrates:

> NIAMH: Every Sunday, we'd put on a CD and we'd all sit down . . . we played together as a family an awful lot.
> JOHN: You learned from the CD at home?
> NIAMH: Yeah, or else he [Bríd and Niamh's father] would say, "Do you know this one?" and "Let's learn this one!"

Ciara, Deirdre, Dermot, and Síle all recounted similar experiences from their home environment.

Also of note was how the majority of interviewees had been exposed to "classical" methods of teaching and learning. Once again, this may have been coincidental, given the small sample size, but it worth noting that a similar pattern was observed in Berrill's recent study of young musicians in the East Galway area (2009). Bríd and Niamh had begun with the Suzuki method in early years, moved on to traditional lessons, and then resumed formal classical training. Niamh in fact now taught classical violin at the Limerick School of Music on an irregular basis. Those who had been exposed to "classical" methods were generally positive about their advantages in regard to literacy (see Keegan 1996), instrumental technique, and posture, and all of the interviewees favored one-to-one over group teaching. (This latter preference appears to be at odds with the general practice of group teaching organized at local branches of Comhaltas Ceoltoirí Éireann.) Although Ciara considered herself strictly a traditional musician, she appreciated the benefits of her classical-influenced fiddle lessons:

> The teacher I went to . . . he would have taught me . . . classical, like to hold it classically, classical scales and stuff like that. How to read music . . . but I didn't *do* classical music. But that was really helpful . . .

As noted earlier, I observed some of Ciara's lessons with children and young teenagers. In each lesson, learning by ear was the primary method used, and there was always a tune or two that was learned by close imitation and repetition. But in keeping with her own initial training, Ciara added some formal instructions on tuning and instrument holding, and handed out sheet music of the pieces *after* they had been played by ear. A similar teaching style for traditional fiddle was reported by Síle.

As with other music styles, internet learning and sharing is a rapidly growing phenomenon in the world of Irish traditional music (Waldron and Veblen 2008). Among the group interviewed, Niamh would have had the most public exposure as a member of Beoga, and she was herself a fan of learning tunes from the internet. Dermot and Johnny had some web exposure through their involvement with Celtic Crossroads, and Dermot also reported that a couple of videos of his *bodhrán* playing had been posted on YouTube. Síle and Stephen were very enthusiastic about YouTube (Síle: "I live in it!") for picking up new tunes, arrangements, and techniques. This virtual community was particularly important for Stephen as he was a totally self-taught musician.

There was much that surprised me while gathering and analyzing the data for this project. The major revelation was the extent and diversity of musical activity among this new generation of traditional musicians. Moreover, the interviews suggested a complex range of perspectives that serve to challenge reductionist assumptions about relations between traditional music, youth, and identity in Ireland.

Initial education in traditional music continues to be firmly rooted in family and in community. At the same time, there are other ways of becoming involved, as in the case of Stephen and Johnny. Young traditional musicians are likely to be exposed to learning and performing in more than one music style; there is also considerable variation within traditional music enculturation as there is a wide spectrum of cultural practice from conservative/"purist" to modern/"fusion." Whatever the formative influences may be, evolving contexts of transmission and social networking afford a wide range of choices—and identities—for the musicians involved. And these are exciting times for young traditional musicians. In addition to the musical and social benefits that were repeatedly articulated by each person I interviewed, it is also apparent that competency in traditional music can lead to opportunities for paid employment, whether on a part-time or full-time basis.

Against these "success" stories it should be borne in mind that access to education in traditional music is not the privilege of all young Irish people, and the joint recollections and perspectives of the interviewees clearly indicate a number of lacunae in current provision for secondary and tertiary music education. On a more positive note, they also highlight social networks and teaching and learning methods that could be adapted in more widespread curriculum development.

Acknowledgments

With many thanks to Johnny, Dermot, Bríd, Niamh, Ciara, Deirdre, Stephen, and Síle.

References

Bernstein, B. 1997. Class and Pedagogies: Visible and Invisible. In *Education, Culture, Economy, and Society,* ed. A. H. Halsey, H. Lauder, P. Brown, and A. Stuart Wells, 59–79. Oxford: Oxford University Press.

Berrill, M. 2009. Pathways to Performance: An Exploration of Musical Growth in the Sociocultural Environment of East Galway. Paper read at the Sixth International Symposium on the Sociology of Music Education. Limerick: Mary Immaculate College, University of Limerick.

Dowling, M. 1999. Composers and Composition. In *The Companion to Irish Traditional Music,* 81–82. Cork: Cork University Press.

Finnegan, R. 1989. *The Hidden Musicians: Music-Making in an English Town.* Cambridge: Cambridge University Press.

Green, L. 2001/02. *How Popular Musicians Learn: A Way Ahead For Music Education.* Aldershot, UK: Ashgate.

———. 2008. *Music, Informal Learning and the School: A New Classroom Pedagogy.* Aldershot, UK: Ashgate.

Hamilton, H. 1999. Session. In *The Companion to Irish Traditional Music,* 345–346. Cork: Cork University Press.

Keegan, N. 1996. Literacy as a Transmission Tool in Irish Traditional Music. In *Irish Musical Studies 4,* ed. P. Devine and H. White, 335–342. Dublin: Four Courts.

Middleton, R. 1990. *Studying Popular Music.* Milton Keynes: Open University Press.

O'Flynn, J. 2009. *The Irishness of Irish Music.* Aldershot, UK: Ashgate.

Ó Laoire, L. 2005. Music. In *The Cambridge Companion to Modern Irish Culture,* ed. Joe Cleary and Claire Connolly, 267–284. Cambridge: Cambridge University Press.

Pitts, S. 2005. *Valuing Musical Participation.* Aldershot, UK: Ashgate.

Smith, C. 2003. The Celtic Guitar: Crossing Cultural Boundaries in the Twentieth Century. In *The Cambridge Companion to the Guitar,* 33–43. Cambridge: Cambridge University Press.

Smyth, G. 2004. Ireland Unplugged: The Roots of Irish Folk/Trad. Con (Fusion). *Irish Studies Review* 12 (1): 87–97.

Waldron, J. 2006. Learning, Teaching and Transmission in the Lives of Two Irish Musicians: An Ethnographic Case Study. *International Journal of Community Music*, 4. At http://www.intljcm.com/articles/Volume%204/Waldron%20Files/Waldron.pdf (accessed 20 May 2010).

———, and K. Veblen. 2008. The Medium is the Message: Cyberspace, Community, and Music Learning in the Irish Traditional Music Virtual Community. *Journal of Music, Technology and Education* 1 (2/3): 99–111.

EIGHTEEN

Fostering a "Musical Say"

Identity, Expression, and Decision Making in a US School Ensemble

SHARON G. DAVIS

The emergence of a musical identity takes place not only through opportunities to listen to and perform music, but also through being involved in expressive decision making concerning a range of musical parameters. Giving children the opportunity to make expressive musical decisions in classroom projects was the impetus for this study, in which students worked together to generate meaning through arrangement, interpretation, and sight-reading. The instances of music-learning described here are drawn from a larger study (Davis 2008) in which I worked as a teacher-researcher to explore the music-learning processes of ten-year-old students in a fifth-grade beginning band class in a US public school. In this classroom, influenced by an earlier study of rock musicians (Davis 2005), I endeavored to foster a learning environment in which students could have a "musical say" in expressive musical decisions within the ensemble. A musical say includes opportunities to contribute in ensemble settings and the development of musical voice through ownership, agency, relevance, and personal expression—and the *investment* of these dynamic and fluid meanings in the ensemble process. As my students worked within this environment, band became more than a performance setting with the conductor at the helm. It became an opportunity for composing, arranging, and improvising through both formal and informal learning processes (Green 2002). Collaboration in small groups provided time for students to develop their ideas and processes for negotiating meaning through musical expression.

In the United States, beginning band programs are not mandatory, and a 2002 National Center for Educational Statistics survey found that only 48 percent of public elementary schools surveyed offered band. Even then, band is typically an elective class, offered to students in grade five or above and taught by a music specialist. The study shared here took place in a suburban elementary school of 370 students that offered beginning band to fifth-grade students. Because of the school district's rich band heritage, these students had been enculturated into the band traditions from their entry into school.

The band was comprised of students from two fifth-grade homeroom classes. Students from each class rehearsed separately, twice weekly (during the school day) for forty-five minutes, and then joined together as one ensemble for dress rehearsals and concerts. This chapter centers on events that occurred in one of those classes as the focus of a case study (Bogdan and Biklen 1998; Bresler and Stake 1992; Stake 1988).

As teacher-researcher I videotaped every rehearsal for six months and invited four students to serve as key informants (Bogdan and Biklen 1998; Bresler and Stake 1992) to capture multiple perspectives. Each informant wore a small microphone attached to a micro-recorder secured in a small waist pack, enabling freedom of movement while capturing all the students' instrumental playing and conversation throughout the rehearsal. I engaged in two semi-structured group interviews with the key informants and one group interview with their mothers. I also interviewed twenty members of the class grouped in instrumental sections. Additional data were collected through observations, reflective field notes, and e-mail correspondence, which served to provide context.

Through data analysis, musical identity emerged as an important theme, largely as a result of my own reflexive pedagogical shift. As I continued to work with the data, I gradually became aware that in my role as a seasoned practitioner, my awareness of my students' musical identities had lived at a subconscious level. Concert dates and the nature of ensemble rehearsals leave little time for the exploration of the identity of individual learners. However, musical identity is omnipresent and evident in these data, influenced by students' recognition of their own competence and achievement, fostered through my conscious desire, as teacher, to provide students with an expressive space—fertile ground for the enrichment of their musical identity and deeper awareness of self.

IDENTITY IN THE MAKING

Wenger (1998: 5) describes identity as one of the key components in learning and an integral part of a community of practice. Identity can be revealed through the ways we discuss "how learning changes who we are and creates personal histories of becoming in the context of our communities." In the community of the study band, students were self-reflective about their growth as musicians over the course of the year, recognizing that playing a band instrument had changed the way they listened to music. Many students commented about the growth in their ability to discriminate instrumental timbre on recordings, indicating that their listening choices had expanded to include a wider variety of music, including songs that featured their instrument. As John described, "You listen to more than just the melody; you listen to the whole picture," and Amy "learned how to *hear* the notes and how to figure them out on the piano and flute." They had become critical listeners, no longer focusing on just melody but recognizing harmony, timbre, and the inner dimensions of music, gravitating toward analysis.

In their process of becoming, they reflected with confidence on their abilities that strengthened their efficacy (Bandura 1997) toward playing music by ear, negotiating notational issues, and employing the necessary strategies, which included reliance on peers. "Before we had an instrument we used to listen to music; now we *play* music" described Tom's personal history of becoming. Engaging with and playing music was central to this growth experience, which focused on the themes of competence and achievement, as individuals and as an ensemble.

The mechanics of learning to play an instrument and read music are part and parcel of being a musician, but what held great meaning for some was the ability to *play music as accurately as possible*. This led to a feeling of achievement, as John described: "When you play well without making mistakes, you feel like you are contributing to the group." For Theo, the audience was the motivation for playing accurately, which gave him a sense of accomplishment. In articulating this process, Theo exposed his evolving identity as a musician.

Polkinghorne (1988: 150) describes identity as a temporal, socially constructed process, identifying narrative as the process through which we configure "personal events into a historical unity which includes not only what one has been but also anticipations of what one will be." Similarly, Wenger (1998: 155) explains identity as a *learning trajectory* and observes that understanding who we are is a result of "incorporat[ing] the past and the future in the very process of negotiating the present."

In *negotiating the present,* students described enjoyable elements of their band experience as "learning songs," "playing the instrument," "learning different notes"; but for Theo it was "listening to what you can actually play, like I never thought I would be good at trumpet." Theo had made steady progress and was one of the best trumpet players in the band, but as his narrative unfolded, he reflected upon his initial feelings of inadequacy and uncertainty about his potential for playing trumpet. He compared himself to those around him and to other musicians in the media and felt he would not reach their level of proficiency. Recognizing his own growth, Theo explained that he felt a sense of accomplishment if he played a song all the way through, "mostly by heart," without making mistakes, because then his audience would understand the music as he understood the music. It was the collective "sound" of the music, not just the notes or rhythms, but the *whole* that had to be expressed to the audience. Theo recognized his progress as a musician and felt "good" about his current abilities. He envisioned himself playing trumpet in high school, projecting a future and *anticipating* what he would be.

The interview process served as a vehicle for students to articulate their understanding of their experience and revealed achievement, competence, and the necessary strategies—all important revelations of their evolving musical identities.

EXPRESSIVE SPACE

Extant literature suggests that playing with expression takes time, musical understanding, and opportunity to experiment and rehearse (Sloboda 1994). Expressive playing requires the ability to weave emotional and intuitive awareness into technical ability (Broomhead 2006) with expressive skills learned through demonstration by musicians or teachers and through teacher feedback (Broomhead 2006; Sloboda 1985). Additionally, teachers must provide what Greene (1991) terms an "aesthetic space." Detaching from the commonplace experiences of life, art comes to be realized in this space, through repeated experiences in which students learn to qualitatively distinguish the properties that determine the art form. Perception plays a pivotal, dynamic function in comprehension, and the role of the teacher is to nurture that perception. "Aesthetic perception," writes Greene, involves the ability to focus and is a "mode of viewing that can only be *personally* undertaken, by an individual present to himself or herself" through an active awareness of "one's consciousness" (Greene 1991: 157).

As a teacher, one of my goals was to cultivate aesthetic space for my students through exploration, discussion, and investment. Learning to play expressively was a process woven into rehearsals from the early stages through engaging with repertoire and through arranging experiences in which students were encouraged to make musical decisions. Small group projects supported this endeavor; one such project involved the song "America." This song, more commonly known in the United States as "My Country, 'tis of Thee," is a popular patriotic piece whose melody is that of the English National anthem, "God Save the Queen." Its familiarity and suitable tonal range made it an ideal piece for the project.

ATTENTION TO TONE-COLOR AND EXPRESSION

To introduce "America," I passed out a unison score with time and key signatures indicated, but no expression marks. Over several rehearsals we discussed possible expressive ideas that could be incorporated into the piece with teacher demonstration used to elicit ideas. We generated a list of qualities that would make a piece of music memorable. Initially, the students' expressive ideas were limited, focused on basic dimensions of music (Wiggins 2009)—for example, simultaneity, correct rhythm and notes, timbral qualities. We then listened to Copland's "Fanfare for the Common Man," guided by a listening map. This compelling piece encapsulated pertinent musical qualities and had the potential to broaden their palette of choices. When the piece ended, they applauded with immediate respect for the music and recognition of its tone and affective qualities. We then revisited our list and added students' new ideas about dynamics, harmony, texture, and other ways to generate affective qualities, including the importance of tone-color, performed so beautifully in the listening example, which added new meaning for these young players. Students then formed small groups of like instruments to work on reconstructing their expressive ideas for the tune "America," with the understanding that we would reconvene and discuss ideas from each group before making collective decisions. While the results of each group experience played a part in the final product, I will focus here on the work of the saxophone section.

MEET THE PLAYERS

John, Mark, and Andy were friends in the saxophone section. They all attended the same church and lived near one another. John sang in the church choir and had the most prior instrumental experience, having studied guitar before saxophone. He had a good ear and was proud that he had read music "since he was in first grade." While his parents and brother had played other instruments, John chose saxophone because he thought it would be more of a "challenge." He identified himself as "the only musical one in the family."

Music was a rich part of Andy's life outside school. His siblings were also school band members, and singing and playing instruments together was an important part of family gatherings. Andy enjoying playing the saxophone and, after a few short weeks, had performed a favorite song he had figured out by ear at home. As a class, we had discussed his process and then applied it in a lesson to learn the same song, with Andy at the helm. Evident in this experience was Andy's strong sense of efficacy (Bandura 1997) about his abilities. Positive peer engagement in the subsequent lesson also contributed to his increasing sense of efficacy, and pedagogically provided a conduit for *a musical say* in the classroom.

McCormick and McPherson (2003: 48) say that performance "is arguably the most important image-forming component of an individual's identity as a musician," indicating that "students' perceptions of self-efficacy . . . play a major role in how they perform." Andy said he felt "proud" about his performance in class, which contributed to his strong sense of agency (Bruner 1996), but it was also his work ethic and process that informed his identity as a musician. Andy was annoyed by playing errors—his own and those made by others—and was therefore constantly evaluating progress and exploring remedies. Singing and humming were constant companions to his musical thinking, and he often answered my questions by singing or humming, captured by the audio-recorder he carried during the study. Playing musically and with expression was Andy's definition of a good musician and he worked toward that end.

Both John and Andy had a strong sense of efficacy about their playing, and they willingly mentored Mark, who had the least experience of the three and whose glaring errors created tension between Andy and Mark, particularly when it drew attention from "the girls" seated nearby.

Example 18.1

THE "AMERICA" PROJECT

While I was explaining the small group project, Andy was already working—looking at me but quietly humming the tune, emphasizing phrases dynamically and fingering silently. After my instructions, Andy immediately addressed Mark, an exuberant look on his face, declaring, "I already have an idea," gesturing and singing the tune incorporating dynamics (see example 18.1). Physical representation was common for Andy (and others) and served as a vehicle for musical thinking (Blair 2008). This process was an "intimate way to know" (Bamberger 1999: 50), sparking expressive musical ideas, and engraving an initial design of personal meaning for Andy. From their initial work together, both Andy and John oriented their ideas and musical thinking kinesthetically, exploring meaning individually, through their bodies with application to their instruments before embarking on discussion and subsequent implementation of the ideas together.

Mark was not always able to perform the agreed-upon expressive markings, which distressed Andy. Andy attempted to use evaluation and recapitalization as mediating tools, but Mark withdrew from the discussions, focusing instead on peripheral behaviors signaling his control. From my vantage point as teacher, the saxophone section seemed to be working well together and I observed a lot of talking, writing, and playing. However, when I listened to the recorded data, I realized that Mark had played a more marginal role in the work process.

Bruner (1996: 36) describes agency as a "goal-directed" activity that implies "skill or know-how." Drawing on Giddens (1979), Carspecken (1996: 128) posits that "all acts are acts of power" linked to the "concept of action." Both Andy and John entered the project with considerable agency about their vision of expression and ability to carry it out. Andy was willing to negotiate with John because he viewed him as a capable peer with similar ideas, but a power struggle occurred when Mark, a less capable player in Andy's eyes, endeavored to implement a conflicting idea. Carspecken (1996: 129) describes "interactive power relations" as occurring "when actors are differentiated in terms of who has most say in determining the course of an interaction and whose definition of the interactive setting holds sway." Mark's input was not respected or negotiated, and yet he was unwilling to be put in a subsidiary role. He positioned himself by demonstrating periphery behaviors and, when the teacher asked the group to perform, he signified his experience of non-participation (Wenger 1998) quietly stating that the ideas were "just Andy's and John's."

Example 18.2

LEARNING TO PLAY EXPRESSIVELY

Over several rehearsals, each group played and discussed its own expressive ideas before we amalgamated them into a collective plan. John was the main spokesperson for the saxophone section, assisted by Andy *and* Mark. Their rendering was much more detailed than those of the other groups (example 18.2). As these decisions were shared publicly, Mark acted as a player, confirming and clarifying John's explanation.

After making additions and edits to our collaborative plan, we performed and assessed our playing and the students wrote the plan into their individual scores.

MARK: But we have it [forte sign] at measure 2.

ANDY: No, it's at the third measure.

MARK: Yeah, there's already an F [*forte* sign] there.

ANDY: OK, it's gonna get gradually louder. That [*forte* sign] means suddenly loud.

MARK: So with the arrow [*crescendo* sign] it's gradually louder, without, it is suddenly loud?

ANDY: Yes.

The concept of *crescendo* had been part of their earlier conflict, but with Andy's help, Mark seemed to have a better understanding of this expressive marking.

This example makes explicit the social nature of learning (Vygotsky 1978) and the centrality of "scaffolding" as a mediational tool in the process (Bruner 1966; Wood, Bruner, and Ross 1976). Vygotsky (1978) identified this as the zone of proximal development (ZPD). Andy and Mark's collaboration is but one of many examples in which Andy provided assistance that enabled Mark's learning, which also contributed to the formation of his identity, an unconscious by-product of his engagement in action (Wenger 1998).

INVESTMENT

In their process of learning and making decisions about how to play "America," these students learned a great deal about expression; further, their attention to articulation improved considerably. Their experience with the Copland piece influenced and revealed their understanding of musical expression. The clarinet section attempted to copy the textural dimensions of the Fanfare by layering their entrances. The percussion section created original rhythm patterns, which were quickly embraced and later played a key role in creating an introductory section for the final arrangement.

Our final version of "America" (example 18.3) evolved over time, influenced through formal rehearsals and the crucial informal sessions together. The piece began with a drum roll followed by the full ensemble entering fanfare style. The main melody was repeated and, in our concert, the audience was invited to sing along the first time; the ensemble observed the fermatas in the final stanza.

Example 18.3

Folkestad (2005: 285) contends that "creative music making and musical identity are two sides of the same coin" in that making music furnishes a locale for which musical identity can be "explored and expressed." The negotiated process of arranging "America" provided an *aesthetic space* on two planes. First in small groups, students were free to explore their expressive ideas and play through their decisions, intensifying the creative process and enhancing meaning through negotiation. This fueled the second plane, which sensitized and empowered students to incorporate concepts such as harmony, improvisation, and ultimately, arranging. Students corporately invested and had *a musical say* in the process.

THE EMERGING SELF

Social interaction within schools exerts a significant role in the development of individuals and the construction of the self. Mead (1934: 155) described the self as a process, emerging through social interaction, with individuals taking on "the attitude of the generalized other" which becomes internally synthesized and manifested through discourse. Agency compels us to learn through social interaction with others, making agency and collaboration an integrated process (Bruner 1996). But skill, writes Bruner, "is the instrument of agency acquired through collaboration. Without skill we are powerless" (1996: 94).

The problem-solving experiences in this band classroom were a source of identity construction in which students engaged in both shared and opposing musical visions, drew upon the strengths of peers, expanded their musical understanding, and sharpened their skills. In a subsequent rehearsal in which students worked in sections to sight-read a new piece of music, John, Andy, Mark, and Jack took turns in leadership roles. John seemed to take the lead when they struggled with rhythm, Andy helped when there was a question about fingerings or note names, and both Mark and Jack evaluated progress and took the lead in pulling the group together to rehearse:

> **JACK:** We have to get a little further than this in the song.
> **MARK:** Let's play this song totally through. One, two, ready, go.
> **JOHN:** Measure 13 is where we are having trouble.
> [They all copy his model followed by short individual asynchronous sessions.]
> **MARK:** Let's start at measure 12.
> **JACK:** One, two, ready, go.

Mark was part of shaping this rehearsal process, and it appeared that his evolving musical identity had developed from his earlier work when his peers had dismissed his ideas. Although he was not as technically able as his peers, he was able to evaluate their progress, demonstrating his competence as valued member of the group. Mark's voice had become an active part of the rehearsals and decision-making processes of the class.

Wenger (1998: 56) notes that "a defining characteristic of participation is the possibility of developing an 'identity of participation,' that is, an identity constituted through relations of participation." While there were moments of tension in the working relationship among the three peers, Mark respected Andy's and John's musical abilities and drew upon their competence. Through musical interaction and dialogue, Mark developed increased agency in his position as a valued member of the section. Mark's suggestions and leadership became more collaborative through processes of "negotiation and compromise," as John mentioned in their interview. Drawing on Mead, Chen (2009: 3) submits that "identity is conceptualized as action as well as a situation in which social actors encounter and develop ways of solving problems in life." The problem-solving lessons shared here provided space for agency and collaboration to sift together the ingredients of identity.

Negotiation and compromise suggest respect and willingness to value one another's input. In our assessment of playing during the sight-reading experience, the students commented on their success and failures in the sectionals that were unassisted by the teacher. In his interview comments, Mark stated that being "friends" helped them work together. Mark's agency to contribute was a direct result of his having developed an "identity of participation" (Wenger 1998) constructed through the relationships of friendship strengthened by the potential of having a musical say.

Beginning band can often be fraught with logistics, rudiments, and foundational measures. These are important considerations in any initial experience but should not serve to cloud the aesthetic experience or crowd out experiences that make this awareness possible. Aesthetic perception, writes Dewey (1934: 195), is found in spaces where "we are carried out beyond ourselves to find ourselves." Working with the substance of expression informs and empowers musicianship, and authentic holistic musical experiences contributed to students' identity of becoming—a musical sense of self.

A salient theme of this study was the awareness that all students came to sectional rehearsals with strong ideas about expressive musical decisions, and my providing the space for them to work in this arena served to enable them to work in a more musical manner, but also birthed a greater creative product through the incorporation of their ideas. Students' ability to have a say in the formal setting of a school ensemble is agentive in nature if teachers foster active engagement and hand over decision-making experiences to the students. Understanding and implementing students' informal music-making processes served to nurture student investment in the classroom and provided opportunities for greater teacher "scaffolding." Additionally, evidence of individual growth in musical identity became more evident in situations where students acted as peer teachers in addition to their role as learners; an avenue for further research.

We have much more to learn about how to foster expressive knowing in beginning instrumentalists. There is room for more creative space in traditional band programs. At core, what is critical is that students are able to engage in processes of music-making, through creating music, performing music, and having a *say* in the expression and creation of music.

References

Bandura, A. 1997. *Self-Efficacy: The Exercise of Control.* New York: W. H. Freeman.

Bamberger, J. 1999. Learning from the Children We Teach. *Bulletin Council for Research in Music Education* 142: 48–74.

Blair, D. August, 2008. Do You Hear What I Hear? Musical Maps and Felt Pathways of Musical Understanding. *Visions of Research in Music Education,* at http://www-usr.rider.edu/~vrme.

Bogdan, R. C., and S. K. Biklen. 1998. *Foundations of Qualitative Research in Education.* 3rd ed. Boston: Allyn and Bacon.

Bresler, L., and R. E. Stake. 1992. Qualitative Research Methodology in Music Education. In *Handbook of Research on Music Teaching and Learning,* ed. R. Colwell, 75–90. Reston, Va.: MENC.

Broomhead, P. 2006. A Study of Instructional Strategies for Teaching Expressive Performance in the Choral Rehearsal. *Bulletin of the Council for Research in Music Education,* 167: 7–20.

Bruner, J. 1966. *Toward a Theory of Instruction.* Cambridge, Mass.: The Belknap Press of Harvard University Press.

———. 1996. *The Culture of Education.* Cambridge, Mass.: Harvard University Press.

Carspecken, P. F. 1996. *Critical Ethnography in Educational Research: A Theoretical and Practical Guide.* New York: Routledge.

Chen, R. 2009. *Early Childhood Identity: Construction, Culture, and the Self.* New York: Peter Lang.

Davis, S. G. 2005, December 8. That Thing You Do! Compositional Processes of a Rock Band. *International Journal of Education and the Arts* 6 (16). At http://ijea.asu.edu/v6n16 / (accessed 20 May 2010).

———. 2008. *Fostering a Musical Say: Enabling Meaning Making and Investment in a Band Class by Connecting to Students' Informal Music Learning Processes.* PhD diss., Oakland University, Rochester, Mich..

Dewey, J. 1934. *Art as Experience.* New York: Perigee Books.

Folkestad, G. 2005. Here, There and Everywhere: Music Education Research in a Globalised World. *Music Education Research* 7 (3): 279–287.

Green, L. 2001/02. *How Popular Musicians Learn: A Way Ahead for Music Education.* Aldershot, UK: Ashgate Press.

Greene, M. 1991. Aesthetic Literacy. In *Aesthetics and Arts Education,* ed. R. Smith and A. Simpson. Urbana and Chicago: University of Illinois Press.

McCormick, J., and G. E. McPherson. 2003. The Role of Self-Efficacy in a Musical Performance Examination: An Exploratory Structural Equation Analysis. *Psychology of Music* 31 (1): 37–51.

Mead, G. H. 1934. *Mind, Self and Society.* Chicago: University of Chicago Press.

Polkinghorne, D. E. 1988. *Narrative Knowing and the Human Sciences.* Albany, N.Y.: SUNY Press.

Sloboda, J. A. 1985. *The Musical Mind.* Oxford: Clarendon Press.

———. 1994. Is Everyone Musical? *The Psychologist* 7 (8): 349–354.

Stake, R.E. 1988. Reading Introduction: Analyzing the Case Study. In *Complementary Methods For Research in Education,* ed. R. M. Jaeger. Washington, DC: American Education Research Association.

Vygotsky, L. S. 1978. *Mind in Society: The Development of Higher Psychological Processes.* Ed. M. Cole, V. John-Steiner, S. Scribner, and E. Souberman. Cambridge, Mass.: Harvard University Press.

Wenger, E. 1998. *Communities of Practice: Learning, Meaning, and Identity.* Cambridge: Cambridge University Press.

Wiggins, J. 2009. *Teaching for Musical Understanding.* 2nd ed. Rochester, Mich.: Center for Applied Research in Musical Understanding.

Wood, D., J. Bruner, and G. Ross. 1976. The Role of Tutoring in Problem Solving. *Journal of Child Psychology and Psychiatry* 17: 89–100.

NINETEEN

Diversity, Identity, and Learning Styles among Students in a Brazilian University

HELOISA FEICHAS

One of the main characteristics of music-making in Brazilian society is that it encompasses a myriad of cultures, traditions, genres, and musical styles, which vary considerably from region to region. In addition to this rich historical legacy, the roles of music in contemporary society are being affected by rapid transformations occurring in the last few decades, particularly with the expansion of the music industry. However, the Brazilian education system has not addressed these changes with the same speed. In particular, the Brazilian School of Music is confined within a traditional system from a European heritage, based on the French conservatoire. Brazilian Schools of Music have been changing slowly, but not necessarily speedily enough to address the growing diversity of aspiring music students' backgrounds and educational needs.

Since the foundation of the first Music School in Brazil, the teaching model has valued the canons of Western classical music, and the acquisition of specific skills such as reading and writing in traditional notation has been a condition of musicianship. For many years, students wishing to pursue a music career at the university had to come "with a strong musical background, obtained in most cases in private schools, since there is no compulsory music education program in primary and secondary schools" (Hentschke and Souza 2004: 103). Entrance to Music School was conditional on passing a demanding exam in which the candidates had to demonstrate that they had a good basis in musical theory, sight-reading, and dictation, and a good level of performance when playing classical music on their instruments. Students with other interests and experiences had no chance of gaining entry because they could not fit into the traditional mold of the conservatoire system. As a result, it was almost impossible for students from alternative backgrounds to get a place at university (Hentschke and Souza 2004: 103).

Recently some changes have occurred due to government guidelines which implemented a huge process of curriculum reform at universities in Brazil. This introduced a process in which the curriculum has more optional courses and fewer compulsory ones. Moreover, the guidelines advocated that some changes should be made in the entrance exam in order to increase the number of students at universities in all subjects. Following this proposed flexibility in the curriculum and the changes to the entrance exam, the number of students looking for a degree at a Music School has been increasing, and it now includes students with experience in popular music. As a result, students in Brazilian higher education come from mixed backgrounds, and this means that they have learned music through different processes. Some students have been trained solely in a classical way, which implies that they have received formal training, whereas others have had experience of informal musical practices through popular music; and others come from a mixture of these backgrounds.

It follows from this that Music Schools have two challenges. The first concerns knowing how to cope with the profile of a student who comes from a background of popular music, since this includes differences in attitudes, values, beliefs, and behavior, as well as musical skills and knowledge, and different educational needs. The second is a consequence of the first and involves rethinking the objectives of the Music School so that they are in tune with the exigencies of life in the twenty-first century. Thus it is crucial to have a discussion about students' identities and to become aware of their views, conflicts, and expectations as well as the kinds of skills and knowledge used when learning music.

This chapter considers the musical identities of students in one Brazilian university Music School, taking into account three different types of background: those who have experienced only classical training, those who have acquired their skills and knowledge mostly through informal learning experiences, and those whose backgrounds contain a mixture of formal and informal learning. The different identities of classical and popular music students, and of those from both types of background, are examined in relation to their different sets of musical values, skills, and knowledge acquired through their formal and informal backgrounds. The musical identities of the students are related to their course choices at the university (either a bachelor's degree course or a music education course), since groups enrolled in different courses acquire particular identities related to the piano, singing, guitar, string, wind, conducting, composition, and music education. Finally, I will consider the role and influence of the Music School environment in shaping and changing students' musical identities.

The discussion is based on findings from a qualitative research study using an ethnographic approach. The research examined students' attitudes toward learning, which implied also understanding their values, beliefs, behavior and identities. The study dealt with 75 first-year students. Among those participants, 40 students were interviewed in detail, and these were divided according to their backgrounds as follows: 7 popular music students, 13 classical, 20 mixed (12 with more emphasis on popular music, and 8 with more emphasis on classical music). Questionnaires and observation were also used. In understanding students' attitudes toward learning at Music School, there is a need to reflect upon new perspectives and possibly offer ideas to change the current approach.

PROCESSES OF LEARNING AND STUDENTS' IDENTITIES

In order to understand the musical identities, values, beliefs, and attitudes of music students in a major Brazilian federal university, it is first necessary to examine their previous learning experiences in formal and informal modes. Then it will be possible to relate those experiences to their musical identities.

The formal mode is based on the values and conceptions of Western classical music, in which a kind of legitimized knowledge that is ready, *a priori*, for students to consume is transmitted through a trained teacher either in such institutions as the school, conservatoire, church, or privately (Green 2001/02). This was the way all the classical students interviewed

had learned. They displayed visual knowledge, since formal music education laid stress on reading and writing skills; they focused on the mastery
of instrumental technique, which led them to manifest an individualist
kind of behavior; moreover, they studied music in a way that separated
theory from practice, which means their theory class was disconnected
from their instrumental lesson. This was a tendency of the formal mode
of teaching music, in a way that compartmentalizes skills and knowledge
regardless of students' experiences. It is worth noticing that for most of
the classical students the process of learning and making music is totally
related to studying music. As they are used to a systematic way of acquiring musical knowledge, the way they make music is closely associated
with the Music Schools' concept.

What I found with popular music students was the opposite. They
possess what the education system has traditionally regarded as "low
status knowledge" (Young 1971: 37): in other words, their literacy skills
are relatively underdeveloped, since they acquired their musical skills
through aural knowledge and memory, playing and copying music by ear.
They also learned by reading chords in songbooks, thus acquiring some
harmonic understanding through a self-taught process, together with the
help of peers who are more experienced. They used creativity through
composing, making arrangements, and improvising; they learned with
peers, acquiring knowledge and skills in group; they did not tend to have
a systematic way of learning or a gradation of curriculum content; they
built their knowledge according to their needs and motivation, which
is associated with more enjoyment. The way they described their initial
process of making music, as well as those characteristics highlighted, has
similarities to the descriptions of Green (2001/02), Cohen (1991), and
Finnegan (1989). Hence, aural knowledge is the most important aspect
of the learning process in informal music.

Besides the classical and popular music students, some "mixed"
students, who had studied mainly formally but who had experience of
popular music as well, displayed characteristics from both formal and
informal modes. I refer to these as the "mixed-classical" group. In other
cases the opposite occurred: that is, students had experienced popular
music initially as informal learners, and then later studied music formally. I refer to these as the "mixed-popular" group. Their learning had
occurred by playing with peers in a band and then looking for a music

school in order to learn music theory. It also occurred when the individuals (having no previous musical learning experience) started the musical learning process through singing in a non-reading choir. Once they had learned how to follow music by ear, they then received some notions about music notation, which motivated them to look for private lessons or learn at a formal music school. Another example is when students started playing within their families in a very informal way, which led them to look for formal instruction later. Through the above means, it is common in Brazilian university music courses to find students with experience from both sides: the freedom of making music informally, followed by the realization that they needed to acquire certain skills, in particular reading and writing, from formal institutions. The mixed-popular group in particular seemed to keep a balance between the practices of both sides, while the mixed-classical group tended to give up some of their informal experiences in order to absorb the demands of classical learning.

GROUP IDENTITIES: RELATING STUDENTS' IDENTITIES WITH THEIR BACKGROUNDS

Nettl (1995: 55) explains that in the United States, "members of music school society identify and classify themselves and the components of their world in a number of ways." There is the concept of central and peripheral in many cases, which are aligned with types of music in the repertoire; Mozart versus Kurt Weil; piano versus guitar; playing music versus reading about music; and even bachelor's versus music education courses. Each of the larger groups of performing musicians had a reason for thinking of themselves as central or uppermost. Nettl (1995: 64) points out that there is a hierarchical structure, with struggles for hegemony between the instruments and instrumental families, such as between winds and strings, and the hegemony of the piano, which is considered the king of all instruments. The piano has for a long time been regarded as an instrument of status and has always been associated with high culture. The piano still occupies "pride of place" in Brazilian Music Schools, holding a glamorous status among the other instruments, and being a piano soloist is high up in the hierarchy of instrumentalist and singers.

PROFILES OF PIANISTS AND SINGERS:
FORMAL BACKGROUND

How this sort of self-identification works becomes clear in an examination of two groups of students from formal backgrounds, in relation to their main performance option: pianists and singers. Piano courses are generally considered to be much more traditional and demanding than other courses at the Music School. Several students mentioned that pianists do not display as much sense of freedom or versatility as other students. For example:

> GUITAR STUDENT: Piano students don't have as much spontaneity as they have a specific and rigid repertoire where they have to read strictly and cannot change anything.

In fact, while pianists develop reading skills as well as other technical issues, aural skills tend to be put aside. Nevertheless there is controversy about pianists' skills. On the one hand, there are students who believe that pianists have more harmonic and aural skills. On the other hand, some pianists interviewed displayed difficulties in harmonic perception, which is surprising given that the piano is a harmonic instrument. One explanation could be related to the stress in reading the notes rather than developing their ears. A pianist plays the chord because it is written, but with no awareness of the meaning of the chord in a harmonic progression.

Singers have similarities with pianists. In terms of skills, singers usually have difficulties in harmony and a lack of awareness, since they normally work with repetition and memory rather than analytical thinking. Both categories have an individualistic tendency. Singers, as soloists, tend to develop a superiority sense and lack of humility; pianists have a lonely attitude, which can be a consequence of the nature of the instrument.

> PIANO STUDENT: The pianist is alone, he plays on his own. He can make chamber music but is very lonely.

Students also mentioned arrogant and competitive attitudes, as well as the formation of cliques, especially with regard to the piano and singing groups. They were considered alienated from the rest, and were often labeled according to the name and status of their teachers. As expressed by one of the students:

CELLO STUDENT: There are many pianists who are alienated from the rest and they form cliques. If you study with Professor X everybody realizes who you are. This is very common with the piano group. It is also common within the singing group, but I've never heard anything similar with the other instruments. I believe that the piano is more traditional.

VOICE STUDENT: I think that pianists close ranks among themselves and form cliques.

PIANO STUDENT: I think that pianists in general are very competitive. When they stand out more than others, they think they are gods and the success goes to their heads, and they underrate other people. There are cliques and rivalry.

Kingsbury (1988: 42) views the clique as a type of social organization in the life of a music conservatoire, and as part of an "intense negotiating of the musical status of both students and teachers." He also points out the aspect of exclusiveness intrinsic to this kind of group.

PROFILE OF GUITAR PLAYERS:
INFORMAL BACKGROUND

Guitar students tended to come from informal backgrounds, and their profile was found to be very different from that of other instrumental groups. The opinions of all students about this group matched this generalization. Guitar players were seen by themselves and by other colleagues to be a bunch of extroverts, and this characteristic was associated with the world of popular music. They tend to have a good harmonic ear, are able to identify harmonic progressions well, and have no problem with rhythms.

FLUTE STUDENT: Guitar players are a very extroverted group, they are used to playing popular music, know harmony very well, and want to show their knowledge in the lectures.

On the other hand, in the words of one guitar student, "the guitar group finds sight-singing and dictation hard." Another said:

GUITAR STUDENT: The instrument determines the difficulty or strengthens the student. For flautists and violinists it is easy to perceive melodies. On the other hand, melodic instrument players have more difficulty in perceiving a sequence of chords. Guitar players, for their part, do it more easily.

Many of the students interviewed mentioned more or less the same characteristics concerning guitarists, which are as follows: guitar players are linked to popular music; they are more interesting and more open; guitar players are always playing in front of the school; they are always together, improvising, playing by ear, or exchanging ideas; they form an extensive group and exchange many things among themselves, playing together and confronting both classical and popular music with the same feelings. Perhaps the instrument helps and allows more flexibility. They have a tendency to work with arrangements that allow them to enter a huge job market. When they complete their course at the Music School, most of them get jobs with popular singers or bands.

PROFILE OF WIND, STRINGS, CONDUCTING, AND COMPOSITION STUDENTS: MIXED BACKGROUNDS

The other instrumental courses, such as those for wind and strings, work in a more homogeneous way. Their students tend to come to the Music School with mixed previous experiences. Their main ambition is to play in orchestras, especially the strings. The wind players also want to play in orchestras, but they have another side which is more connected with popular music, normally joining big bands or other popular ensembles. Thus they have more options in the labor market. The saxophone course is different from the rest: the students work equally well with popular and classical music. The instrument allows this approach because it has a very limited classical repertoire and has an important role in popular and jazz. The clarinet and double bass are also versatile, as well as the saxophone and guitar.

Conducting and composition students also tended to come from mixed backgrounds. In the conducting course there are many students seeking positions in choir conducting, especially the students from churches, since orchestras in Brazil are hard to win a place in. Each church has a choir, which is an important area for training new conductors. Thus it is a good option for students seeking jobs. The students in the composition course are totally different from other students. They are more engaged, aware, and active politically. They take part in the political side of the institution, organizing the students' union and fighting for their rights. Their presence is felt at the school, where they are organizing events and writing newspaper articles about the university.

DIFFERENCES BETWEEN BACHELOR AND MUSIC EDUCATION STUDENTS: FORMAL VS. INFORMAL

There are many differences between students in the bachelor's course and those in the music education course. As the focus is quite different in both courses, there will be certain characteristics for each group that define its identity. These characteristics were often stereotyped as strongly held beliefs, which to some extent were based on a distorted or even prejudicial view. For example, there is a general belief that students who enter the music education course have "less theoretical knowledge" and less talent or abilities as performers than those registered in the bachelor's composition or instrumental courses. To what extent these suppositions are backed up by evidence would take further study; however, here are a number of reasons for these differences dating from the recent past.

Until recently the entrance exam used to be quite explicitly "easier" for the music education course. Thus the students' skills in reading and writing were of a lower standard than students from the bachelor's courses. Additionally, they were asked to play pieces on their instruments that cannot be compared with the high level demanded from bachelor's candidates. Currently, following changes in the curriculum, the entrance exam is almost exactly the same, which means that all the students must show evidence of the same level of theoretical knowledge and skills. However, the weight of tradition extolling the greater demands and excellence of bachelor's courses still prevails, which means that, for the musical community, studying an instrument and doing the entrance exam in instrumental studies requires a "deeper musical knowledge" and "greater instrumental skill."

This is an example of the type of knowledge that the musical community considers "deeper" and "better," insofar as it makes clear that what counts as musical knowledge and as a strong musical basis is related to the technical sphere of the instrument, and to reading and writing skills. As music education students did not need to show a high level of instrumental technique or a high standard in theoretical subjects, they were always considered inferior. In other words, many people believed that they do not have enough talent, though this is not stated explicitly. The criteria employed to "measure" their musical knowledge were not based on their musicality in a broad sense, but rather on their being able to demonstrate good sight-singing and dictation, and to perform well the pieces from the required repertoire. Thus skills such as improvisation or playing by ear were overlooked.

Similarly, Roberts (1990) notes in his research in Canada that there are differences between music education students and performance students, and raises the issue of "talent" and how it is constructed. In my study, music education students listed the reasons they have chosen the music education stream rather than the performance stream as follows: their nerves are not strong enough; they do not want to practice as much as is needed; they really want to teach anyway; they are interested in a wider variety of musical activities; and so on.

It is possible to associate an informal background (popular music students) with a tendency to opt for the music education course, while those from a formal background (classical students) seek bachelor's/instrumental courses. According to the music-student community, there are some further clear, and interesting, distinctions between these groups: music education students are considered to be "free," to be more relaxed, and to have more diverse musical experiences through singing in choirs and playing in bands.

> GUITAR STUDENT: In the aural training class I notice that students doing Music Education are more open-minded. They try to make contacts with their peers and are not competitive or superior.

> CELLO STUDENT: People from music education come from a world that is totally different from those doing the bachelor's course. If you compare people from both courses, they have different mentalities.

The free and relaxed profile has to do with the fact that they do not spend their time practicing just one instrument as the bachelor's students have to do. They are more prepared to make up music, their creativity is released, and they are not so self-critical, as they feel less trapped; they have more open minds and try to make contact with their peers and are not competitive or superior; although they are not so good in reading and writing music, they are very hard workers, serious, and eager to learn. On the other hand classical students are considered to have good sight-reading skills, but to feel more imprisoned and tied to their scores; they are also known as having concrete aims related to playing their instruments well and prefer more practical and dynamic activities. They are very hard workers as they have to learn and practice a huge program of pieces for their instruments, chamber music, and orchestra practices.

The idea that "those who do not play are faux-musicians" was also found in Roberts's (1990) discussion of the position of inferiority faced by some music education students, and the superiority of performance to theoretical subjects. One of his findings regards a feeling among the bachelor's students that they are wasting time doing courses in the area of musicology and theory. More common was the notion that these academic courses about music actually interfered with the ability to concentrate on more important performing activities, and were seen as an intrusion into the time needed for valuable playing. Nettl (1995: 56) mentioned a similar prejudice among the musicians in his research. He states that "among the activities, performance is seen as central by the music school society, and there are those who perform and those who don't. The grouping and status are encapsulated by a frequently heard maxim: 'those who can, do; the rest teach [or write books]'" (1995: 56).

Within the musical community there are different profiles related to the students' choice of the music education rather than the bachelor's course. First there are students who really want to be music teachers, which means they are in the right place. However other cases occur: there is a type of student who thinks about getting money quickly with a degree in music education; and another type who knows a bit about an instrument, like the piano or guitar, and tries out the music education course because it is thought to be less "heavy" than the bachelor's. Although this group thinks it is an easier course, once inside the course they find it hard and demanding, especially the theoretical disciplines. Some students start with music education and when the course ends, switch to the bachelor's course, so that they can keep on either studying an instrument, composing, or conducting. There is also the type that drops out from the bachelor's course because they feel they cannot cope with the difficulties of the instrumental demands, and change to the music education course so they can get a degree in music. Students who have a low profile in the bachelor's course are often persuaded to change to music education, which will open up more opportunities in their professional life. This category of student is often found in the piano course, since the bachelor's piano course is designed to turn a pianist into a concert player.

In looking at the students' identities, it is important to understand that overall these characteristics do not concern people in an individual sense, but are part of the general *conception* of the group in which they are a part. If they wish to be part of that particular group, the students must act in accordance with the "rules," which represent the identity of the group. When they are out of the group they do not necessarily behave in the same way, and may of course profess different views.

The classical and popular students can crudely be viewed as opposites. They have their own identity in the same way that groups related to different instruments acquire particular identities. However, despite all the above, I found that the students recognize that they can benefit from living together. Most students believe it is possible to learn from each other, as each has strengths as well as weaknesses. Thus it is valuable and desirable to integrate characteristics of popular and classical music students within the Music School system. The challenge is how to put this into practice. The findings point to some conflicts, which can be related to the role and influence of the Music School environment in shaping and changing students' musical identities.

The teaching methods at the Music School tend to fit all the students into the same mold. The School has its accepted content and pattern of knowledge and the students must fit and adapt into this. As a result students tend to abandon their previous knowledge in order to grasp that of the School. Consequently it affects their identities. In the first place, the popular students run the risk of losing many qualities and feeling inferior; moreover, the system of knowledge legitimized by the Music School imposes a barrier that prohibits them from drawing on whatever they knew beforehand. It is difficult for those with informal experiences to make a connection between what they know already and what they are learning—in other words, to construct a bridge between their previous experience and the musical patterns of the Music School. In ignoring students' identities and previous backgrounds and trying to fit all into the same mold, the School will contribute to the reproduction of the same styles and thus perpetuate the traditional model.

However, a "pedagogy of integration" could be developed in which the teacher's role would be more as a facilitator. As many educators are arguing today, a music teacher is one who should mediate students' processes of learning, helping them to acquire knowledge and taking into account what they bring as their existing experience, rather than one who should dictate contents that are pre-established by the curriculum. A music teacher must enlarge students' views and experiences, allowing encounters with a broad range of musical styles and genres from different periods and cultures. This diversity will benefit students by presenting an open mind and relativistic perception of music rather than the absolute beliefs that certain music is superior to other kinds. Encouraging the creativity of students is crucial for their learning processes. Teachers should be able to take all the opportunities in a class for asking students to make music creatively by both improvising and composing, and also to develop the skills involved in group music-making. Assessment processes should involve students in an active way. Once they are assessed they should be informed about the criteria used. They should also be asked to assess themselves so that they can develop more awareness and responsibilities about their own processes, rather than waiting to receive a "paternal" judgment by teachers.

This would be an attempt to design a model that integrates formal and informal modes of learning, that ultimately represents an integration of classical and popular music students, or of students from both formal and informal backgrounds. In this way the diversity of students could be respected and their musical identities would change naturally as part of any learning process, rather than being either imposed or destroyed.

References

Cohen, S. 1991. *Rock Culture in Liverpool.* Oxford: Clarendon Press.
Finnegan, R. 1989. *The Hidden Musicians.* Cambridge: University Press.
Green, L. 2001/02. *How Popular Musicians Learn.* Aldershot, UK: Ashgate.
Hentschke, L., and Souza, J. 2004. Musicianship and Music Education in Brazil: a Brief Perspective. In *Musicianship in the 21st Century: Issues, Trends and Possibilities,* ed. Sam Leong. Sidney: Australian Music Centre.

Kingsbury, H. 1988. *Music, Talent and Performance.* Philadelphia: Temple University Press.

Nettl, B. 1995. *Heartland Excursions. Ethnomusicological Reflections on Schools of Music.* Urbana: University of Illinois Press.

Roberts, B. 1990. Social Construction of Talent by Canadian University Music Education Majors. *Canadian Journal of Research in Music Education* 32 (2): 62–73.

Young, M. F. D. 1971. An Approach to the Study of Curricula as Socially Organized Knowledge. In *Knowledge and Control: New Directions for the Sociology of Education,* ed. M. F. D. Young, 19–46. London: Collier-Macmillan.

TWENTY

SIMPhonic Island: Exploring Musical Identity and Learning in Virtual Space

SHERI E. JAFFURS

She's been working on a new composition combining digital loops and midi instruments in her music technology class and is anxious to perform it. After checking the settings she goes to the virtual theater, takes a seat at the virtual piano, and waits for the class to begin. Soon the avatar teacher and other avatar students appear. The performance will be broadcast so that later any other avatars who stop by the theater can listen. The instructor announces that the performance will begin and that a question/answer session will follow. Suddenly, music fills the room, the talking stops, and the avatars turn to face the stage.

The story above is from my field notes describing a student's experience in an online class that takes place in a virtual setting, SIMPhonic Island, http://simphonicisland.wordpress.com/, located in the Metaverse. The term Metaverse was first introduced in Stephenson's *Snow Crash* (1992: 24). I define the Metaverse as a virtual embodied world. Usually associated with gaming, this world allows players to access a website and experience a virtual three-dimensional space where they can interact with others. The students in the story were enrolled in an online high school music technology course I taught in the spring term of 2009. Students and I scheduled synchronous meetings, and after logging into the text-based program Second Life on their computers, we were transported to a three-dimensional virtual world for multiple users. The students had logged in from their homes and could listen, record, stream music, instant message, and talk via headsets and microphones as they maneuvered their virtual embodied representative, their avatar, on SIMPhonic Island. Students control their avatar's movements to walk, run, and even fly, meeting with other avatars to discuss creating their music, collaborating, and broadcasting. Second Life (SL) was launched in 2003 and is available for any user eighteen years of age or older. SIMPhonic Island is located on the Teen Grid of Second Life. The Teen Grid (TG) is an area in Second Life for any teen thirteen to seventeen years old. There are two types of Teen Grid–sponsored projects, public and private. Public projects are open to anyone age thirteen to seventeen who has created an account on the Teen Grid. These accounts are free. SIMPhonic Island, like many of the other education projects, is a private project. Information about the public Teen Grid can be found at http://teen.secondlife.com/.

The course, titled Music in Cyberspace, is offered to high school students in a Midwest school district in the United States. The term cyberspace is "conceptualized as a net, matrix, Metaverse and universally, as a place constructed out of information" (Jordan 1999: 26). The course's premier objective is to create a musical identity in a virtual world. The examination of garage musicians working in and out of informal and formal music venues led me to speculate as to how we form musical identities and the importance of venue. Discovering the many resources available to students outside the walls of the school revealed some of the nature of these venues. How the groups interacted with no one in charge and the connections they made between experiences in and out of school were important to their music development.

In my study of garage musicians (Jaffurs 2007), the participants credited their parents, school music teachers, and private music teachers as being a part of their success as musicians. Several of their parents, while not actively part of the rehearsals, were former garage musicians themselves; they purchased the equipment and owned the garage (their venue was actually a basement). Hargreaves and Marshall (2003: 263–274) stipulated that the extent of the control and the style and genre of music chosen are necessary for the creation of these contexts. An important characteristic of what could be described as a third arena of learning, or Hargreaves and

Marshall's (2003: 266) term, "third environment," is the "extra learning" that occurs outside of the formal venue. This extra learning is vital. It is self-motivated learning for learning's sake. Categorizing the differences between informal and formal venues on a continuum led the author to discover where these two may intersect and revealed an opportunity for a unique venue. What are the possibilities that a virtual venue, a place with no walls, offers? What could such a venue offer to music educators and their students? If the third environment, or borrowing from Heath, the "third learning environment" (2001: 10–17) is the venue outside of the school where extra learning occurs, then perhaps the virtual venue could be delineated within the third environment.

Underpinning the importance of venue for musicians is the idea that many young performers of popular music identify themselves as musicians, not as students learning to become musicians (Green 2001). Popular forms of music play a central role in the lifestyle of most teenagers, and indeed constitute a "'badge of identity' for many of them" (Tarrant, North, and Hargreaves 2001: 565–581). Understanding how we perceive musical identity may give us a deeper understanding of the many facets of musicians. Additionally, a course that encourages and fosters the development of a musical identity in a virtual simulation, not school simulation, for "out of school activities and roles" (Regelski 2004: 15) may be highly motivating. Many music educators may understand the importance of developing the musical skills and achievements necessary to be a musician but may not have thought about the broader perspective, the musical identity that each student defines for themselves.

CREATING SIMPHONIC ISLAND
AND MUSIC IN CYBERSPACE

After a series of presentations between the fall of 2007 and fall of 2008 on the opportunities a virtual online music technology course could offer high school students, I was granted financial support from the district to pursue the course offering. The application process and development of an island within Second Life involved an extensive application and development process. The complete education project had to be defined. Because the Teen Grid is for teens, any adult over the age of eighteen who would be working and mentoring the students in the project would be asked to submit cleared criminal background checks. In the fall of 2008, a virtual island on the Teen Grid of Second Life was purchased by a Midwest K–12 public school from Linden Labs. After submitting the application and subsequently receiving approval for the project, the virtual island on the Teen Grid was purchased and the pilot course was officially launched.

There were many things to do to prepare SIMPhonic Island for the student avatars. Although not your typical schoolhouse, the layout of the island had to be developed and actually "built." Building in Second Life is 3-D modeling. On its website, Second Life states that "highly flexible building tools allow manipulation of geometric primitives" (http://second life.com/whatis/building.php).

Based on recommendations from other educators working in Second Life, we contacted and hired a young virtual architect to design and build SIMPhonic Island. The island's design and construction took approximately six months. It included a virtual theater, coffee house, class building, forest, beach, boat dock, and a garage. The course Music in Cyberspace was open to any high school student in the entire district, and students could register and take the course for high school fine arts credit. The course objectives were stated as the following: to develop a musical identity in a virtual world and a personal goal for individual musicianship and technology skills. Moodle (http://moodle.org/), a free open source content management system (CMS), was contacted and a request for a work site was granted. Each Moodle site is a template with wikis, blogs, discussion boards, or forums that instructors and students can manipulate and design.

In the spring semester the island was ready for occupancy. The course was listed on the district webpage, and principals, counselors, and secondary music teachers were sent information about how students could register for the course. Five students enrolled in the ten-week course. Students who registered for Music in Cyberspace were asked to choose a name for their avatar. The district provided, on loan, a midi keyboard and headset and a secure password for access to the program. The students' avatars can access SIMPhonic Island, but no other island, in the Teen Grid. All of the students enrolled in the course used their home computers.

Describing an In World (virtual venue) experience can be complex, due to the fact that there are many layers of activities embedded in some of the statements. For example, the phrases "logging in" and "rezzing onto" SIMPhonic Island in Second Life signify that you turn on your computer and connect to the internet. Second Life is a web-based, not a stand-alone, program, and web-based programs require continual internet connection. Once you have a server available, you click open the program that you have previously downloaded and find the tabs to enter the first name, last name, and password of your avatar. Immediately the screen begins to change, shifting to display an area on SIMPhonic Island. A white cloud appears and a doll-like woman begins to take on a form. After a minute or two your avatar is standing on the island. Your avatar has just "rezzed" (just come online, from the verb "resurrected"). The narrative that follows describes a class session from the perspective of a student who logs onto SIMPhonic Island.

Using the mouse and the up and down arrows on the keyboard, my avatar can walk, run, sit down, turn around, and fly. The garage has a car on a lift and you can take it for a spin if you like, but it can be difficult to park and I always run into trees or campfires over by the beach and forest. There are different instruments hanging on the walls of the garage. I find a keyboard here, and put it in my avatar's inventory so it is a mere click away when I need it. Before anyone else arrives I usually change my appearance a little. I can make my avatar tall or short; change my clothes, my hair style and color, anything I would like. I then check the settings on my midi set-up and the connection to the stream that we use to broadcast on the island. I wonder if anyone else is here now for our meeting, and I click on the "communicate" button and notice that the instructor, Lucy, is on the island. Avatars can create groups with other avatars. We are members of the SIMPhonic Musicians group and can send and leave notes to each other about meetings and assignments. Lucy sends me a message that she is over at the theater so I fly over that way. From the air I notice that we have a new boat over by the beach that'll be fun to take for a ride. Once inside the theater, I join in the conversation about digitally altering our performances. I have some questions about streaming live and recorded streaming. I hope I can get some feedback from other students here today about the loops I added to my composition. After the session today, I have a softball practice, then I'm going to go back to SIMPhonic tonight and look for the notes Lucy said she'll leave about the next week's assignments.

This "netnographic" investigation was an online ethnographic study. A netnography "adapts the traditional, in-person ethnographic research techniques of anthropology" (Jupp 2006: 193) to the online computer-mediated venue. The study took place at the end of the pilot year for the Music in Cyberspace course. Three students, whose avatars were named respectively Fleet (age seventeen), Rain, and Trinity (both sixteen years old), accepted a request to participate in the study. These students gave permission for the author to use the avatar name they used when taking the course. Rain and Trinity attended the same high school, and Fleet attended another high school in the same district. Each participant and their parents signed consent and assent forms granting permission for participation in the study. I conducted the interviews online, appearing as a teacher-avatar whom I named Lucy Joles. Five questions pertaining to identity development were sent to the participants prior to the interview:

1. Describe your identity on SIMPhonic Island.
2. How is this identity different from your identity in real life?
3. How does the time it took you to develop your identity In World (the virtual venue) differ from that development in real life?
4. Describe your musical experiences on SIMPhonic Island.
5. How did your participation on SIMPhonic Island enable you to create a musical identity?

The questions were meant to start the students thinking about musical identity. The interview would be open-ended and focus on the perceptions the students had regarding their musical identity in the virtual world.

FLEET'S MUSICAL IDENTITY

Among all of the activities humans possess as means by which to create such a powerful sense of identity and community, music may be among the most personal and the most meaningful. (Herbert and Campbell 2000: 14–22)

The first interview took place on SIMPhonic Island with Fleet. Fleet improvised and composed for solo guitar and created a repertoire of music to perform. He was an accomplished guitarist and singer and knew a great deal about audio recording. He shared his knowledge with the other students in the course; they would often ask if he was available for advice about audio or other technical issues. Lucy (author and instructor) met Fleet in the theater area of SIMPhonic Island. The text below is from the instant messaging during the interview.

> LUCY: What do you think your musical identity is?
> FLEET: Define identity?
> LUCY: I'm going to ask you to lead me by your responses.
> FLEET: My musical identity is depending on my emotions at the point in time. It's a way to convey emotions, much stronger than anything else can. Music is what emotions sound like. So in a sense my music identity varies from day to day, but it's always a way to let go and see what things I can develop from ideas, concepts, and emotions in my brain into audible form that allows people to connect with me on a level not normally reached.

Fleet asks for a concrete definition for identity, but then goes on quite fluently to describe his musical identity as fluid. Gracyk (2004: 13) stated that adolescents' "search for a coherent self-understanding is a challenge because that self-understanding is no longer tied to concrete thinking." Fleet's comment is twofold; first he feels that his musical identity is in flux, changing day to day. Secondly, as O'Neill (in Macdonald, Hargreaves, and Meill 2002) points out, the older individual will focus more on the "psychological characteristics" and less on the physical characteristics.

> LUCY: So the most important "image" you'd like others to "hear" from you, that defines Fleet or your real life identity, is your emotion and the connection it has to your music?
> FLEET: And establishing that same connection to other people.
> LUCY: Helping them understand it?
> FLEET: Kind of, just more connecting to that same emotion.
> LUCY: How do you know this happens?
> FLEET: I assume that people listen to music a lot of the time because they can connect to it. That's why people listen to the music they do. And that's what I do. I assume others are similar.
> LUCY: You've mentioned many times that your best music is what you do in a live performance. Is there a connection between this and your desire to connect with listeners through the emotions elicited from your music?

> FLEET: I guess it's sort of more pure, uncut, and what music is in its natural form, not over-processed but it develops a deeper connection. I think some of that is lost in the translation of the recording process; that being said, recording still definitely has its place and time.

DeNora (in Bennett, Shank, and Toynbee 2006: 145) refers to the process of "finding the me in music" as visible through the personal decisions and ways we create and listen to music. Fleet is sensitive to music's power to evoke feeling but also understands it as a vessel for his own emotions. Fleet places value on the music he is creating; his passion shines through his statements (Green 2008). In addition, his statements demonstrate an observation about the way children develop their identity (O'Neill 2002). Young children look to objective views of what they do, what instruments they play, music classes they take. Older children tend to look inward and become more reflective about themselves and the views of others around them.

RAIN'S AND TRINITY'S MUSICAL IDENTITIES

Rain and Trinity attend the same school and know each other. They both studied classical piano and are accomplished pianists. They were interviewed at the same time at their request. When Lucy arrived on SIM-Phonic for the interview, they had created an area with seating so that the three avatars could sit down in "cushiony" chairs, with a rug, coffee table, and even a plant. So, virtually, the three sat down, got comfortable, and discussed identity.

> TRINITY: I think that it [musical identity] is what you feel like about music, what kind of music you like. I would say that I don't really have a defined style. I like a mixture of different music styles. I do find myself preferring lyrical music pieces to fast and happy ones. Later on I got the opportunity to play more modern pieces, and that really allowed me to enjoy playing and to start finding out what music I liked.
> LUCY: So you discovered music that touched you in a different way than what you'd been studying with your teacher?
> TRINITY: I was able to better relate to it because I had heard it before and could associate it with a movie and emotions.
> LUCY: How does your music play a role in your identity?

TRINITY: Well, even playing the piano is something that I feel separates me from many people. So I feel that it gives me some individuality, and just playing the piano makes me who I am.

LUCY: Is expressing emotion the most difficult thing in terms of your musicianship?

TRINITY: I like to understand it almost analyze it . . . I want to make other people feel the same way as I do about the piece . . . especially when I am playing it on the piano.

LUCY: Why is that important to you?

RAIN: You can express how you feel and get people to understand.

TRINITY: I like to really bond with whatever I am playing or listening to. I think that music can teach people so much, it is so great for expressing emotions and really coming in contact with what you believe. I would love to be the one who makes people think about what music means to them, to be able to use music to help people find their real emotions.

Trinity's and Rain's understanding of musical identity was similar to Fleet's concepts of self-identity. However, if musical identity was on a continuum as a single, objective idea on one end and a fluid, always changing subjective idea on the other, Trinity's and Rain's responses would be more of an objective view. They want to be identified by the instruments they play, the style and genre of music they enjoy and compose, and overall as musicians. They enjoy the expressive nature of the "modern" (popular) music and define themselves as unique in comparison to many others who do not possess musical skills.

LUCY: Discuss identity in relation to SIMPhonic Island?

RAIN: OK, we created our avatars.

TRINITY: We created our avatars and gave them distinct features thus making them individuals, and then creating music and expressing ourselves helped us to further create our identity.

RAIN: Your individuality as time goes by becomes your identity.

A VIRTUAL IDENTITY

All three participants in this study had a great deal to say about the virtual venue for creating a musical identity. There was contradiction between the world as embodied and real, and yet, a feeling that there was some barrier between the real person and their online presence.

> LUCY: Do you see any differences between the ability to develop a musical identity in a virtual world as opposed to a real world experience?
>
> TRINITY: We based our music around what our avatars, what we liked, so their individuality turned into their musical identity.
>
> RAIN: You have more opportunities in a virtual world.
>
> TRINITY: u not only have more technology to make music but it is also much more comforting to know that you are in the cyberspace and not in real world. It gave me a sense of security and that security allowed me to open myself up and really create music that I liked and to not hold anything back.
>
> LUCY: What holds you back from doing that in real life (RL)?
>
> RAIN: There is more pressure from the surroundings, and you don't have as much time as you need.
>
> TRINITY: and even just the stress of performing, and I don't like people to see my work while it is in progress.
>
> RAIN: If you are in your home it's much easier.
>
> Trinity: and being able to put on those headphones and hear only you made it much more comforting to me.
>
> LUCY: you felt less performance anxiety
>
> TRINITY: yes
>
> RAIN: yep!
>
> LUCY: Would you feel more inclined to perform in RL now that you have in SL (Second Life)?
>
> RAIN: I love to perform but I don't think so.
>
> TRINITY: I love performing in RL even though it is very stressful, and I on the contrary do think that it would make me more inclined to perform in RL.
>
> TRINITY: On SIMPhonic Island, my goal for my identity was to make it as close to what I am like in RL as possible. To make it seem like all the experiences that my avatar was experiencing . . . I think these experiences were quite realistic, because you get to interact with other people. I mean the fact that you fly is not realistic but it just makes it more interesting.

Fleet's focus was similar, but even more specific to the potential of a level playing field that a virtual world offers.

> **LUCY:** What about the virtual world we've created here. Did you find it useful for a musical identity?
>
> **FLEET:** In Second Life a person could develop an entirely different identity or person than they could be in real life. For people from everywhere to come and appreciate music for what it is, without labels or preconceived perceptions of what and who the performer is, and if there is indeed perceptions of who they are, it is up to the performer to decide how they want to identify themselves to people. People are too scared of what people think of them, and being judged by people they can't escape from, so a lot of people are not at all who they seem to appear as in RL as they are in SL.
>
> **LUCY:** SL can help us reach others all over the world. We refer to this as a democratic teaching environment. I agree that it helps us to study and learn in a venue where the playing field is leveled. Do you think that the identity you created on SIMPhonic helped you personally?
>
> **FLEET:** The identity in SIMPhonic is still me, just with a different outer image, I never want to pretend to be something I'm not.
>
> **LUCY:** What does the virtual venue provide for you?
>
> **FLEET:** An outlet for a wider range of audience, and an extended potential fan base than if you were stuck playing a coffeehouse in your own community. Do whatever you want, don't limit yourself in any way.

And though we transgress the physical as we have known it, we do not eliminate our bodies from cyberspace but reinvent them. (Jordan 1999: 2)

Lysloff (in Lysloff and Gay 2003: 395) described the internet as a "deserted metropolis where I find traces of life everywhere, but no people, no living bodies." With Web 2.0 and the ability to create content, internet ghost towns disappeared and the Metaverse was born and continues to grow. However, as with any teaching and learning venue, there are positive and negative impacts. Many find the virtual world totally immersive, drawing you back time and time again. However, there are those who do not find it compelling and are turned away by what they may believe to be a hidden compliance. SIMPhonic Island is still unchartered, and virtual venues like it should be investigated further. Turkle (2009) suggests that we remain open but always with a critical eye. It is easy to veer away from the focus of this learning venue, musical study, and become immersed in the simulation. Like a shiny toy, some may put it away before the task is completed.

Questioning how a musical identity is created in a virtual world, and why we teach music in a virtual world may improve our understanding of music education. Turkle (2009: 40) asks what it is that simulations want and concludes that simulations do not want to "replace the real but to reveal it." While not the primary focus of this chapter, the relevance of an online virtual world probably crossed the mind of many readers. I have heard more than once that music performance is lost in an online course. My endeavor here was to reach as far into the virtual world as I could to enable students to perform and potentially connect across the globe. Why couldn't a group of musicians gig together in the Metaverse? It has some complications, but if we can fly over to a theater for a performance created by students anywhere in the world, then as Fleet said, "do whatever you want, don't limit yourself in any way."

This study also suggested that the context of a virtual world may break down the perception of "our music" and "their music." Trinity mentioned that once she was allowed to play "modern music" she could "enjoy playing and to start finding out what music I liked." Discourses such as this may help us construct our identity. Music teachers may benefit from similar conversations with their students.

I concluded in a prior study (Jaffurs 2007) that going to the homes of my students, getting to know their families and pets, was a powerful way to create meaning and connections. I wondered how this would ever be possible. We can do this virtually and learn with our students individually and in groups in new and creative ways, as we may never have done before. I met with two of the students in this study one time and never met in person the third, yet I have learned a great deal about their musical identities and practices, and with no preconceived labels or preconceived perceptions of what and who the performer was before he or she rezzed into the garage on SIMPhonic Island.

References

SIMPhonic [cited 8/25/2009 2009]. Available at http://simphonic.socialminds.co.uk (accessed 23 May 2010).

Bennett, A., B. Shank, and J. Toynbee. 2006. *The Popular Music Studies Reader.* New York: Routledge.

Gracyk, T. 2004. Does Everyone Have a Musical Identity? Reflections on Musical Identities. *Action, Criticism, and Theory for Music Education* 3 (1). At http://act.maydaygroup .org/articles/Gracyk3_1.pdf (accessed 23 May 2010).

Green, L. 2008. *Music, Informal Learning and the School: A New Classroom Pedagogy.* Aldershot, UK: Ashgate.

———. 2001/02. *How Popular Musicians Learn: A Way Ahead for Music Education.* Aldershot, UK: Ashgate.

Hargreaves, D. J., and N. A. Marshall. 2003. Developing Identities in Music Education. *Music Education Research* 5 (11): 263–274.

Heath, S. B. 2001. Three's Not a Crowd: Plans, Roles, and Focus in the Arts. *Educational Researcher* 30 (7): 10–17.

Herbert, D. G., and P. Shehan-Campbell. 2000. Rock Music in American Schools: Positions and Practices Since the 1960s. *International Journal of Music Education* 36: 14–22.

Jaffurs, S. E. 2007. Lessons from a Garage Band: Informal Venues for Music Making. PhD diss, Michigan State University.

Jordan, T. 1999. Cyberpower: The Culture and Politics of Cyberspace and the Internet. In *The Culture and Politics of Cyberspace and the Internet.* New York: Routledge.

Jupp, V. 2006. *The Sage Dictionary of Social Research Method.* Thousand Oaks, Calif.: Sage Publications.

Lysloff, R. and L. Gay, eds. 2003. *Music and Technoculture.* Middletown, Conn.: Wesleyan University Press.

Macdonald, R., D. J. Hargreaves, and D. Meill, eds. 2002. *Musical Identities.* Oxford: Oxford University Press.

Regelski, T. 2004. *Teaching General Music in Grades 4–8.* New York: Oxford University Press.

Tarrant, M., A. North, and D. J. Hargreaves. 2001. Social Categorization, Self-Esteem, and the Estimated Musical Preferences of Male Adolescents'. In *Journal of Social Psychology* 141 (5): 565–581.

Turkle, S. 2009. *Simulation and its Discontents.* Cambridge, Mass.: MIT Press.

Contributors

John Baily is Emeritus Professor of Ethnomusicology and Head of the Afghanistan Music Unit at Goldsmiths College, University of London. His research has focused mainly on the music of Afghanistan, though he has also carried out extensive research with the Gujarati Muslim Khalifa Jamat in the UK, with fieldwork in Bradford, Leicester, and Nuneaton. He is currently working on a monograph titled *War, Exile, and the Global Circulation of Afghanistan's Music.*

Charles Byrne is Senior Lecturer in the Faculty of Education, University of Strathclyde, Scotland. He has published articles in the *British Journal of Music Education,* the *International Journal of Music Education, Psychology of Music,* and *Music Education Research,* and chapters in a number of edited books. With Mark Sheridan, he has authored articles on Gaelic music and the oral tradition of Scotland's music and culture.

Sharon G. Davis is Adjunct-Lecturer in Music Education at Oakland University in Rochester, Michigan, and a general music teacher at Cool Spring Elementary School in Leesburg, Virginia. She has published in the *International Journal of Education and the Arts* and *Research Studies in Music Education* and recently authored a chapter on instrumental learning and performance in the elementary school for the forthcoming *Oxford Handbook of Music Education.*

Zoe Dionyssiou is Lecturer in Music Education at the Department of Music, Ionian University, based in Corfu. Her research focuses on Greek music education, especially the teaching of Greek folk music; globalization and its effects on music education; problems and profiles of future music teachers during their teaching practice as university students; cross-disciplinary music curriculum issues; and the integration of poetry, movement, and the arts in the music education curriculum.

Peter Dunbar-Hall teaches in the Music Education Unit of the University of Sydney Conservatorium of Music in Australia. He performs regularly as a member of the Sydney-based Balinese gamelan, *Sekaa Gong Tirta Sinar.* Among his publications are the books *Deadly Sounds, Deadly Places: Contemporary Aboriginal Music in Australia* and *Strella Wislon: The Career of an Australian Singer,* and a DVD documentary on Balinese shadow puppet theater, *Di depan dan di belakang kelir* (*Before and Behind the Screen*).

Robert Faulkner is Assistant Professor of Music at the University of Western Australia, where he is presently engaged in an Australian Research Council project with Gary McPherson and Jane Davidson titled *Music in Our Lives*— a longitudinal study of young people's musical experiences from primary school to adulthood. Previously, he lived for more than twenty years in Iceland and worked in music education and community music.

Heloisa Feichas is a lecturer in the School of Music of the Federal University of Minas Gerais, Brazil. She has worked in cooperation with the Music School of Pitea, Lulea University, Sweden (Boomtown Project), and with the Connect Project, Guildhall School of Music and Drama, London. For nearly twenty years, Feichas has taught children, adolescents, and undergraduate students in Brazil, exploring new teaching methods in which creativity, improvisation, and popular music are key words.

Eva Georgii-Hemming is Associate Professor at the School of Music, Theater, and Art, Örebro University, Sweden. Recent publications include articles in the journals *British Journal of Music Education, Research Studies in Music Education, Music Education Research,* and *Nordic Research in Music Education.* Her research interests include investigating the concepts of knowledge and narrative; the value and role of music in education, as well as in people's lives outside education; and the relationship between theory and practice in music education.

Lucy Green is Professor of Music Education at the London University Institute of Education, UK. She has lectured around the world and serves on the editorial boards of a number of journals, including *Music Education Research, Radical Musicology, Popular Music,* the *British Journal of Music Education,* and *Research Studies in Music Education.* She is author of *Music on Deaf Ears* (1988/2008), *Music, Gender, Education* (1997), *How Popular Musicians Learn* (2001/02), and *Music, Informal Learning and the School: A New Classroom Pedagogy* (2008), as well as numerous articles and book chapters.

Sophie Grimmer has worked as a soloist in the UK and abroad, performing lead roles in opera (English National Opera) and theater (Royal National Theatre) under directors such as Sir Peter Hall, Simon McBurney, and David Freeman. In concert she has performed premieres with many ensembles, including the Brodsky Quartet. Sophie also works extensively in music education, as Vocal Professor (Trinity College of Music, London); creative director/workshop leader for music education projects (London Sinfonietta, Glyndebourne, Spitalfields Festival); and is presently completing an Arts and Humanities Research Council–funded PhD at the Institute of Education, London, examining the development of skill for solo vocal performance in the classical Karnatic tradition of South India.

Susan Harrop-Allin lectures in the Wits Schools of Arts and the School of Education at the University of the Witwatersrand in Johannesburg, teaching music education, music history, research, and ethnomusicology. She has been involved in community music outreach and development in South Africa for twenty years and performs as an accompanist and chamber musician. Harrop-Allin also trains arts and culture teachers and has coauthored several textbooks in this field. She is on the editorial board of the *International Journal of Community Music* and is a director of the Johannesburg Youth Orchestra Company.

Sheri E. Jaffurs is Lecturer in Music Education at the University of Michigan, Flint, and a kindergarten through twelfth grade music teacher with Farmington Public School District, Michigan. Her publications include "Music in Cyberspace: Exploring Models in Alternative Approaches in

Music Education: Case Studies from the Field" (with B. A. Younkers) and "The Impact of Informal Music Learning Practices in the Classroom, or How I Learned to Teach from a Garage Band," in the *International Journal of Music Education*.

Sidsel Karlsen is Professor of Music Education at Hedmark University College in Hamar, Norway, and postdoctoral researcher at the Sibelius Academy in Helsinki, Finland. Recent publications include articles in the *International Journal of Music Education*, the *International Journal of Community Music*, and the *British Journal of Music Education*. She is also a contributor to international anthologies such as *Exploring Social Justice: How Music Education Might Matter* (2009) and *Sociology and Music Education* (2010).

Kyoko Koizumi is Associate Professor of Social Information Studies at Otsuma Women's University, Tokyo, Japan. Her publications include chapters in *Terror Tracks: Music, Sound and Horror Cinema* (2009) and *Drawn to Sound: Music, Sound and Animation Cinema* (2010). She serves on the editorial board of the online journal *Screen Sound Journal*. Her latest paper, titled "An Animated Partnership: Joe Hisaishi's Musical Contributions to Hayao Miyazaki's Films," is included in Rebecca Coyle, ed., *Drawn to Sound: Music, Sound and Animation Cinema* (2010).

Roe-Min Kok is Assistant Professor and Chair of the Musicology Area at McGill University. Coeditor of *Rethinking Schumann* (2010) and *Musical Childhoods and the Cultures of Youth* (2006), she has published articles, essays, and reviews in, among others, *Gender-Handbuch Musik*, *Acta musicologica*, *Music & Letters*, *19th-Century Music Review*, *The World of Music*, and *Studien zur Wertungsforschung*. She serves on the editorial board of the *Journal for the History of Childhood and Youth*, and is a member of the Interdisciplinary Initiatives Committee of the German Studies Association.

Kathryn Marsh is Associate Professor and Chair of Music Education at the Sydney Conservatorium of Music, University of Sydney. She is author of *The Musical Playground: Global Tradition and Change in Children's Songs and Games* (2009), winner of the Folklore Society's Katherine Briggs

Award. She serves on editorial and advisory boards of the *International Journal of Music Education*, *Research Studies in Music Education*, and the *British Journal of Music Education*.

Annie On Nei Mok is a Senior Teaching Fellow in the Department of Cultural and Creative Arts of the Hong Kong Institute of Education. Mok specializes in music pedagogy, current issues in music education, and musicianship. Her recent research projects include Teaching Cantonese Opera in Schools, Interdisciplinary and Integrative Arts Research and Pedagogy, and Outcome-based Assessment in Creative Arts and Physical Education.

John O'Flynn is Senior Lecturer and Head of Music at St. Patrick's College, Dublin City University, Ireland. Since 2007, he has served on the editorial board of *Music Education Research*. His recent publications include contributions to the *Continuum Encyclopaedia of Popular Music of the World* (2003) and to the forthcoming *Encyclopaedia of Music in Ireland*. He is author of *The Irishness of Irish Music* (2009) and is currently coediting a volume of essays on music and identity in Ireland.

Avra Pieridou-Skoutella is Lecturer in Music Education and Ethnomusicology at Arte Music Academy, Cyprus, and is coordinator and music educator of the Cyprus Symphonic Orchestra's early childhood educational programs. She is author of *Kypriaká Paradosiaká Trayoúdia yia Paidiá: Mésa apó tin Mousikī Paidagogikī* [*Cypriot Traditional Songs for Children: Through Music Education Practices*], which includes a CD of traditional children's singing, song books, and a music education book. The publication is included in the country's public educational system.

Stephanie Pitts is Senior Lecturer in Music at the University of Sheffield. Her publications include *A Century of Change in Music Education* (2000), *Valuing Musical Participation* (2005), and *Music and Mind in Everyday Life*, with Eric Clarke and Nicola Dibben (2010). With Gordon Cox, she was coeditor of the *British Journal of Music Education* from 2002–2007, and she has written and reviewed for journals including *International Journal of Education and the Arts*, *Music Education Research*, and *Music and Letters*.

Trevor Wiggins is Director of Music at University College Falmouth, United Kingdom, where he teaches Ghanaian drums and xylophone. He has made audio and video recordings in Ghana that have been released commercially and placed in archive collections internationally. He has published books, articles, and CDs on topics such as music pedagogy, ethnomusicology, and world music. Wiggins is currently editing the *Oxford Handbook of Children's Musical Cultures* (forthcoming).

Index

CPSIA information can be obtained at www.ICGtesting.com
Printed in the USA
LVOW040402200912

299567LV00003B/2/P